LOVE HUNGER

OTHER BOOKS IN THE MINIRTH-MEIER SERIES

Worry-Free Living
Love Is a Choice
The Lies We Believe

LOVE HUNGER

Dr. Frank Minirth
Dr. Paul Meier
Dr. Robert Hemfelt
Dr. Sharon Sneed
Don Hawkins

Thomas Nelson Publishers
Nashville

In order to protect the privacy of the doctors' clients, stories recorded in the book are composite illustrations from the case histories of several individuals.

Published in Nashville, Tennessee, by Thomas Nelson, Inc., and distributed in Canada by Lawson Falle, Ltd., Cambridge, Ontario.

Printed in the United States of America.

Scripture quotations are from THE NEW KING JAMES VERSION of the Bible. Copyright © 1979, 1980, 1982, Thomas Nelson, Inc., Publishers.

Library of Congress Cataloging-in-Publication Data

Love hunger : recovery for food codependency / Robert Hemfelt, Sharon Sneed . . . [et al].
    p. cm.
  ISBN 0-8407-7455-9
   1. Compulsive eating. 2. Co-dependence (Psychology) I. Hemfelt, Robert II. Sneed, Sharon.
RC552.C65L68 1990
616.85'26—dc20   89-49702
                                           CIP

— ACKNOWLEDGMENTS —

THE AUTHORS are grateful to the friends, family members, and working companions whose contributions and assistance have made the publication of *Love Hunger* possible. We are especially thankful for Susan Hemfelt, Mary Alice Minirth, Jan Meier, and David Sneed. Many thanks also to Donna Crowe, whose writing craftsmanship transformed the authors' notes and transcripts into manuscript form; Janet Thoma, for her encouragement, support, and editorial expertise; Glenna Sterling Weatherly, for her friendship and her hours of typing; Vicky Warren and Kathy Short, for their assistance at all stages of copy. And finally, to those who participated in recipe formulations and testing: Ernestine Meadows, Shelley McAfee, Maxine McAfee, Pat Cavalier, Debra Evans (Director of Lake Austin Resort), and Georgia Butler (caterer, Austin, Texas); and Shannon, Lauren, and Jonathan Sneed, who tried many of the recipes as their evening meals—even with the recipes that weren't quite "bookers," they remained gracious and supportive.

CONTENTS

PART ONE: Understanding the Problem

PART TWO: Ten Pathways to Recovery

PART THREE: Love Hunger Cookbook

PART FOUR: Appendices

PART ONE

UNDERSTANDING THE PROBLEM

1

WHEN IS A BINGE A BINGE?

ANYONE WATCHING Ralph Yoland preparing to go to work that morning would have seen a slim, attractive, thirty-five-year-old man and judged him the picture of success. But inside, Ralph felt anything but successful as he battled the monsters he had been fighting for seventeen years.

Would this be the day he slipped off his maintenance program and spiraled back up to 220 pounds, only to have to lose it all again? He had been at his ideal weight for two weeks now, but was the crazy roller-coaster ride he had been on most of his adult life about to start again? He gave a final brush to his smooth, blond hair and a last adjustment to his neat, pin-striped tie. As he turned from his mirror, the image in the glass shouted after him, "What if this is the day—the day they *really* find out who you are? You've kept them fooled through four promotions in eight years, but when they find out what you're *really* like, you'll get the sack."

Determinedly he repeated the steps from his Overeaters Anonymous program, "I admitted that I was powerless over my food compulsion—that my life had become unmanageable. I came to believe that a Power greater than myself could restore me to sanity. I made a decision. . . ."

Ralph completed all twelve steps before he poured his cup of black coffee and turned to his refrigerator for skim milk to pour over his raisin bran. He smiled at the sign he had taped to his refrigerator door. Big red letters asked him, "WHAT'S EATING YOU?"

The monsters that had eaten at him for so long were quiet but not gone. Only daily, if not hourly, maintenance kept them in control. Would he ever be truly free?

Or would Barbara Jamison?

Ralph and Barbara, a heavy-set woman of 185 pounds, would

seem to be two very different people. Certainly no one watching Barbara later that day would have thought her to be a picture of confidence and success. Barbara had made certain no one could see her that afternoon. In fact, even though she was alone in her apartment, she had locked her bedroom door. Plopping onto the middle of her bed, she began ripping the bags open and savoring their contents: chocolate creams, extra-crispy fried chicken, creamy crab salad, a yet-unopened box of doughnuts, and french fried potatoes.

She always had to have french fries when she binged. They had been her first binge food when she was eleven and climbed out her bedroom window after her drunken father had locked her in her room. French fries had been the first real food she returned to after the numerous fad diets she embarked on in high school. French fries from the Kampus Korner drive-in in college—downed before she raced back to the dorm to stick her head over the lavatory and get rid of it all in the binge-purge cycle of her college years. Then came Tom and their troubled marriage. . . . Well, at least since he'd moved out, it was easier to hide her binging, even though the ravenous monster seemed to demand feeding more often when she was alone.

At last the monster seemed to be stilled, and with the carton still half full, Barbara was able to put her spoon down. She was too miserable for any more movement. With a sweep of her arm she brushed the leftovers from her bed and leaned back. Her last prayer before sinking into oblivion was, "Dear God, where will it end?"

Barbara and Ralph are compulsive overeaters whose addiction to food became so intense they needed counseling in the Minirth-Meier Clinic's inpatient hospital treatment center in Dallas, Texas.

WHAT IS COMPULSIVE EATING?

"But doesn't everyone overeat sometimes?" you may be wondering. "I always eat until I'm uncomfortable at Christmas." "I binged in college—before exams, when I broke up with my boyfriend, when my roommate got a care package." "Sure I've gone on diets and then gained it back—plus a little." "Does that mean I need counseling?"

One of the difficulties in working with food issues is these grey areas. It's much easier when dealing with alcohol or drug addictions—either you drink or you don't, you're either drug-free or you aren't—but everyone has to eat something, and the lines of what's too much are highly individualized.

Our definition of a compulsive overeater is not some fixed

weight limit or percentage, such as someone who is thirty pounds over normal weight. We concentrate, instead, on the subconscious causes of this obsessive behavior.

We define compulsive overeaters as people who are eating to satisfy emotional hungers, hungers of which they may or may not be aware. The compulsive overeater may be a few pounds or a few hundred pounds overweight. The issue is not how much the person weighs, but rather his or her reasons for eating.

The compulsive overeater may be addicted to food just as the alcoholic is addicted to alcohol or the workaholic is addicted to work. This strong emotional reliance on something on the outside to make one feel good on the inside is called "codependency." Unless the causes of this behavior are identified, the person will never be free from a codependent relationship with food.

THREE EATING DISORDERS

Compulsive overeating, like that of Barbara and Ralph, is just one type of eating disorder. Two other types are anorexia and bulimia.

Anorexia is chronic self-starvation to more than twenty percent below the ideal body weight. Anorexia is an eater's attempt to control something in his or her environment—a rigid, authoritarian father, for example—by controlling food. Often anorexics are so hungry for love that they stop trying to fill their hunger. Their fasting anesthetizes the pain of love hunger. *Bulimia* is compulsive overeating to fill love hunger, then purging the food out in an attempt to purge out pain. The purging is done with self induced vomiting, laxatives, or diet pills. Bulimics then feel empty, so they binge again; then they feel guilty, so they purge again.

Although the emotional dynamics of all three eating disorders and the principles of recovery are similar, this book is focused on the compulsive overeater, and for the sake of simplicity, most of our references will be directed to this disorder. Anorexics and bulimics, however, share many emotional dynamics with compulsive overeaters, and we invite all who suffer from any eating disorder to walk our pathways to recovery. It is important to emphasize that anorexia and bulimia are serious, life-threatening problems, and if you identify yourself in one of these categories, you must seek medical help as well.

A SHORT QUIZ

If you're trying to decide whether or not you're a compulsive eater, ask yourself the following questions:

Do you eat when you're angry?

Do you eat to comfort yourself in times of crisis and tension?

Do you eat to stave off boredom?

Do you lie to yourself and others about how much you have eaten or when you ate?

Do you hide food away for yourself?

Are you embarrassed about your physical appearance?

Are you 20 percent or more over your medically recommended weight?

Have significant people in your life expressed concern about your eating patterns?

Has your weight fluctuated by more than ten pounds in the past six months?

Do you fear your eating is out of control?

If you found yourself answering yes to several of these questions and identifying to some degree with Barbara or Ralph, you are a compulsive overeater. The Minirth-Meier Clinic treats many overeaters, and this book is written by four doctors associated with the clinic. Dr. Frank Minirth and Dr. Paul Meier, the founders of the clinic (one of the largest counseling clinics in the United States, with regional offices in Texas, California, Washington, D.C., and Illinois), are psychiatrists who also have theology degrees. They treat patients from a psychological, medical, and spiritual perspective. Dr. Robert Hemfelt is a psychologist, who specializes in obsessive-compulsive behavior and directs our group therapy program at the Dallas clinic. Dr. Sharon Sneed is a practicing nutrition consultant with the Minirth-Meier Clinic who has helped thousands of patients with various health problems associated with improper diet. Don Hawkins has helped provide insight from his more than twenty years of pastoral counseling. The clinic's program for compulsive eaters brings together medical, psychological, spiritual, and diet components.

Whether you are a first-time-recovery patient like Barbara or a successful dieter at your goal weight like Ralph, we invite you to come along on their journeys with the doctors at the Minirth-Meier Clinic and our unique methods for dealing with eating disorders.

We do not offer easy answers—the problem is too complex for that. But there are answers. And there is comfort in understanding the complexity of the problem. If you, like a majority of Americans, have repeatedly gone on diets and fallen off, an understanding that this is not a single problem that "just requires a little more will-power" is a key to understanding why so many past attempts to conquer the problem have failed—and why the multifaceted approach at Minirth-Meier can succeed.

Two years ago, when Ralph first came to our clinic weighing 230 pounds, we helped him to understand the factors that contributed to his overeating and the self-propelling force of the addiction cycle, which we will look at in the first section of this book. Then Ralph walked through the ten interweaving footpaths to recovery, which are found in the second section. At the same time he worked with Dr. Sharon Sneed to understand the medical complications related to obesity and dieting. She put him on her "easy-to-live-with" eating program so that he could drop off the pounds as he followed the pathways to emotional and spiritual health. He revised his meals to include some of the 165 healthful, easy-to-prepare recipes, which are in the third section.

Once we felt that Ralph was beginning to recover from the emotional causes of his overeating, we asked him to share his seventeen-year off-again/on-again battle with food with the other members of his therapy group. He was hesitant, as many patients are. Although he had spoken words of encouragement to others in the group during the last months, he had never told them the long history of his addiction. We knew the tapes that were running through his mind. The old "demons" laughed: "Ha, just wait till they hear about *that*." "They won't want you in the group when they know." "You've fooled them so far, but now it's all over—ha, ha. . . ."

RALPH'S PROMISE TO THE GROUP—AND TO YOU

That evening Ralph took a deep breath, tugged at his white French cuffs to be certain they showed an even half inch under his jacket sleeves, and walked into the clinic. His heart sank as he saw that all seventeen members of his therapy group were there, seated in straight rows of beige folding chairs. Ralph tried to take comfort in the fact that over half of them had already shared their stories with the group, but his "demons" prodded thoughts like, "Yeah, but they haven't heard anything like yours yet."

The preliminaries were a blur, and suddenly, Ralph was standing in front of the group, talking: "My father was an alcoholic. My mother was so depressed she ricocheted in and out of mental hospitals until she finally just stayed in one. Dad left me with my grandma in New Mexico. . . ."

Now the talking came easier, as Ralph saw in front of him not the therapy group, but Gran's shanty, where he waited in the old days for the welfare checks to come. "Gran never left the house; I ran all the errands for her. She never had anything to give me, but she would always cook for me. If I stayed out until three in the morning, when I came in, she'd get up and fix beans and eggs." He could see Gran, her tousled gray hair scraggling down the back of her house-coat from which the pink flowers had faded long ago.

But the only comfort Gran could give him brought its own problems. It was bad enough being teased at school because he owned only one pair of pants, which he wore until they literally fell apart, but then the taunts increased as his pudgy stomach strained at the buttons of his shirt and bits of skin showed where his clothing didn't quite meet.

"When I was sixteen, I lied about my age and ran off and joined the army. Only instead of sending me to boot camp, they sent me to the fat farm, where they spent six weeks getting the weight off me: running miles, working long hours, eating little. The weight came off. Then boot camp—no weight gain there." Members of the group who had been in the service laughed as they identified with that.

"Then I went overseas. In Nam I was introduced to drugs. When the war ended I came back to the States feeling lonelier than ever, eating more than ever, and being addicted to drugs. At least I found solace for my isolation. I joined a motorcycle gang." There was an audible gasp in the room. It couldn't be possible, this man who stood before them—trim, literate, successful—a member of "The Brothers Speed"?

Ralph grinned at their reaction; he enjoyed this part. Reaching into his pocket he pulled out a snapshot of himself at three hundred pounds, greasy blond hair hanging to his shoulders, wearing a metal-studded leather jacket and boots, sitting astride his black Harley-Davidson. He passed it around.

"But that didn't really do it for me. So I married Tina. Her dad used to beat her up all the time, so I guess she thought it was pretty normal when I came home high on drugs or booze. But the marriage didn't last long, and I decided if I was going to do anything with my life before I woke up dead in a ditch some morning, I'd better get a decent job. I got a haircut, dieted down to my ideal weight—it didn't take me long because the army had taught me what a ten-mile run on an empty stomach could accomplish—and bought a cheap but decent suit. I got a job doing punch cards for a computer company. I didn't have much in the way of formal educa-tion, but I took to the electronics stuff and rose pretty fast in the business: serviceman, supervisor, manager. I was still doing drugs weekends and evenings, just being sure my head was clear by morn-ing so I could show up for work.

"And I kept getting into these difficult relationships with women—two or three at a time. It was like my need to overeat—I could never get enough. Dr. Meier helped me to see just recently that I wanted two or three women at a time so that I would never have to get too emotionally intimate with any one woman." Two heads on the back row nodded. Ralph relaxed a bit—someone understood. Not everyone thought he was crazy—even if the story sounded it.

"I learned that I was eating to fill a vacuum the doctors call love hunger, created by my messed-up childhood. I learned how the pain of that love hunger caused low self-esteem that got me on the addiction cycle. And I learned all the pathways I have to walk to reach the full recovery I've committed to."

Ralph glanced at the clock on the wall. Could he really have been talking that long? Surely he should sit down. But the group didn't seem restless. Some were even leaning forward on their chairs as if they were anxious to hear more. Well, he might as well finish. He wiped his forehead. "Well, that's the story of the human yo-yo. I've probably been up and down on my weight between ten and twenty times, once every year or two since I was seventeen. But this time it's going to be different because I'm not just dealing with food, not just treating the symptom. This time I'm working with the feelings that result from my childhood and the guilt over the drugs and alcohol, dealing with core issues. And I'm trying to learn how to achieve maintenance—a lifetime of victory—but I'm here to tell you, that's the tough part.

"Getting the weight off was no problem with Dr. Sneed's help, and because I do everything obsessively, I lost my weight in the first four weeks." Everyone in the room groaned. Ralph grinned. "Yeah, I know. Everyone in the program hates me. But I still have to keep going to these meetings, and that's kind of hard. I don't want to go, but if I don't, there's no guarantee it's going to stay off. I've got to listen to somebody else, get somebody else to feed me information instead of my own head because my head tells me, 'Oh, never mind, Ralph. Everything's OK.' But it isn't yet.

"And, hey, you guys, I know I've talked too long, and you've been such great listeners, but I just wanta tell you, it's worth it. Getting your life together, reaching recovery—it's tough, but it's worth it. And you deserve it. You deserve to like yourself. You deserve to be happy.

"Being overweight is me being abusive to myself. And I don't have the answers for me, but there are people out there who do. Sometimes we have to use outside people to help us recover from drugs and alcohol and abusive families. Getting help from other people is scary, but it's also fun and rewarding. And remember— just keep telling yourself you're worth it. Every day, if you really

believe you deserve to be healthy and happy, then you'll make it—
one day at a time."

To Ralph's overwhelming surprise, each person in the room
came up to hug him or to shake hands. They had heard all about the
real him, and they loved him anyway.

2

I KNOW I BINGE— I WANT TO KNOW WHY

THE DOCTOR'S office with its gray carpet, oak furniture, and potted palm in the corner was obviously intended to be relaxing. But Barbara couldn't relax. There was no way in the world she was going to tell the doctors at the Minirth-Meier Clinic about last night's binge. It was bad enough knowing about it herself. Somehow saying it out loud would make it all real, something that actually happened—not just the bad dream she hoped it was. And at the back of her mind was the thought, *If I don't talk much, I can get out of here quicker, and then I can EAT.*

For a while the conversation was easy and pleasant, just getting-acquainted stuff like you might exchange at a rather stiff, boring party. She readily admitted to her depression since Tom had moved out two months ago after four years of marriage, and she talked a great deal about the boredom of her checking job at the discount store. "I've wanted to be an artist since my earliest memories. I majored in art in college and had a job I enjoyed as a window decorator for a department store for a while. What I really wanted was to be an interior decorator . . . but that never worked out. . . ." Her voice trailed off.

Then, right there in that quiet space, Dr. Hemfelt dropped the bomb with his soft, gentle voice. "I understand you're depressed and a lot of things aren't working out the way you'd hoped. Has your weight been a factor in this, do you think?"

Barbara shrugged and tried to keep the belligerent tone out of her voice. "Well, obviously I need to lose a few pounds. Of course, I am big boned. But if I had a happy marriage or an interesting job, I'm sure I'd slim down."

Dr. Hemfelt leaned back in his chair and put his fingertips together. "Unfair as it is, there are many myths and stereotypes about overweight people. I'm sure you've heard them." He ticked them off on his fingers: "Overweight people are lazy; overweight people are nonsexual; overweight people are jolly; overweight people aren't intelligent or efficient; overweight people are weak-willed. And overweight people themselves buy into a lot of the myths: Ultra-slim is both necessary and beautiful. My family is overweight, so I must be overweight. A diet has to be exotic and punishing to be effective. I can never keep weight off—I'll always be heavy."

Barbara grimaced. *Heard* them all? She'd *lived* them all—even *believed* most of them.

You may have too. Perhaps you didn't have to work through the checklist in Chapter 1 to decide you are a binge eater. Or perhaps after reading it, you now realize you are, but you don't know why. What is that nameless monster that drives you to eat a whole package of cookies before you're even home from the grocery store?

Overeaters need to understand the dynamics that cause their eating compulsion before they can begin to change this addiction. Let's look at twelve common reasons for compulsive overeating so that you can identify the specific factors that are influencing you.

1. OVEREATERS MAY RESPOND COMPULSIVELY TO CULTURAL PRESSURES

Some overeaters feel stress because they are constantly bombarded by cultural pressures to "Eat, eat, eat" or "Get slim, slim, slim!" Never before in history have so much time, money, and energy gone into urging people to eat and yet at the same time demanding that they be slim. Psychiatrists call these push/pull messages, double-bind messages, paradox messages, or best of all: "crazy-making messages." And these crazy-making messages have led us to become the most food-obsessed, obesity-plagued society in the world. In spite of the fact that Twiggy was English, the obsession with skinniness and the other side of the coin, the obsession with food, are peculiarly American diseases. In order to resist these lies, we need to understand the multifaceted nature of these pressures, so we discuss them with our patients during one of their initial visits, as we did with Barbara.

A CULTURAL ADDICTION

A traveler just returned from a month in Great Britain told us, "I didn't see any fat people. Oh, lots of people who need to lose ten pounds, but if they have really huge people over there, they're home eating; they aren't out on the streets. The only truly obese people you see on the streets are American tourists."

And a patient who has become aware of the role cultural pressures have played in her obsession with food said, "I've been watching a lot of English TV shows. You know, their actresses look more real. Some of them are a little bit big around the middle. Some of them don't have flawless complexions. I even saw one with short fingernails last night."

The next time you watch television, notice what you're being bombarded with. Keep a note pad handy and jot down the images: full-screen-sized hamburgers followed by french fries floating in the air, skinny people drinking diet sodas, ten ultrasvelte actresses, and one pudgy actress—she didn't get the man.

As convenient as it is to point the finger at television and the American media, however, other cultural culprits are at work, also.

Dr. Sneed says, "We have turned the horn of plenty into the barrel of excess." It's very, very hard to live in the American culture where there's a fast-food restaurant on every corner and to resist the temptation to overeat. We can go in and buy two thousand calories for two dollars, and it tastes good. Trying to control your weight under those circumstances comes down to consciously deciding to reject a lot of the values you see around you—probably a majority of them. And that's not easy. It's tough to say, "I'm different. I don't value what everyone else values." And it's tough to make that decision stick when you are constantly bombarded with popular values.

The food system in the U.S. has changed so dramatically in the last fifty years that it's difficult to eat normally. Dr. Sneed points to studies on how many meals are eaten outside the home. During the last fifty years this has gone from one or less per month, to at least one per day per family. If you want to make money, buy stock in a fast food chain. This has undoubtedly turned a lot of people who were not compulsive eaters into obsessives because the food is so readily accessible. This cultural phenomenon has also produced a lot of secret eaters, especially people who eat in their cars.

When you think about it, it's a miracle there's anyone out there who isn't a compulsive eater. The list of things that don't work seems endless: Fad diets don't work; starvation doesn't work; diet pills don't work; wearing special clothing to melt off calories doesn't work; reducing machines don't work; laxatives don't work. . . . People bring a lot of "magical thinking" to diet programs. "If I can just find the right diet—the magic formula—my weight will just slip away."

Yes, Barbara could identify with all that. And after a lifetime of living with those signals, *anything* could trigger her desire to eat. And with all the failure she'd experienced, *anything* could discourage her. She smiled and relaxed a bit as Dr. Hemfelt mentioned the second reason for compulsive overeating.

2. OVEREATERS MAY SUBCONSCIOUSLY DESIRE ADDED POUNDS TO PROTECT THEMSELVES FROM LOVE AND INTIMACY

We see people in our clinic who subconsciously want a protective fat pad. This impulse frequently occurs after a traumatic event such as a broken engagement or after a mate has run off with another person and the eater doesn't want to have to deal with personal sexuality. Also, childhood fears of intimacy and adult ambivalence toward sexual intimacy can trigger the need for insulation.

Many compulsive overeaters make an effort to deny, repress, or obscure sexuality. The more one overeats, the less conspicuous become some of the body's sexual areas. And if one is heavy enough, either due to aesthetics or to simple mechanics, sexual activity becomes unpleasant, if not impossible. As we will see later, this was part of the reason for Barbara's compulsion.

An extension of using food as a denial of sexuality is using food for intimacy avoidance. This works in two ways. First of all, if our obsession with food demands emotional energy (either by our overeating or by our trying to fight a compulsion to eat), the amount of energy available to give to a relationship is limited. An extreme example of this was Mary, a bulimic we were treating in the hospital. Mary had only been married for two years, and she loved her husband in spite of problems in the marriage. But by the time she gorged herself and then immediately purged seven or eight times a day, she had no physical or emotional energy left to put into her marriage. Secondly, the overeater can get so fat he isn't interested in sex and others are not tempted to initiate sexual intimacy.

Roller-coaster eaters, those who are forever losing and gaining twenty or thirty pounds, worry before every meal, *What should I eat? What shouldn't I eat?* If they are cautious about what they eat, they may still be hungry afterward and obsessed with that. If they overeat, they may be obsessed with guilt. This endless obsession with food starts to crowd out other life issues, including other people, which may, in fact, be the eater's subconscious goal.

3. OVEREATERS MAY USE FOOD TO SATISFY THEIR NEED FOR IMMEDIATE GRATIFICATION

We're all born self-centered. We feel as if we're the whole world until about eighteen months of age when we figure out we're separated from our mothers. The older we get, the more we are drawn out of our self-centeredness by loving parents who discipline us and set an example. But if children aren't disciplined and aren't given good role models, they'll continue to want instant gratification. So whenever they want food, they eat. They indulge themselves and become overweight.

Selfishness often leads to an exaggerated sense of competition. Even children who are otherwise nice to their siblings will compete for food. They yell, "Hey! That's *my* cookie!" even if there are three more on the plate. The instinct for food is so basic that people will subconsciously compete for food by taking larger portions than they want. This would be especially true of those who grew up in a poor family, as Ralph did, where the food supply was limited, but it's not confined to them.

People reared in families that provide good nurturing and good role models outgrow this natural selfishness. But growing up in a dysfunctional family with a lack of adequate gratification in childhood will leave a person ungratified in adulthood. These people try for self-managed gratification and turn to food because it provides instant gratification. Anyone who grew up in a dysfunctional family will have double difficulties here because he or she will have great emotional hunger and also will lack good self-gratification skills. The person who doesn't know how to provide self-gratification by building relationships or developing creative hobbies will repeatedly turn to the cookie jar for gratification.

We have found this cause of overeating to be particularly difficult to detect because people often cover selfishness with a veneer of unselfishness. Many overt people-pleasers who work all day helping people in hospitals, in schools, or at home will then binge in private for self-gratification.

4. OVEREATERS MAY USE FOOD AS A TRANQUILIZER

Many people use food as a tranquilizer. When these people have anxiety, they eat; their blood sugar level rises, and they feel relaxed. The pituitary gland is sometimes called the master gland because it controls all the organs in the body. Yet there is another gland called the hypothalamus that controls the pituitary gland. Right in the middle of the hypothalamus (in the very center of the brain) is the satiety center. The blood runs through that center. The satiety center picks up our blood sugar level and tells us if we are satisfied and comfortable or if we are hungry.

For most people this works fine. But there are also millions of nerves coming from all the other parts of the brain to and from the hypothalamus, and when some people get nervous, their satiety center says, "You're hungry." In reality, they may not actually be hungry, but if they eat and their blood sugar level gets higher, they relax. Of course, they feel guilty about overeating, and then the cycle starts all over again.

A second way that food acts as a tranquilizer is that each time a person eats, the brain stimulates some of the neurochemicals, the endorphins, which are natural painkillers, relaxants, and pleasure stimulators. Endorphins are somewhat similar to the narcotic drugs that produce these results. The difference is that they are a natural, God-given part of our mechanism, and certain activities stimulate them; such as, laughter, sexual excitement, eating, and aerobic exercise. So after a person has eaten, there is a true state of anesthesia.

This tranquilized state is normal and healthy. But the compulsive overeater may have become dependent on his own endorphins and the state of food-induced pleasure. That is why a true food addict may go through six or eight meals a day, like a drug addict having to go out and get one more fix.

5. OVEREATERS MAY CONCENTRATE ON THEIR DESIRE FOR FOOD TO AVOID FACING PROBLEMS

Many people in our eating disorder unit at the hospital suffer from anxiety. Now we aren't talking here about a specific fear—worry about the final exam next week, worry about the pay raise you're going to ask for tomorrow and may not get. We're talking about a persistent, vague anxiety: fear of the unknown. Anxiety is fear of finding out the truth about one's own hidden thoughts, feelings, or motives. For example, overeaters might have rage toward a parent but refuse to acknowledge it because that would mean admitting that the parent isn't perfect. If this person has based his self-worth on his parents' acceptance (which one shouldn't do, but most people do), the anger at a parent would mean lowering his own opinion of himself.

Joey was an example of one who ate to avoid insight. He grew up with a selfish father, who had his own business. The father used Joey as "slave labor" from early childhood on, making him work from after school until ten o'clock at night. Joey wanted to have a high opinion of his father and to think his father loved him so that he in turn could feel a sense of self-worth. So Joey worked his heart out, telling himself that his father was really great and that Dad was doing this because he loved Joey and wanted to be with him. In reality his father was sociopathically selfish and was using Joey.

Whenever Joey saw a TV show with a selfish father or witnessed an incident with a selfish father in public, he became overwhelmed with a desire to eat. But he never put two and two together. He would eat to stifle his own rage and to keep from having to look at the truth.

6. OVEREATERS MAY EAT TO PUNISH THEMSELVES OR OTHERS

People also eat compulsively to punish themselves or others. A number of our patients are really angry at themselves for something they have done—cheating on a test, going too far sexually—and so they go through life bearing a load of false guilt and punishing themselves by overeating and being overweight. When they're overweight, they can hate themselves for the weight, which may be less painful than getting in touch with their anger toward themselves because of their mistake. They get obese not only to punish themselves by being overweight, but in order to use the weight as a scapegoat. This is an extension of eating to avoid insight.

"I don't deserve to be pretty. As long as I keep this weight on, I can punish myself," Sherri, a formerly beautiful teenager, told Dr. Hemfelt. Sherri was polyaddicted—an alcoholic, a sexual addict, a rageaholic, a compulsive spender, and a compulsive eater. She was in recovery to some degree from all her addictions except her weight. She was sober; her spending was under control; she was faithful in her marriage; and her temper was controlled. Her compulsion for food was the toughest of all. She gained eighty-five pounds with her pregnancy and had lost only half that weight six months after the baby's birth.

"I know I'm punishing myself for the bad feelings I had growing up," she said, recalling her childhood with an alcoholic parent. "And I'm probably punishing myself for all the years I acted out the other addictions. It's a way to pay a price for the guilt I carried. I look in my mirror and say, 'You don't deserve to be pretty. You need to be punished. You need to be blemished.'"

We liken this attitude to making installment payments on a revolving charge account. The guilt-sufferer feels, "If I just stay fat and unhappy the next ten years, then magically I'll have paid the guilt debt. I'll have paid off my revolving charge account."

Other people want to punish their mates. When most of us are dating and engaged we think, *Boy, what a good deal I'm getting.* We think we're getting somebody who's better than ourselves. Once we get married and share the same small spaces and argue over which channel to watch or what restaurant to go to, we reverse our decision and think, *I could have done better. I made a mistake.* We all tend to deny our own faults and see faults in others. A mature person works through this natural tendency and decides, *I've got faults; my mate's got faults. We deserve each other.*

People who don't reach this conclusion may continue to think, *I got a raw deal; he's not as nice as I thought he was going to be.* These people might decide to get even with their spouses by putting on weight.

7. OVEREATERS MAY EAT TO RELIEVE DEPRESSION OR STRESS

EATING TO RELIEVE DEPRESSION

Eating to relieve depression can likewise cause obesity. In the history of the clinic, we have treated thousands of people for depression on an outpatient and inpatient basis. The majority of those people suffer from repressed anger and their unconscious desire to get vengeance, frequently on themselves. Many of them are perfectionists, who inwardly resent themselves for not being better. Holding a grudge against ourselves is a sin. So it's an emotional and a spiritual problem. And it's also a physical problem. When we hold resentment against God, others, or ourselves, serotonin and norepinephrine are depleted in our brain cells. These are the chemicals that move across the synapses from one cell to the next, the chemicals that we think with, move with. When these are depleted, people lose energy and motivation.

This depletion of brain chemicals can cause people to gain weight because they become inactive while continuing to eat at their former levels. Of the people who develop a serotonin or norepinephrine depletion, many will lose their appetites and some may even develop anorexia. But for the remainder, this biochemical change will produce the opposite—increased appetite, and they will overeat.

In the case of repressed anger, we have both a chemical basis and an emotional basis for overeating. Many people literally stuff their anger—they keep it down by putting food on top of it. The process is similar to packing in wadding when loading a cannon—and the results can be just as explosive.

EATING TO RELIEVE STRESS

Other people are overweight because they have repressed hostility from their childhood or from current stress. These people chew constantly to sublimate their subconsciously repressed hostility. They frequently develop Temporomandibular Joint Syndrome (TMJ), a joint disease of the jaw. (People can also inherit TMJ.) These are the nice, overly conscientious people who do most of the work in their school, service club, or church. They repress anger because anger is not an acceptable emotion for nice people. So they grind their teeth in their sleep and spend their waking hours chewing on things: potato chips, ice, pencils, steak. They're looking for an oral sublimation of their hostility. Then they feel guilty and angry at themselves for overeating and the cycle starts again.

8. OVEREATERS MAY EAT TO REBEL AGAINST THEMSELVES OR OTHERS

People can become so tired and frustrated with trying to live up to a perfect body image or follow the rules or follow a diet that they may use overeating as a radical push against this pressure. Mitzy, for example, was a perfectionistic housekeeper whose home was always spick-and span, everything precisely in its place. Her children were always polite and well groomed. Beautifully prepared food was always on the table on schedule. Her own compulsive eating pattern was her one way to step out from all that regimentation.

Tanya, on the other hand, rebelled against perfection imposed from the outside. Her husband was rigid and legalistic, and she lived up to his standards in every other area. They were both high achievers: he, a lawyer; she, a CPA. They owned an expensive home, drove the right kinds of cars, had successful friends—the perfect yuppie couple.

After several unsuccessful attempts at dieting on her own, Tanya's husband sent her to us for counseling. We discovered that she had repressed anger from a childhood lived under an authoritarian, perfectionistic father and anger at her husband who was repeating the pattern. She twice smashed her husband's black and gold Volvo in our parking lot when she was coming for counseling. Yet she denied her anger, denied her rebellion, and denied that she was

12 COMMON REASONS
FOR COMPULSIVE EATING

1. Overeaters may respond compulsively to cultural pressures.

2. Overeaters may subconsciously desire added pounds to protect themselves from love and intimacy.

3. Overeaters may use food to satisfy their need for immediate gratification.

4. Overeaters may use food as a tranquilizer.

5. Overeaters may concentrate on their desire for food to avoid facing their problems.

6. Overeaters may eat to punish themselves or others.

7. Overeaters may eat to relieve depression or stress.

8. Overeaters may eat to rebel against themselves or others.

9. Overeaters may eat to express their need to control their circumstances.

10. Overeaters may have a faulty perception of their body image.

11. Overeaters may have emotional feelings about food, which were developed at their parents' dinner table.

12. Overeaters use food as a nurturer to satisfy their love hunger.

reacting against perfectionism. She acted out her anger by damaging her husband's car, rather than express it by saying to her husband, "I don't want to be in counseling."

People also binge eat to get revenge on parents. Many parents will say, "Be sure to eat." "Clean up your plate." "Finish your orange juice." Or the exact opposite: "Stay a good weight." "Don't make a pig of yourself." "Cut down on sugar." Teenagers especially like to rebel and use eating as a way to counter their parents' demands. Both anorexia and compulsive overeating are profound ways of saying, "No!" when eaters don't feel they can say it directly.

9. OVEREATERS MAY EAT TO EXPRESS THEIR NEED TO CONTROL THEIR CIRCUMSTANCES

Control is a major issue, especially to the perfectionist. Most perfectionists are oldest children who grew up in a home where they were overly controlled. In fact, many of the people we treat for obsessive-compulsive disorders are oldest children who have been overly controlled by new parents, anxious to do a good job. A majority of people who excel in science, music, or professional athletics are firstborns. Fifteen out of the first sixteen American astronauts were firstborns who were perfectionistic enough to make it to the moon and back. Perfectionism can be a great asset for the individual and for society, but it can also lead to disorders such as compulsive eating.

Control is also a big issue for a child growing up in an unhealthy family. In a dysfunctional family with an alcoholic parent or where there are sexual, physical, or emotional abuses, the child grows up learning to be scared. In defense, they take control of their lives to protect themselves from pain.

As the child grows older, there are only a few battlegrounds where they can practice their control. Money is one of them, so they work on being in control of money—hoarding and becoming misers or spending everything they can get their hands on. It's not unusual for a binge eater to become a binge spender or a compulsive gambler.

Or frequently, food becomes the battleground where the perfectionistic person seeks to be the boss over something. In reality, binge eaters aren't in control because the food is in control and is killing them. But they feel as if they're the boss.

Brian's mother uses food as a control issue in her overly perfectionistic attempt to raise a model child. It's questionable whether Brian is truly hyperactive or not, but his mother has him on an extremely regimented Feingold diet where he can have no preservatives and no artificial color, no additives of any kind, in his food. She scans every package of food she buys. Brian can't go to birthday parties. He can't eat at other people's houses. He can't eat hot lunches at school. The more rigidly the mother tries to control his life, the more hyperactive Brian becomes. And the more hyperactive he becomes, the more tightly she clamps down on his eating. The mother thinks she's regulating Brian's food, whereas she's actually imposing her compulsivity on the child. Food and nutrition have very little to do with his behavior. And as a result of food being used as a control, Brian will very probably grow up to have an eating disorder.

Ironically, most compulsive overeaters are overdisciplined. They tell themselves, "If I just had more willpower I could beat this food issue. I could make that diet work with a little more will-power." Yet willpower is not the answer. Believing you can solve the problem with just a little more self-control often leads to binge eating each time this faulty approach fails.

10. OVEREATERS MAY HAVE A FAULTY PERCEPTION OF THEIR BODY IMAGE

A faulty perception of body image can make a person overeat or undereat compulsively. This is always the case with anorexics, for example. They can never see themselves accurately. None of us sees the self with entire accuracy, but eating-disordered persons really have no idea how they look. One patient of ours weighed nearly four hundred pounds. The man said, "Well, yes, I am a little overweight. I suppose I really should get back on my diet and lose a few pounds this summer."

Another patient, who is now working her way out of codependency and a serious eating disorder, cannot recognize her own photographs. She will go through the family snapshot album and ask, "Who is standing next to Uncle Jim in that picture?"

Our patient Sherri, however, was finally motivated to deal with the weight she had gained and failed to lose after pregnancy when she saw the photographs from her child's christening. Seeing herself in the mirror every day did not tell her how serious her problem was, but seeing pictures of herself standing next to other people startled her into taking action.

The more serious an eating addiction is, the less accurately a person sees himself. This denial, or inability to see the truth, will allow a compulsive overeater to continue to gorge himself or an anorexic to starve herself to death.

11. OVEREATERS MAY HAVE EMOTIONAL FEELINGS ABOUT FOOD, WHICH WERE DEVELOPED AT THEIR PARENTS' DINNER TABLE

We often ask our patients about the "table manners" around their parents' dinner table; we try to discover the emotional tone at mealtime. Did family members abuse each other? Did members of your family overeat? Did they use food as a medication? Or did they use food to celebrate? If patients answer yes to any one of these questions, their families' attitude toward food may have contributed to their overeating.

THE DINNER TABLE AS A BATTLEGROUND

A frightening case example is Justin, who grew up in a home where the dinner table was a shooting gallery. Each night his father would sarcastically put down a certain child. In a shooting gallery atmosphere the child thinks, *My nurturance is not going to come from Mom and Dad. So I'll dig into the food for my emotional as well as my physical sustenance.*

The tension Justin experienced at the dinner table caused his stomach to generate so much acidity that the acid began to bubble back up out of his stomach and burn his esophagus. Later, as an adult, he had to have surgery to tighten the flap on his stomach to prevent this.

THE "YOU MUST EAT" SYNDROME

Obsessive parents who insist on perfectly clean plates often contribute to an adult's food compulsivity. Vicky vividly recalls times when she could not or would not eat the food and her mother forced her to sit at the table for hours. The rest of the family would leave and go on with their activities while Vicky sat there and cried. Of course, by then, there was no way her body could digest the food. This was repeated frequently in Vicky's growing-up years, and in therapy as an adult, she realized it was a major factor leading to her eating compulsion, for while she wanted to rebel against Mom, she was also receiving a powerful, hypnotic message: "You must eat. You must eat. You must eat."

"FOOD IS FOR CELEBRATING"

Food is often part of a family celebration. In and of itself, this isn't bad, but for the compulsive eater, the ceremonies can escalate to become a daily ritual. Most true food addicts, like the alcoholic, will eat for solace when they are feeling bad and eat to celebrate: A thirty-two-ounce steak when I get fired; a thirty-two-ounce steak when I get a raise.

THE "YOU DID GOOD, MOM!" SYNDROME

Some people overeat to please their parents. Dr. Paul Meier shares his own story here. "I grew up in a German home. My mother was a wonderful cook, and still is, at age eighty, a wonderful cook. And, like good old-world eaters, we put butter on everything. Sometimes I used to *food my butter* rather than *butter my food*.

"Mom was a homemaker who spent a lot of her time cooking really fine meals and desserts when all four of us kids were at home. She was pleased to see us enjoy her cooking. If I asked for seconds or thirds, that made her happy. My request said to her, 'Mom, you did good.'

"So I grew up overeating to please my mom. It wasn't anything she consciously desired or that I consciously desired, but it became a type of codependency."

12. OVEREATERS USE FOOD AS A NURTURER TO SATISFY THEIR LOVE HUNGER

The twelfth cause of overeating is: *Overeaters use food as a nurturer to satisfy their love hunger.* Since this is an underlying cause of *all* compulsive overeating, we will devote the entire next chapter to the major step of learning to feed your hungry heart.

CHAPTER

3

FEEDING THE HUNGRY HEART

"DO YOU think you could treat yourself to one of the clinic's group therapy sessions tonight?" Dr. Hemfelt asked Barbara Jamison.

Barbara sighed. She'd been coming for counseling for three weeks now, and every time the question was the same. And every time her response had been the same: "No, I just don't really think I could do that."

That afternoon her answer changed. We had helped Barbara to understand the numerous causes of her compulsive overeating, some of which began in her childhood. She was able to say, "I've got a serious problem" rather than, "Yeah, I eat a little too much because I've been depressed lately."

"Oh, all right," she answered. "What time does this fat fanci ers' fellowship meet?"

Even though we told Barbara the exact time of the meeting, she arrived ten minutes late. She quickly took a seat near an attractive, sandy-haired young woman who gave her a smile of genuine warmth. But there was no chance for them to speak because a tall, blond woman named Adrian was just being introduced as an "alumnus" of the group who had agreed to return to share her story. Adrian was tall, nearly six feet, Barbara guessed, with broad shoulders and a large frame, but not at all fat. She looked great in her gray-and-red dress and her sleek page-boy hair style.

Adrian plunged right into her story without preliminaries: "My father was passively abusive. That means he never abused me physically, he never abused me verbally; he abused me passively by doing nothing. In all of my growing-up years, my father never once hugged me, held me, played with me, or spent any time with me. To the very best of my memory, my father never even spoke my first name.

"And Mother just sort of ignored the whole thing—whatever it was. To this day I don't know if my father had been an abused child or if he wanted a son and so rejected his daughter. I can only make guesses. I kept on desperately wondering, *What's so defective with me that my own father won't say my name?* I remember lying awake at night, staring at the black void of my ceiling, trying and trying to figure out what I'd done wrong. Wondering if it was possible to be a monster and not know it.

"I worked harder and harder to please: I became Mother's helper, took over the cooking. I took care of my little brother. I got good grades in school. When I grew up I became a teacher and began writing children's stories. And all the time my weight problem was getting worse and worse.

"When I got more than 250 pounds overweight I turned to medical procedures. First I had an intestinal bypass where they removed a large part of my intestine. I dropped about 50 to 75 pounds with that, then just sort of stuck, so I had my stomach stapled. I got down to being only about 80 pounds overweight, so I thought I had my weight problem under control. After all, I was the slimmest I'd been in years. But you know what? Losing all that weight didn't make me feel a bit better inside. Oh, it was easier to move around, I slept better, and it was nice to be able to sit in a normal chair, but those were just externals. Inside I wasn't any happier.

"Actually a lot of old angers that I had been keeping down with overeating began to erupt. Physically, I just couldn't stuff my anger down with food because my stomach had been stapled to a size that couldn't accept it. So the rage surfaced, and I would have these terrible temper explosions at my husband. . . ."

Here Adrian was interrupted by an expression of surprise from her audience. She grinned. "Oh, yes, I was married. Hard to believe, isn't it? Of course, I wasn't 250 pounds overweight when Dick and I were married, but I was on my way. Dick always has been a very mellow, accepting sort of person. And even when I was erupting with these terrible tantrums, I don't think it upset him as much as it did me. I mean, here I was, a woman who wrote gentle children's stories, my husband was my best friend and a nice guy, and my behavior was totally baffling and unacceptable.

"In therapy later, I learned that deep inside me was this great quantity of hurt, and below that hurt was an even greater quantity of anger. But I'd never allowed myself to deal with the hurt or the anger because I had literally stuffed those feelings with food—pushed them down until I had no idea they were there. But then I couldn't stuff enough food in to keep the rage down, and it all boiled out. I would be fine for days or maybe weeks, and then one day Dick would walk into the room, and I'd have this look on my face, and I would literally attack him and scratch him and hit him. Once the anger was out, I was as baffled as Dick, and I'd apologize to him. I'd be better for a while, but then it would happen again.

"We were beginning to think maybe I was demon possessed. And that's when I came in for therapy, with a group very much like this, only we were all hospital patients, people whose conditions were so serious they were immediately life-threatening to themselves or to others, or people who needed to be taken out of a bad situation for therapeutic reasons. There were several bulimics, anorexics, and drug abusers in our group.

"Well, anyway, a part of me wanted to be in the hospital and realized I was getting help. But as my therapy made me dig into these pockets of pain, a part of me wanted to run away—to get out of there. So one morning I simply ran out of the hospital and down the highway. For my own protection, the hospital staff called the local police to help find me.

"Now, you've got to get this picture: My hair was long then, and fuzzy-curly, I weighed well over two hundred pounds, and I was wearing this nightie with blue and purple flowers and fuzzy pink slippers. Well, this nice young policeman—he couldn't have been more than twenty-two, and about two-thirds my size—was the one who found me. I turned all my rage on him. I gave this sort of snorting yell and charged right at him. Fortunately he sidestepped or I'd have flattened him. He had the courage to chase me, and at one point he got hold of my wrists. I kicked him in the shins and broke free. The next time he came for me I stampeded right under his arm with my head down like a mad bull rushing a toreador. This was right by Highway 75 during rush-hour traffic, and people were honking their horns at me. Then I think I had some idea of hiding behind a tree—but of course, no tree could hide me. Finally, his partner arrived to help him, and they got me back to the hospital."

Adrian and her listeners all stopped to laugh at the images her story had conjured up. After a few moments she added, still chuckling, "So I guess the moral of that is, if you want to run away, have the sense to put on slacks and running shoes first. But really, I was just so angry. I can still feel the intensity of all that boiling up in me. And I was so afraid to face it that the only thing I knew to do was to run.

"When I saw this policeman, it was like an ultimate authority figure that had to be resisted. Once I calmed down, I worked through that crisis and realized that I needed and wanted to stay in the hospital. Working with the doctors here—Dr. Minirth and Dr. Meier and Dr. Hemfelt—I finally learned that I could trust men.

They weren't all like my father, and I learned that people really do care about me—that I'm worth caring about.

"This all happened a year ago. So today is an anniversary for me."

She was interrupted here by applause and cries of, "Congratulations!" "Happy anniversary!"

"Thank you. Only maybe I should call it a birthday because I truly feel like a new woman. You see, for the first time in my life I really dealt with the foundation of my problem, not just the symptoms."

The group applauded again. Then, in the general discussion that followed Adrian's speech, Barbara's neighbor turned to her. "Hi, I'm Ginger. She had a great story, huh?"

Barbara nodded. "Yeah, she sure did. And she looks fabulous—so pulled together—can't imagine her doing that wild scene with the policeman." Barbara paused and probably would have remained silent if Ginger's smile hadn't been so encouraging. "But you know, to be honest, I don't really get this relationship stuff they talk about around here. I mean, I'm fat because I overeat. Every book I ever read said it's a simple matter of mathematics: if you take in more calories than you burn, you'll store it as fat. So what's the big deal about whether my father ever spoke my name or not?"

"Yeah, I felt like that at first too. I mean, when Dr. Meier gave me this relationship survey to work through, I said, 'Hey, that doesn't have anything to do with food!' and he just gave me that slow grin of his and said, 'Yeah, I know. But I want to get to know you a little better. So tell me a little about Mom and Dad and what it was like growing up. . . .'"

Surely this woman couldn't have had a messed up life like Adrian's, Barbara thought as she wondered what Ginger's story was.

As if Ginger had read Barbara's thoughts, she continued, "I guess my story isn't as dramatic as the one we just heard—I never did a bullfight scene with a policeman. But all my weight problems and my marriage problems came from junk in my childhood.

"The whole thing was, my parents never gave me permission to leave home emotionally. There was a lot of codependency in our family. . . ." She interrupted herself with a laugh. "Spend enough time around psychologists and you start talking like one. But my father is very authoritarian, and Mama has a big-time weight problem. Real big-time. So my father had me on a rigid diet and exercise program all my childhood, and Mama told me all her marital problems, and I was the scapegoat for everybody's problems. Dr. Meier said that, emotionally, I was functioning like a surrogate spouse to both of them.

"My brother married and left home—no problem. But I never could manage to leave for very long. I made two really bad marriages and never moved more than a couple of miles from home."

Barbara blinked. She truly appreciated Ginger's openness and friendliness, but her story just added to the confusion. "I can see that was very difficult for you, but I still don't see what it had to do with your eating problem."

"Well, I ate to defy my father—what the doctors call a control issue—and I ate to keep Mama happy, and I ate to protect myself from men. And then, just before school started every year—I'm a history teacher—I'd go to Weight Watchers and lose a bunch, which I'd gain back by the end of the year. Then I'd start all over again. But all the time I was—am—aware of my biological clock ticking. I want a good marriage. I want a home. I want children. Here I am thirty-five years old, and I'm having trouble leaving home."

The meeting was breaking up. Barbara nodded as if she understood; but she wasn't at all sure she did.

"Here, it's time to go, but let me show you this. It's really helping me." Ginger pulled a 3x5 card from her purse. "I carry this with me all the time to remind myself that eating can't solve my emotional problems. No matter how much food I stuff into my stomach when I'm feeling angry at my parents or longing for a husband and children, food will never reach my heart and satisfy its hunger."

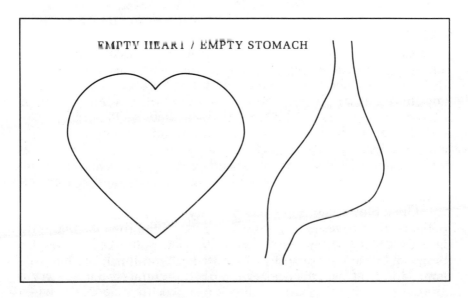

EMPTY HEART / EMPTY STOMACH

LOVE HUNGER

If your problem, as with approximately 90 percent of our patients, is rooted in a multigenerational dysfunction, then you may be walking around with a vacuum in your heart, which is illustrated by our empty heart/empty stomach model, the illustration on the 3x5 card that Ginger showed to Barbara (see p. 37). Every human infant is born with a need to be loved. Children with emotionally available parents, will, throughout their growing-up years, have their hearts filled, and then as adults they can fill others' hearts.

But children like Ginger, who are deprived of a heart-filling childhood, will walk around with empty hearts (emotional vacuums waiting to be filled, waiting to suck, pull, shove something into them) by the time they reach late childhood or adolescence. If food is chosen as the agent of addiction, these people begin feeding their gullets, just like an animal feeding its gullet with no consideration of the aesthetic pleasures of taste.

People with heart hunger will stuff their stomachs, either constantly or periodically, in an attempt to fill their hearts, but no matter what they put into or force out of their stomachs, (in the case of the anorexic or bulimic), none of it touches the heart. In fact, the more effort and energy they direct toward their stomachs, the less emotional and psychic energy they can invest in those things that could legitimately fill their hearts. Chapter 10 in the recovery section will present positive ways to fill your heart.

So if either of two things have happened to you: If you have come from a dysfunctional family (where, for example, one parent was an alcoholic or rigidly authoritarian), you may have entered adulthood with an empty heart. Or if you came from a normal family, but in adulthood encountered enormous setbacks, such as a disappointing marriage, a job failure, a death in the family, or a serious illness, you may now have an emotional deficit. This deficit can even be caused by the exhaustion and constant giving required by good things in your life: nurturing an active, growing family; career success that demands more and more of you; volunteer work that swells to take so much of your energy that you have no time left to recharge your own batteries.

Often the simple empty heart/empty stomach model causes our patients like Ginger to say, "Now I see it! All the time the real hunger is over here in the heart. I see now that no matter how much I binge or purge the stomach, it's never going to touch my heart issues." Many of the patients put the diagram on a card and carry it around with them, as Ginger did. We suggest they look at it when they feel a desire to overeat and then ask themselves: *Is my stomach hungry, or is my heart hungry?* And they often look at this diagram in counseling to help them remember: *When I'm addressing my heart issues, I'm also addressing my eating disorder issues.*

Our empty heart/empty stomach model is the core of most eating disorders, while a small percentage is primarily caused by physical, chemical, or metabolic problems. Only your physician can determine if you are one of this minority. We recommend you have a physical examination and discuss this possibility with your doctor.

SURVEYING YOUR RELATIONSHIPS

Now that Barbara has come to understand the delicate interweaving between food and relationships, she, just like you, our reader, is ready to take a close, detailed look at all areas of her life, past and present. The list we gave her to work through looked something like the one on pages 46 and 47 and, after talking about it for a while, we asked her to take the survey home, think about it, and answer the questions, as deeply and as truthfully as possible in a journal.

"Don't try to edit or map out your answers," we told her. "Just ask yourself a question—tell your subconscious mind you want to get at the truth. Then write nonstop for as long as you can on each question. Don't worry whether or not you're making sense; just keep your pencil moving. If the only thing that comes to your mind is a shopping list, write it down—get it out of the way; then the deeper answer hiding behind it will emerge. You should probably be able to write without stopping for about ten minutes at a stretch. Remember, no editing. If your pencil is moving, you're doing it right."

RELATIONSHIPS WITH FAMILY OF ORIGIN

The first area of your relationships to survey is your family of origin—the family you grew up in, whether your biological parents raised you or you were adopted, either legally or informally. Or did you live in the same house with your biological parents or one parent, but were really raised by a grandparent, babysitter, or older sibling? Or were you the parent in your home, even to your own biological parents, as Ginger was?

Besides recalling who performed these roles, how did you feel about them? Do you have happy memories? Or are you filled with rage or despair when you remember how you were treated?

Although unpleasant, it's particularly important to explore

your unhappy memories. There are three types of abuse you need to understand in order to evaluate whether or not your family of origin was dysfunctional.

Active abuse is the easiest to identify because it is violent and often leaves physical marks. Active abuse includes beatings, sexual violation, verbal or emotional violence, or rigid overcontrol.

Passive abuse is harder to identify because it consists of acts of omission rather than acts of commission. You need to look for what was missing. To develop into healthy adults, children must receive time, attention, and affection from their parents. If any of these qualities was missing or compromised in your family of origin, then there was passive abuse.

The *tyranny of the "isms"* in a home creates its own abusive situation which may have elements of both active and passive abuse. The "isms" we refer to include alcoholism, rageaholism, workaholism, perfectionism—any all-consuming behavior of the parents that denied the children time, attention, and affection or that led to beatings or overcontrol.

RELATIONSHIPS WITH MEMBERS OF THE OPPOSITE SEX

Being able to see repetitious patterns in your relationships with the opposite sex is one of the most valuable discoveries you can make. One of the most devastating patterns is codependency, in which one seeks to gain identity and worth through the approval of a partner. For many of our patients recognizing codependency with the opposite sex is a life-changing experience, which provides insight into their codependent relationship with food. One woman in her forties told us as she smiled her first real smile of excitement since she had entered therapy, "I can see it! For the first time in my life, I see it on paper. I've never—never picked a man that gave to me. I never realized that before. I mean, I knew there was pain, but I didn't understand it. Now I see the pattern that time after time I picked men who needed to be taken care of—who were caught up in their own worlds—and I tried to win their approval, but they never gave love or approval to me."

Think about your relations with members of the opposite sex. Think as far back as you can. It's especially important to focus on your first dating experiences, probably about junior high age. These first experiences likely were your first venture in intimacy outside the family of origin. Your choice of dating companions might have seemed to be a matter of accident or luck, but really subtle influences were at work. Early dating experiences are an attempt to transplant intimacy from the family of origin to a larger circle, and one will subconsciously choose situations similar to those in the home. Did you choose fun, caring companions who could give to you and share freely, or did you choose codependent or abusive companions? Simply list all the names that come to mind as you think back through these relationships from adolescence through young adulthood, up to the present. Then, in journal form, sketch out what you remember about each particular relationship. What was enjoyable? What was painful? Are there repeating factors?

RELATIONSHIPS WITH FAMILY MEMBERS AND FRIENDS

Now take a close look at your current family relationships. In your mind's eye, put your hand on the doorknob of your home. How do you feel about walking through that door? Are you walking into a warm, fun, safe place? Or does your stomach knot up?

If you are married, focus on your relationship with your spouse. One patient of ours who is married to an alcoholic found this to be a particularly revealing exercise. "I pushed the garage door opener," she said, "and I realized that I relax if Ed's car is gone. If it's there, my stomach tightens up."

When discussing with patients this part of their relationships, we often ask, "To whom are you married?" This always evokes a double take, especially if the spouse is sitting in the office.

Yet the question is not simply one of identification. We are asking, "Where is the greatest intensity of your emotional commitment?" Is your greatest emotional commitment to your spouse? To a parent or a child? To your job? Or to food? Love hunger can be used to build a warm, secure marriage, and that's good. Too often, however, we see cases in which it has led to overbonding with a parent or a child or something outside the marriage relationship or even something nonhuman, like food.

The tightest love bond needs to be between spouses. This, then, creates a secure atmosphere for the children. In any home where the spouses are not truly married to each other, there will be dysfunction. This is an especially important area for compulsive overeaters because there is always some degree to which the food-obsessive person is married to food.

Besides looking at your relationships with those living in your home such as spouse, children, roommate, or elderly parents, look at your friendships. Who are your close friends? What do you do for them? What do they do for you? It's very common for patients to respond to this question with blank stares and astonished silences. A great many compulsive eaters have allowed food to consume their lives so fully that they have no room for normal friendships. It's important, also, to understand that even in the best of marriages, each partner needs healthy outside friendships. It's great to consider your spouse your best friend, but the wife also needs a good female friend she can share with, and the husband needs a male friend to enjoy activities with.

RELATIONSHIPS WITH AUTHORITY FIGURES

When we asked Ralph, the roller-coaster overeater, to inventory his relationship with his boss, he found a repetitive pattern.

"Every time I got a promotion," he told us, "I'd go on an eating binge. You see, I'd tell myself, deep down inside, *I'm not worth it. If they really knew who I was, they wouldn't give me this job.* And so it would set me off—I'd go into deep depression over guilt feelings that *I'm not who they really think I am,* and then I'd start acting out all my diseases, and the weight would spiral back up.

"Then I'd go out the back door and go in for treatment. Go out and stay gone for six or eight weeks. And then I'd come back, and they'd say, 'Where have you been?' And I wouldn't answer, and they'd say, 'Everything OK?' and I'd say, "Yeah, thanks.' And usually it was too late to pull back the promotion. I thought they should, and I offered to step down, but they said no.

"But every time they talk promotion, I think, 'They're setting me up. They want to promote me so they can fire me.' And I go out and binge eat—especially in the last three years since I've been drug- and alcohol-free. Food's the only one of my addictions I can act out in. Around the office they didn't really know what was going on, but the fluctuations in my weight were obvious. Some of the fellows started calling me Yo-yo—I guess that sort of fits anyway, since my last name is Yoland."

Look back through the relationships in your life, and survey the authority figures. Some of this will be repetitious of the first point we surveyed, but this time think of these people as authority figures, rather than in parental, nurturing roles. How was control maintained in your home or classroom or on your teams? Were you disciplined in a loving way? Or were you punished harshly in anger?

To evaluate the authority in your home, you need to understand that authority can be abused in two ways. Undercontrol by parents who ignore a child is as abusive as overcontrol from tyrannical parents. We offer our patients four guidelines to determine whether or not they received abusive discipline.

1. Was there any tissue damage? Were you spanked hard enough to leave bruises or to raise welts?

2. Did the discipline come out of a power struggle arising from the parent's insecurity?

3. Was there any humiliation involved in the punishment? Forcing a child to pull down his pants to receive a spanking in a shopping mall is abusive.

4. Was the punishment disproportionate? An anorexic patient told us, "The punishment never fit the crime. Once I was grounded for two weeks for refusing to eat the crust on a piece of cream pie."

Other aspects of your family of origin besides discipline may affect your relationships with authority figures. An example is a compulsive-eating patient of ours who is an airline executive. He does very well initially in a new position, but "then all the backbiting and power-jockeying start to get to me until I just can't take it any more," he said. In doing his relationship survey he discovered that these paranoid feelings came from growing up with siblings who were continually tattling to gain their parents' favor.

RELATIONSHIP WITH YOURSELF

Now we come to the hardest part of the survey. Take a look at your relationship with yourself. How do you see you? What kind of a friend are you to yourself? As an old music hall line asks, "Would you want to join a club that would accept you as a member?"

This part of the survey is critical because elements of low self-esteem will begin to show up. When Ralph recalled how the taunting of his classmates made him feel like a withered bean plant, he immediately saw how his relationship with himself and his low self-esteem had started him out on the addiction cycle.

One of the major reasons patients come to us for counseling is that they want better relationships with other people. The building block is: I've got to have a good relationship with myself before I can have a good relationship with people. I've got to have a good relationship with people before I can have a good relationship with food.

Often a food addict will come to us and say, "Just break my addiction. Let me make peace with food." We can't do that. We've got to identify the food problems and then go down through all the layers to get to the core issues. To help our patients do this, we often assign two exercises. First, take a clean sheet of paper and complete this sentence as fully as you can: "I don't like me because . . ." An honest assessment of the answer will be helpful in two ways. It may bring up valid areas where self-improvement is needed, but more importantly, it will show areas of unnecessary self-blame.

Now, on another sheet of paper, write a letter of introduction for yourself, commending yourself to a new person you will be meeting. Generously list all of your positive qualities. In this exercise give yourself full permission to lay aside all self-criticism. If possible read out loud this list of attributes to a trusted friend or recovery companion. This sharing may seem awkward, but it is a powerful means of reinforcing your new self-perceptions.

This part of the survey is crucial to your recovery. For at least one patient, it was life and death. Dr. Upton was a fine pediatrician who had saved the lives of many children, but his overweight was so extreme that it was medically defined as morbid obesity. In surveying his relationship with himself, Dr. Upton saw that because his parents never seemed to like him, he never learned to like himself. "I suddenly realized that it was OK for me to save others—to help them live—but that I disliked myself so intensely that I didn't believe I had a right to live. I've been committing suicide with obesity." This insight was the turning point in the doctor's recovery.

Popular recovery writer and speaker John Bradshaw says, "You are the only person you will never leave or lose," so you must have a good relationship with yourself.

RELATIONSHIPS WITH FOOD

This brings us to relationships with food. Has food been a friend to you? Most food addicts will talk about food the way drug addicts talk about drugs: "I hate it. I hate what it's done to me. But it's also my best friend. I can't live without it." In your journal, note how food has been a friend and/or an enemy.

It is often important for patients to approach this part of the survey as they did their relationships with the opposite sex, by beginning with their earliest memories.

Look for the progression of your eating addiction. Our patient Sally is a patterncard example of progressive addiction. During Sally's childhood, her mother had a mild tendency to use food as a nurturer, but overall Sally had a healthy relationship with food. As an adolescent, Sally began using food as a form of recreation, but she was active and had a high metabolism, so she remained slim. In college she began using food as a coping mechanism for the stress of grades and boys. Long hours of sitting while studying also contributed to the beginnings of her overweight problem. In early marriage Sally turned to food as a partner to compensate for the absence of a traveling-salesman husband. Now in middle age, Sally finds herself eating out of anger. Self-hatred has led her into a full-blown eating addiction.

Remember that your feelings about (and your activities with) food form a relationship as real as any relationship with another person. Your relationship with food affects all your people relationships—including your relationship with yourself. What are the recurring patterns of your relationship with food? When patients frame their eating history in terms of a relationship and chart it out like the course of a friendship or a marriage, they suddenly see patterns, and footpaths to recovery can be built on recognized patterns.

RELATIONSHIP WITH YOUR BODY

Seventh, you need to inventory your relationship with your own body. Again, go back in time and ask yourself, how did I see my body as a child? How did people around me view my body? It is interesting to think about how people respond to a toddler's self-discovery. When the three-month-old, sitting in his infant seat, discovers his toes, Daddy runs for the movie camera, and Mama applauds as Junior kicks his feet in delight. When Junior discovers his own ear and goos and gurgles, the family responds with corresponding oohs and aahs. But when Junior walks in without his diaper on to show what he's discovered, there is dismay. So what were the body messages you received as you grew up?

Then in adolescence and puberty, what did you hear about your body? What were you told about sexuality and body shape and body size? Were you told that if you're not large here or small here, you're not a real man or a real woman? We see many women in our hospital unit—beautiful women physically and emotionally—who had one body part that wasn't the way their parent thought it should be. They were told, "You're not a woman. You're not sexual. No man could want you." To a child or teenager, such messages come with the weight of gospel truth.

Then in your college or post high-school years, when perhaps you were dating more seriously and in the working world, what kind of messages did you get about whether or not you measured up physically? And, most importantly, in marriage, ask yourself: *Do I feel my body is OK? Have I made peace with my body? Does my spouse affirm my physical appearance?*

We tell our patients to ask themselves, *Am I disembodied?* Obesity and anorexia are ways to leave your body, to abandon control and ownership. Most patients have to give this concept considerable thought, but then they will tell us, "I feel like I've been walking around in shoes that are too big for me. When I turn a corner, my body doesn't really turn with me. I don't fit." On the other hand, something we frequently hear from recovered patients is, "I feel as if I'm back in my body again."

Do you have a sense of being at war with your body? Only when peace is declared can the healing begin.

MY RELATIONSHIP SURVEY

1. *Family of Origin.* During my growing-up years, what were my relationships with my biological parents? Adoptive parents? Grandparents? Surrogate parents such as teachers or coaches? Other extended family members? Siblings? Was there active or passive abuse in my home? Was there an "ism" like alcoholism or rageaholism that rampaged through my home?

2. *Members of the Opposite Sex.* Beginning with junior high or earlier, who were my close friends of the opposite sex? What do I remember about each relationship? What was enjoyable? What was painful? What situations repeat?

3. *Current Family.* What are my relationships with my spouse? My children? Anyone else living in the home? My close friends? Is my current home a warm, safe, nurturing place?

4. *Authority Figures.* What were my relationships with authority figures in the past? In the present? Parents? Teachers? Coaches? Military officers? Doctors? Employers? Do I have a constant feeling that authority figures are just waiting for me to make a mistake? Are people out to get me? How do I respond to criticism, real or imagined? Have I served in an authority capacity myself? How did I feel about it? Was my church atmosphere a loving one or rigidly authoritarian? How do I feel about God as an authority figure?

5. *Myself.* How do I feel about myself? What kind of friend am I to myself? Would I pick me as a best friend? Have I acknowledged that I must have a good relationship with myself before I can build a good relationship with others?

6. *Food.* How do I feel about food? Has it been a friend? An enemy? What was food like in childhood? What was my relationship with food as a teenager? How did I get along with food in college? How did that relationship change when I got married? Am I punishing myself with food? What different roles has food played in my life from childhood to the present? In recent years has food come to assume an increasingly important role in my life? Am I addicted to food?

7. *My Body.* How did I feel about my body as a child? What was I told about my body as a child? Was it OK to be the gender I am? Or did Dad want a boy and I turned out to be a girl, or vice versa? What kind of sex education did I receive in adolescence and puberty? How do I feel about my body now? Am I living comfortably inside my own body? Am I using food to wrap a protective layer of insulation around my body, especially to insulate my sexual features?

8. *God.* What was I taught about God as a child? How do I feel about a Higher Power now? Do I see God as a source of unconditional love, or do I view God as a source of judgment and criticism? Have I formed a personal relationship with God to permit Him to live and move intimately in my daily life?

RELATIONSHIP WITH GOD

Finally, inventory your relationship with God—with the One who is so central to many successful recovery programs for addictions.

Ralph admitted to us, "I have a lot of trouble with all the spirituality stuff in the twelve-step programs. I say the twelve steps every day, but you know, that third step, about making a decision to turn our will and our lives over to the care of God—well, I'd never prayed before in my life.

"Now I do every morning, but it's hard to understand how this applies to my whole life. It was easy enough to apply it to my drugs and alcohol, but I'm just starting to apply it to my food issues. I know it's something I've got to work on, but it's so new to me. And I know there's a whole lot of power that I can tap into—I've proven it by getting off drugs. Now I've got to prove it with controlling food— then apply it to my work—that would be progress. But it's a big change to allow God into my life in any form."

Working The Twelve Steps of the Overeaters Anonymous (OA) program requires inventorying your relationship with God in several areas: Do you believe there is a Power greater than yourself who can restore you to sanity? Have you made a decision to turn your will over to God? Have you admitted to God the wrongs you have done? Are you ready to have God remove your shortcomings? Have you sought through prayer, Bible reading, and meditation to improve your conscious contact with God?

As you work through this relationship survey, you will see many points where relationships dovetail in your life, such as, "Oh, I see—my relationships with my family of origin affected my relationships with authority figures, which now affect my relationships with my spouse. . . ." This was how it worked for Barbara.

For once, the papers surrounding Barbara on her bed were not discarded food wrappers. Long yellow sheets of her relationship inventories filled rapidly with unearthed memories as her pencil moved across the page: Little Timmy in the third grade. Except for his occasional bouts of calling her names on the playground, they ignored each other at school. But because his back yard joined hers with only a scraggly hedge between, it was natural to run to him whenever her father locked her in her room, or later, when she used that exit route to escape his drunken rages. And it seemed she never went out the window without fifteen cents in her hand—Mother always gave her money when she couldn't give her anything else— and Barbara and Timmy would scamper up the street to the drive-in. They could get a large order of fries for fifteen cents in those days. Barbara paused in her writing to lick her fingers, as if the salt still clung.

And then the pencil flew again as she remembered a hurt that must have lain buried for more than twenty-five years. Timmy took off as soon as the fries were gone. He was captain of his Mighty Mites team, and he'd go to practice, requiring her to scramble her way back through the window alone, now feeling abandoned by Timmy as well as by her parents.

Dating as a teenager? She paused and tried to remember. She couldn't think of one boy's name to list. There must have been boys in her classes, but she couldn't name one. Oh, their class president—was he Fred? Yeah, Fred, but she couldn't put a last name with it. All she could remember was turning away every time she came near him in the school corridor. She hadn't thought for years of how terrified she had been at that age of members of the opposite sex. She just remembered being shy and working very, very hard in her classes, especially art classes.

And then college. She left home, and for the first time in her life could live free of physical fear of her father. Maybe that was what had made her feel free to become friends with Calvin. Besides, he was going to be a preacher, so he would be safe. A preacher couldn't be an alcoholic. Yes, if she went back far enough—to the early days with Calvin when she thought she'd found a man who could fill the place her father never had—she remembered there had been some good times. She had felt so fulfilled she hadn't even binged. Not until the pressures of exam week when Calvin caught her coming out of Kampus Korner with a triple order of fries. It was probably the guilty look on her face that ruined her attempt to pass them off as being for a whole study group.

That was her first encounter with the legalistic approach to eating control. Calvin told her, "Now I want you to throw those fries in the garbage and pray for forgiveness right now." Barbara couldn't believe that she could still recall his words. She could even still see his long finger pointing at the garbage can and his bony wrist sticking out beyond the sleeve of his sweater.

From then on, she never left Kampus Korner without looking both ways, and she began purging meals even when she didn't overeat. Because the sermons continued: "God requires good stewardship. Wasting food when millions are starving is sin. Besides, a preacher's wife must look good. It's a good witness, and it helps His image." Did he really *say* that? Or was it just the message she perceived? Either way, she became very adept at sneaking, and the only time he suspected her of purging, she successfully invented a case of flu.

Her hand tired of writing. Barbara looked back over her last paragraph. So was that why she hadn't darkened the door of a church since she left college? What the doctor said about relationships' dovetailing was true. Now she wondered, *Had everyone at that school been as coldly legalistic as Calvin?* Was God really like that? Would God have abandoned her as Calvin did, or did she just assume she was unacceptable after . . . ? She began to write again.

Now she looked at the word that jumped out at her from the page. *Abandoned.* She'd said that about Timmy too. And her father. Her father *abandoned* her for alcohol. Timmy *abandoned* her for baseball. Calvin *abandoned* her for God—after she tutored him through six credits of English literature and he didn't need her anymore.

And then Tom. She thought she really had her life together when she met Tom. She had her bachelor of arts degree and a dream job decorating windows in a big department store. Next stop, a special course in interior decorating, and who could tell—maybe her own shop someday? And she wasn't even overeating much. Weight Watchers worked well when she stayed with it, and she loved her job so much she had other things to think about besides food. But Tom said she couldn't work after they were married. He was rising rapidly as a pharmaceutical salesman, and in his company the wives were expected to attend all the medical conventions with their husbands, to help entertain the doctors, and to be free to travel to frequent sales conferences. He'd never get where he wanted in the company if she didn't play the game with him. Tom was everything her father and Timmy and Calvin hadn't been. She'd willingly give up more than her career for him. Two weeks after the wedding he suggested she lose ten pounds and get three new dresses before the next medical convention.

But that would be all right. She could still paint and sketch at home. And as soon as they had children, she would have a wonderful time doing craft projects with her children. Only Tom didn't want children because he worked so hard and was tired when he came home at night. He wanted it quiet, and he wanted Barbara to be free for him. And she had been a good wife and done her job and seen him through three major promotions before the eating compulsion got out of control again. When she was twenty-five pounds overweight, she couldn't help his career anymore, so he moved out. Abandoned her.

Barbara's pencil quit writing and started sketching—the first "artwork" she'd done in years. She drew a rainbow with clouds at either end and a few last drops of rain falling on a flower bed below. This was her rainbow experience. All the men she'd ever known had used her and abandoned her, and she'd turned to food for comfort. Every time! She was sure she had some watercolors at the back of her cupboard. She wanted to paint her rainbow.

THERE'S NO SINGLE THREAD

As you have seen, the twelve causes of compulsive eating are intertwined and overlapping. It's a rare overeater who could point to just one item on the list, like cultural pressures, and say, "That's me; that's my problem. There's nothing else to it."

In group therapy we often use the example of a beach ball with its slashes of bright colors. We hold up the beach ball to a group sitting in a circle and ask, "What color is it?" People on one side will say, "It's red," while people on the other side will say, "It's yellow." Those to the left will shout, "Blue," and those across from them declare, "Green." Each answer is legitimate; each group is accurately reporting what it sees. But people need to see all sides of the beach ball in order to answer the question accurately.

Eating disorders are like that beach ball. Paul Meier says, "There are many different aspects to my compulsion. Part of my reason for gaining weight when I got older was the fact that my metabolism slowed down, and part of it was selfishness, a desire to gratify myself when I was feeling sorry for myself for having to study so much in medical school. And part of it was my subconscious desire to please my mother."

Doing your relationship survey should have helped you, like Barbara, to understand why you have a void inside you that you have been trying to fill with compulsive eating. Now you need to understand the whole addiction cycle, which begins with love hunger.

4

UNDERSTANDING THE ADDICTION CYCLE

STEPHANIE GREEN walked into Dr. Hemfelt's office with the somnolent gait of a sleepwalker, her eyes glazed, her voice a slow monotone. Her husband, Bob, was right behind her. Well over six feet tall and weighing hundreds of pounds, Bob brushed both sides of the door frame. He made his way straight to the blue wingback chair that partnered the one Stephanie sat drowsing in. In spite of the chair's ample proportions, Bob barely fit into it.

"Well now, Doctor, I don't rightly know why those insurance people sent us here. I don't mind telling y'all that the day that semi truck killed our Joe Bob was the darkest day of our lives. But Mother here and me don't need none of your counseling."

Stephanie rolled her stiffly permed, blonde head. "I freely admit that Joe Bob was our favorite—even if we do have three other children. And it was a terrible blow at first. Terrible. But then I found Madame Baize."

"Madame Baize?" Dr. Hemfelt looked at his notes. The Greens had been to another counselor and had discontinued abruptly, but the name was not Baize.

"Madame Baize is a sensitive—an intuitive—you know, a psychic. And she made me see that Joe Bob is happy. He chose to die this way so I could have the insurance money." She gave a wavery sigh. "It's so like that poor dear boy to be so thoughtful of his mama and his papa. In all his twenty-three years, he never gave us no trouble. And when he married that sweet Sharon Jean they just kept right on living at home with us. You know she and the baby were in the car with Joe Bob. . . ."

Stephanie's voice drifted off, and she settled back into the corner of her chair.

Bob continued the story. "Yep, that's right. And Mama and me, we figure the best way we can spend this money Joe Bob got for us from the insurance company is to use it on the family. We got a plot of land out Austin way, and we're gonna build us a nice big house and a house for each of our kids right around it so we can all be together the way Joe Bob would want it."

Stephanie roused herself from her stupor. "Just like the family of J. R. Ewing. We're gonna have our family all together just like at Southfork on *Dallas*. The first time I saw that show I knew what I wanted."

Dr. Hemfelt cleared his throat. "I see from this form you filled out that your children have their own families. What if they don't want to live together?"

For the first time that morning, Stephanie opened her eyes. "Well, why wouldn't they want to, pray tell!"

The conversation continued, full of Madame Baize's psychic revelations and Stephanie Green's dreams to recreate the TV show, *Dallas*, but never was there a mention of the most obvious problems in these people's lives: Stephanie's prescription drug addiction and Bob's three-hundred-plus pounds.

"Now, Mr. and Mrs. Green, if I were a medical doctor and you had come to me with a broken arm, I would have taken an X-ray first because I'd need to know what was happening inside before I could help you. What I need now is an X-ray of your family. I need to talk to your other children."

The Greens agreed, and Bob struggled to his feet.

The picture of the Green family that developed over the next three or four weeks was one of multiple, long-standing addictions. This was Stephanie's fourth marriage. When she was younger she had been an alcoholic and had frequently abandoned her children. When the children were young and needed a mother's nurturing with food, love, and spiritual support, she pushed them away. Now that they were grown and could nurture her narcissistic personality, she wanted them back.

Beth, the daughter, had succumbed easily to this emotional blackmail. Living in near poverty in a trailer house with two small children and a gambler husband, she said, "I'll do whatever you want."

Billy, the second son, was uncommunicative and didn't seem to care much.

But Larry, the oldest child, nearing his thirtieth birthday, gave evidence of possessing the backbone to break out of this codependent cycle. He shook his head at the doctor's question. "No, the accident didn't trigger Mom's pill popping or Dad's eating binges. Oh, maybe they turned a little more to their food and pills—after all, they depended on Joe and Sharon for everything. The kids even lived with them for a while after they were married. Then when the baby came and they moved to their own apartment, they went shopping together several times a week. The folks paid the bills, and Joe and Sharon just went along. Of course, they were both on drugs too."

Now it was Dr. Hemfelt's turn to shake his head. "And in all this time, has anyone ever confronted your parents with their addictions? Have they ever admitted there was a problem?"

Larry laughed. "You kiddin'? Can you imagine what it'd be like to get my dad mad at you? I'd sooner stand in front of a mad bull elephant!"

Dr. Hemfelt grimaced. "Well, Larry, you've hit on it exactly. We often call a problem like this 'the elephant in the living room.' The elephant is parked right there in the middle of the living room, and no one talks about it. Instead, everyone steps around it. And yet it's an enormous intrusion right there in the heart of the family."

Larry gave an ironic laugh. "Boy, is that an apt metaphor in this case. And I'll give you another one. Y'all remember the story of the emperor's new clothes? Well, I'm not going to be the one to tell the emperor he's naked."

On the Greens' next visit, Dr. Hemfelt knew it was time for him to confront the elephant sitting in his blue chair. There is always a critical time in therapy when the therapist has to act like a mirror for his patient—to hold the mirror up and say, "This is what I see. Are you willing to deal with it?"

"Bob, do you believe your weight is a factor in the depression and family problems you have told me about?"

Bob shrugged. "Well, I know how to control my weight. Most of it comes from drinking. I'll just cut back on my beer, and the weight'll come off."

Stephanie didn't bat an eye.

The doctor was not to be put off by Bob's evasion. "Bob, I'm afraid the situation is much more serious than that. I need to tell you what I see here. I see food addiction, chemical addiction, relationship addiction, and money addiction. Now all of these are very serious, but they can be conquered. The addiction cycle can be broken. But first you have to admit they exist. If you want help, you'll have to stop denying you're addicted."

The elephant in the living room didn't thunder. He just breathed very, very heavily as he lumbered to his feet and moseyed out the door, with Stephanie sleepwalking behind him.

BREAKING THROUGH DENIAL

Denial isn't always as dramatic or as impenetrable as in the case of the Greens, but some form of denial is always present in an addiction cycle. Denial keeps the addiction cycle going. Denial keeps a person from seeing the elephant in the living room. Denial makes it impossible for a doctor to help an addict or for an addict to help himself.

Most people, even those who readily admit that they have a problem, don't understand the depth of an eating compulsion. The paradox of the situation is that while food is a problem, it is not the real issue. People identify their problem as food when it really might be codependency or love hunger or depression. And in an inverted way, admitting to the food addiction can be its own form of denial, a denial of the deeper problem. "If I can just lose fifty pounds, my marriage problems will disappear." The first stop on the road map to recovery must be breaking through denial.

THE MIRROR ON THE WALL

If you were in therapy, at some point the therapist would endeavor to serve as a mirror to you and say, "This is what I see."

Eating-disordered persons will see themselves as heavier or lighter than they are—and that is a part of denial, a key aspect of addiction. Consider the alcohol-addicted person. He never really thinks he's drunk. An alcoholic treatment center will automatically multiply whatever amount a patient says he's been drinking by a factor of three. If the patient says, "I've been having five or six beers a night," the treatment center assumes that probably means fifteen. Any addiction destroys the person's ability to see objectively.

And this applies equally to the undereater and the overeater. When an eighty-five-pound patient tells her therapist, "I need to lose a little more weight," he will say, "I realize you can't see this, and my saying it won't help, but we need to establish that you are dangerously emaciated." (TO MAKE THIN, AS BY STARVATION OR ILLNESS)

We all remember the story of Snow White. The mirror on the wall did not lie to the wicked queen, and she was driven to attempted murder in her rage. But the truth spoken by your human mirror need not be a threatening, enraging enemy. The truth can be your key to recovery. Knowing the truth about food can free you of your bondage to it.

So although the wicked queen let the truth of her mirror drive her to murder, and Bob Green stalked out of therapy when confronted with a mirror that showed his multiple addictions, you can use the truth about your own addictions to break through denial. Bob's son, Larry, is doing just that. Happily, he continues in therapy and is making progress on breaking out of the codependency cycle he was trapped in.

Let's pause to understand the complex nature of the addiction cycle you are battling. Remember, we promised answers that work, not easy answers. Take comfort in the fact that this problem will be conquerable when we face all the truth.

UNDERSTANDING THE ADDICTION CYCLE

Understanding a problem is always the first step to conquering it. When Ralph, whom his fellow workers nicknamed the "Yo-yo Man," came to us for help with his food addiction, he still did not understand the six-step downward spiral of an addiction, even though he had his alcoholism under control with the help of Alcoholics Anonymous.

1. LOVE HUNGER

We explained to Ralph that love hunger is the trigger mechanism that sets off the addiction cycle like the first domino in a circle of dominoes, with each stage bumping into the next to continue the spiral. A circle of dominoes would all fall, however, and then be finished, but in the addiction cycle, the stages continue to go around and around, bumping one another and leading the addict deeper and deeper into the addiction.

As you saw while doing your relationship survey in the last chapter, love hunger most often begins in childhood. Anyone from a dysfunctional family is likely to enter adulthood with love hunger, but one can get on the addiction cycle later in life as well. A disastrous love affair, a severe disappointment, a trauma at work, a disfiguring disease—any of these things can trigger the falling dominoes.

2. LOW SELF-ESTEEM (Emotional Pain)

Low self-esteem is a symptom of having experienced a love-hungry childhood. Low self-esteem is felt as pain, and one searches for an anesthetic to dull the agony of the crashing dominoes.

As soon as we explained this to Ralph he understood what we were talking about. "Yeah, how well I know. You know, just last week I dreamed I was back in the third grade, and the kids were laughing at my clothes. I can still feel myself shrinking inside."

3. THE ADDICTIVE AGENT (Food as an Anesthetic)

In searching for a way to make the pain bearable, people turn to a narcotic agent that will anesthetize their pain, even for a short period of time. For some it's alcohol; for others, drugs or sex or rage or spending. For still others—those to whom this book is dedicated—it's food.

In Chapter 2 we explained how food can act as a tranquilizer, either simply by raising blood sugar levels or by increasing the output of the neurochemicals known as endorphins. And we explained how an obsession with food and dieting can be used to block out having to cope mentally or emotionally with other factors in one's life. A person doing this is using food as a hypnotic agent. Finally, there is the ultimate extreme of using food as an anesthetic—eating until one passes out. This is exactly the same as the alcoholic who drinks until he passes out because the earlier stages of euphoria and numbness aren't enough to ease his pain.

In addition, food is not only an anesthetic, but also the fuel that perpetuates the cycle with the pain of its consequences. The overeater turns to food as an anesthetic to kill the pain and at the same time uses food as a means of self-punishment to generate pain. This dual function of food can cause an addiction to continue like a feedback belt. The more people eat to kill the pain, the more they inflict punishment on themselves.

We have long condemned the drinker but condoned the compulsive overeater. "After all," people say, "we all eat—especially at church dinners, and eating doesn't impair your actions." It is true that normally one can overeat and still drive a car, but there are published case studies of compulsive eaters who binge while driving and suddenly find themselves in a town miles off their route.

Whether or not the food addict reaches that extreme stage, however, he must realize that he is as emotionally impaired as the alcoholic. In fact, emotionally, eating might be even worse. With most alcoholics there are times when they are not drunk. Many alcoholics binge drink with long dry spells in between. But the food addicts have very few times when they aren't food obsessed. It is not at all uncommon for a binge eater to indulge daily or several times a day in his narcotic agent—and to be constantly thinking about it between times. Even times of dieting and weight loss involve a mental obsession with the absence of food.

Ralph's face lit and we could see that he had reached a new level of understanding. "Yeah, I see. My yo-yo eating was just like the dry spells with my drinking. And then I'd fall off the wagon with one or the other—or maybe both." He paused a moment to think. "Food as an anesthetic . . . ," he nodded. "Yeah, I knew I sometimes drank to forget. I never realized I ate for the same reason . . . but it's true. If I concentrated long enough on Grandma's beans and eggs, the taunting voices would fade.

"And later on—I don't think I ever visited my mother in that mental hospital without going on a major binge afterwards. What a losing game—the food does make you forget for a while; but when you wake up you've got the painful memories back, plus the guilt from what you've just done to yourself."

Eating is, however, not the only oral addiction. Compulsive talking is another, as is compulsive chewing—which may be tobacco, gum, or teeth grinding. Smoking, verbal aggression—a compulsive need to dominate a conversation—profanity, biting sarcasm, biting humor, or compulsive lying: all are oral attempts to satisfy an inner craving.

When we mentioned these multiple addictions to Ralph, he shook his head. "Boy, I was trying to ride three ferris wheels at once—or maybe occupy three seats on the same one. I never realized that my drugs, alcohol, and food were really all the same problem." He was quiet for a moment. "But I see it now. When the kids tormented me, I'd go home to Grandma, and she'd feed me. Years later, when no one was calling me names, I was still eating and drinking because I was still on the ferris wheel."

With the cycle of addiction bumping out of control, the overeater begins to experience the consequences.

4. CONSEQUENCES

Obesity makes life less satisfying. The overweight person finds activities severely restricted. Sports and physical recreation become uncomfortable, difficult, and finally impossible. This is its own vicious circle. Travel, too, becomes restricted, if not impossible, as the person is unable to fit comfortably into bus or airplane seats. And in less extreme cases, even light housework or the simple climbing of stairs may be "too much work to be worth the effort." In Chapter 5 we will give a detailed discussion of the medical dangers of overweight. Here, let us just say that the effects of obesity on your health are disastrous, and prolonged overeating is certain to shorten your life.

Over and over, patients have reported job discrimination resulting from their obesity. Statistical research demonstrates that obese people are less likely to be hired, to be promoted, or to receive raises. Remember earlier when we discussed the myths surrounding obesity—"Overweight people are lazy. Overweight people are inefficient. Overweight people are dumb." Unfair as it is, these myths abound and result in drastically smaller paychecks for obese people.

As if this weren't enough, obese people also suffer interpersonal rejection in romantic relationships, in friendships, and frequently even within the family. All this impels the dominoes to fall faster as self-esteem sinks even lower.

We can't stress the consequences of interpersonal rejection strongly enough. Loneliness brings us more patients than any other consequence of obesity. Think back through your relationship survey. Ask yourself, *Do I isolate and pull back from people? Do people pull back from me?*

We waited for Ralph's response to our discussion of the consequences of his addiction. "I guess I was lucky on this one—the army took me and got the flab off. The Brothers Speed didn't care. And my boss at the computer company thinks more of me than I think of myself. Oh—" He stopped so abruptly his head jerked up. "That's it, isn't it? I'm buying into those myths when I don't trust myself to take a promotion, aren't I? Funny, it's harder to change what you think of yourself than what others think of you."

We agreed with Ralph's analysis, because it is the internal consequences of the spiral that accelerate the addict into guilt and shame.

5. GUILT/SHAME

People caught in the addiction cycle are under the burden of false, self-imposed guilt and its darker aspect, shame. Parents can often start a child into the shame mode by repeatedly saying, "You should be ashamed of yourself." "You don't deserve that treat." "Shame on you." But the serious, even dangerous point is reached when the person tells himself, *I don't deserve to be happy. I don't deserve to be sexual. I don't deserve to be healthy. I don't deserve financial security.*

Ralph continued our list from his own experience: "I don't deserve to be successful. I don't deserve that promotion."

Shame can result from either false guilt, things over which we had no control, such as poverty, or carried guilt, such as when the child of an alcoholic carries the guilt for the alcoholic parent. Overeaters have a double burden of guilt to carry because they have the shame of the obesity and the overeating itself, plus the old shame from their family of origin. The two flood in together, and the shame is overpowering. The tremendous impact of a shame burden can be illustrated by the fact that most doctors believe that at some level all addictions are shame-based.

The final progression of the colliding dominoes is that as guilt, both false and carried, crashes into shame, the two pick up force and result in self-hatred.

6. SELF-HATRED

Oedipus Rex, who carried the guilt of bringing disaster upon his people and the shame of having committed unknowing incest with his mother, shows that self-hatred leads to self-destructive acts. As the Greek king gouged his eyes out with his own hands in an attempt to punish himself, an addict at this stage of the cycle will literally turn against himself. The obsessed person feels the false guilt, and the shame becomes unbearable. He must confess it and thereby dump it on someone else or carry it inside and dump it, with increasing weight, on himself. And here the self-hater will turn against himself and make self-destructive decisions. From the "I don't deserve to be happy" of the shame stage, the addict now passes to "I don't deserve to live."

"I knew I was lucky to be alive from the purely physical standpoint—the way I'd abused my body," Ralph said. "But when I rode my Harley on crazy courses at speeds that even scared the Brothers, I never realized it was an emotional death wish."

We sometimes call addictions emotional cancer. With cancer the body's own growth process turns against itself and begins to eat away at its own tissue. Emotional cancer can be just as destructive, just as fatal.

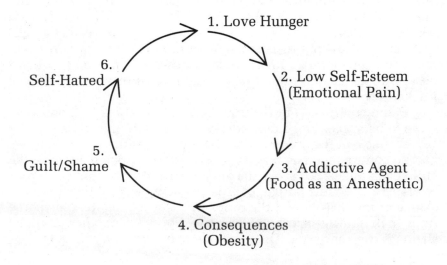

1. Love Hunger

6. Self-Hatred

2. Low Self-Esteem
(Emotional Pain)

5. Guilt/Shame

3. Addictive Agent
(Food as an Anesthetic)

4. Consequences
(Obesity)

The more shame addicts bear, the more they tell themselves, *I have no right to direct my anger at others,* so they turn it back on themselves. This self-hatred carves out a hungry place in the addict's emotional heart, enlarging the love hunger cavity and bumping its way around for another fall of the dominoes.

Reaching an understanding of the addiction cycle is often a rainbow experience. When the light of understanding breaks through the dark clouds of fear and depression and fills the sky with its many-faceted lights, the patient often says, "Oh, I see! That's exactly the endless cycle I've been on—and I didn't know what was happening to me. Now I know why I've never been able to get off."

And the most reassuring part of this life-changing understanding is the patients' knowledge that they are not crazy or abnormal. This is the inevitable working of the cycle. Patients can see that if they've been dealing with only one or two points of the cycle, usually #2 (the addictive agent—food), it's no wonder they've never recovered.

A person may say, "I take the pledge. No more fattening food for me." But if a person deals with only a single point on the cycle, the other points (consequences of years of disordered eating, love hunger, guilt and shame, self-hatred) continue to build up until the pain is so great that they will have to dip back again into the addictive agent.

This can be particularly difficult for a person with a strong Christian background. They will come to point #4 (guilt/shame) and say, "I'll just pray for God to take away my guilt and shame and that will magically take away my compulsive eating." It's true that God will deal with the guilt that all humans are born with as members of a fallen race. But this is only one point on the cycle, and if the other five points aren't dealt with, the person will be caught back in the cycle again.

"Dealing with the addictive agent, as you call it, was never much of a problem for me," Ralph said. "Once I decided to quit chemicals or food, I could go cold turkey. But I don't know whether that meant I was lucky or not. Maybe that made it harder for me to see all the emotional stuff. Now that you've explained it, though, it makes perfect sense."

We gave Ralph a chart of the addiction cycle to take home so that he could continue his self-analysis as hidden memories surfaced. We urged him just to let this happen, neither to force the memories up, nor to suppress the painful ones. This self-understanding would be the basis for his recovery, so it must not be rushed.

THE STAGES OF BINGE EATING

Just as the addiction cycle is a crazy spiral, so is the act of bingeing itself. Compulsive eating, as with most addictions, tends to be chronic and progressive. It may start somewhat innocuously, but over months and years of time, there is an inexorable progression. The bingeing may have started out just as recreation or maybe to celebrate something. Then people begin to binge on weekends, then nightly, and somewhere in the addiction progression, they realize they're bingeing constantly.

This is not an absolute pattern. Just as with alcoholics, some people remain periodic binge eaters. They may eat moderately for days or weeks, then go on a food "drunk," then moderate for days and weeks, then fall off the wagon again. But the most common pattern is that of the steady downward spiral.

This was the case with Barbara, who began overeating in childhood to assuage fear and isolation. Under the pressure of college life, these periods of bingeing and purging became more serious. Then, in her marriage, the progression which had been slow, spanning months and years, suddenly accelerated. In the year before Tom left her, her weight skyrocketed and Barbara isolated herself. In Chapter 1 we saw Barbara in the rapid, late-stage progression of an eating addiction; she had crossed over the top of the roller coaster, and her downhill plunge was out of control.

The accelerating factors of the addiction cycle we just described were primarily emotional, but binge eating can also be physical. Nutritionist Dr. Sharon Sneed reminds us that after the age of twenty-five, one's basal metabolic rate (BMR) drops 2 percent every ten years. For example, if people existed on 2,000 calories a day when they were twenty, by the time they got to be fifty, they would need to be down to 1,880 calories per day to maintain their weight. Lowering our calorie intake by 120 calories a day may not seem like much, but 100 calories a day multiplies into ten pounds by the end of a year.

Dr. Paul Meier, who is dieting his way back to his ideal weight, says this was his problem. "I'm about six-foot-five. In college I was ten to fifteen pounds underweight, and no matter what I ate, I couldn't gain weight. My friends teased me about being too thin. So I took a weightlifting course, ate protein pills, and got my weight up and maintained it as long as I was active in sports. When I went to medical school, I sat and studied a hundred hours a week and put on about ten pounds a year."

A common problem for women is the myth that "I can't lose

weight after pregnancy." In fact, the expectant mother simply got used to eating two to three hundred more calories a day during pregnancy, and probably four or five hundred a day more during lactation if she nursed her baby. She has developed a habit of eating more, and breaking the habit is difficult.

These simple habits can cause binge eating. Many patients get depressed that with advancing age and changing concerns, weight, which never used to be a problem, suddenly seems out of control. This discouragement can lead to lowered self-esteem, which, if coupled with stresses in the home or on the job, can cause the person who was not formerly a compulsive eater to develop emotional hang-ups about food and enter the first stages of the bingeing cycle.

SPECIAL ADDICTIVE TRIGGERS

Any addiction has its triggers—substances or situations that cause an uncontrollable "rush," demanding that the addict engage in the narcotic agent or act. For the food addict, sugar and chocolate are the most common trigger foods, although there can be individual triggers, such as Barbara's craving for French fries.

SUGAR

Of all mood-altering, addictive foods, sugar is the most common, both in the sense that it affects the largest number of people and in the sense that it is most abundant in the American diet. Consider the unnecessary prevalence of sugar in candy, breakfast cereals, processed foods, children's food products, soft drinks, and snack foods, just to mention a few.

And exacerbating the problem of sugar's ubiquitousness is its especially potent mood-altering properties. Many people will say that sugar, more than any other food, medicates depression and boredom and also supplies a surge of energy. Unfortunately, these alluring results are short-lived: the body rapidly metabolizes glucose, so the body demands even more sugar, and the addiction spirals.

Most people have long recognized sugar as an "upper." But the newest studies show that sugar can also be a sedative. Mary, a kindergarten teacher, came to Dr. Sneed with her problem: "I'm responsible for a whole roomful of five-year-olds, and after lunch I can't stay awake. Yesterday I actually dozed off and ten minutes later found them finger painting with the tempera paints."

Dr. Sneed asked the teacher to do a food inventory for one week, and the doctor then identified the villain as the orange juice

Mary regularly had for lunch. "A glass of natural orange juice contains a pretty stiff dose of sugar," Dr. Sneed explained. "Orange juice is fructose. Table sugar contains half fructose, half glucose. The glucose is absorbed extremely fast—that's called active transport. The fructose, which is the sugar found in fruit, is absorbed by a process called passive diffusion. So fructose enters the blood stream in a slower, more controlled rate."

Sharon Sneed explains that "There's not a lot of hard, scientific evidence that the more sugar you eat, the more you want, but some nutritionists feel that when all the data are in, this theory may be valid. In the meantime, it's important to understand that, chemically speaking, sugar is sugar. And whether it's honey, brown sugar, white sugar, turbinado sugar, molasses, or even apple juice, it's wise to control your sugar intake and watch out for any mood-altering or other physical effects it may have on your own individual metabolism."

Many people in Overeaters Anonymous identify sugar as a trigger food. They may not be rigid about any other part of their diet, but they've discovered they have to abstain from sugar. The more they eat, the more they want. Once they dip back into sugar, they're back on the slippery slope of the addiction cycle again.

CHOCOLATE

Chocolate is the second most common trigger food, and some fascinating studies are being done on this substance. The term people most frequently use in describing their feelings about chocolate is *love:* "I love chocolate." And we've all had fun laughing over the chocolate lovers' calendar, which says "You know you're a chocoholic if you dab fudge sauce on all your pulse points. You know you're a chocoholic if you consider chocolate the fourth basic food group. You know you're a chocoholic if you lie awake at night worried about the world chocolate shortage."

Interestingly enough, science now supports the use of the verb *love*. The New York State Psychiatric Institute released a study by Dr. Donald Klein and Dr. Michael Liebowitz which shows that a body in love produces a chemical called phenylethylamine. Chocolate is loaded with phenylethylamine. So when someone says they *love* chocolate, they aren't just speaking metaphorically.

And another study, which Dr. Sharon Sneed quotes in her book on premenstrual stress, indicates that women who crave chocolate just before their periods may actually be craving the large amounts of magnesium that chocolate contains. In these cases, taking magnesium supplements seems to decrease the chocolate craving.

SITUATIONS

The compulsive eater must also identify and guard against trigger situations, which can kick off a binge. We will talk in more length later about how to handle these situations. For now, you need to identify the situations that may be affecting your eating patterns.

Most compulsive eaters put family gatherings, especially at holiday time, at the head of their danger list. Many myths surround family eating, such as the often unspoken idea that "The family that overeats together stays together" and the more often spoken motto, "We meet to eat." For someone from a dysfunctional family, holidays, such as Mother's Day and Father's Day, can be incredibly hard to handle. One patient reported attending Overeaters Anonymous on the Monday after Mother's Day: "There were two groups of us: Those who were smiling and those who were groaning. I handled it pretty well. I thought about the holiday ahead of time, even role-played it with my doctor. I knew what I was going to say and what I was going to eat. It wasn't too bad. About half the room agreed with me. The others said, 'Well, it was pretty awful. I lost it. But I'll do better next year.' "

Parties and award banquets, especially those centered on one's job or professional organization, can be a special danger because of the peer pressure to eat, drink, and celebrate—after all, the boss is paying for it. In reality, the overeater pays for it by bearing the consequences.

Simply driving past a fast food place can be a trigger. If your route home from school or work (when you may be tired, hungry, or depressed anyway) takes you past a drive in you can't resist, you need to consider several alternatives. Change your route. Try car pooling or using public transportation. Eat a light, nutritious snack before starting out. Or try listening to a tape, especially one of the narrated books, either fiction or nonfiction, that will take your mind off the trigger. A friend of ours has used this method to refresh her memory of all the English classics and at the same time lost fifteen pounds. Dr. Meier listens to tapes of the New King James Bible.

The trigger function of TV ads we discussed in Chapter 2 can also apply to radio ads and commercials on the movie screen. To the sight and sound triggers of these ads, we need to add the scent trigger, especially that of popcorn in the movie theatre. A college friend of ours used to vow that his favorite theatre sprayed the place with "Essence of Popcorn" before every showing. A food smell can be a powerful trigger: fried chicken, coffee, pizza.

Finally, grocery shopping can be a treacherous trigger. The situation couldn't be more tempting: The food set out in attractive displays, according to the best marketing techniques. The buyer required to walk up and down the aisles perusing the shelves, plus the preconditioned notion that it's OK to buy; in fact, I must buy—it's my duty to take food home. Several techniques can make the grocery store a less dangerous place for a compulsive eater: First, never go shopping on an empty stomach. If you must market at the end of a work day, eat a light snack first. Second, make a list *and stick to it*. This will save you money on your grocery budget as well as keeping you from fattening impulse items. Third, if the kids tend to beg for cookies and treats, leave them home or drop them off at a friend's house. You don't need that kind of pressure. And finally, if it's too much for you, have your mate or friend market for you or with you. This won't be forever—just until you've broken out of the addiction cycle.

Most of our readers, like most of our patients, have probably seen themselves on some of these pages and are now eager to go on to recovery. But if you are saying, "Yeah, I can see that there are a lot of sick people out there, and this will probably be a big help to them, but not me—I'm just a happy eater. I overeat because I enjoy it. I don't need this psychology stuff," we invite you to probe deeper. There may be old hurts, old problems that have lain dormant so long that you aren't aware of them, but whose roots are strangling your progress with weight control.

Dr. Sneed says, "Whenever a patient says to me, 'I'm just a happy eater,' I acknowledge, 'OK, that may be the case.' But I feel that I've done a disservice to the patient if I don't really probe to see if there's something behind the mask. Besides, the threats of obesity to physical health are so severe that even a 'happy eater' should be concerned."

Anyone who has grown up in an alcoholic home or a workaholic home or a perfectionistic home—in other words, any home where there was any dysfunction—will be left with a scar that we call love hunger. And the love hunger must be satisfied and the empty heart filled, before the addiction can be broken.

While trapped in the addiction cycle, all the addict knows to do is to turn the pain against himself. In the second part of this book, the recovery section, we will show you how to discharge the pain and feed the love hunger in healthy ways.

PART TWO

TEN PATHWAYS
TO
RECOVERY

5

PATH ONE: PREPARING TO SUCCEED

ONE OF the most delightful activities of a trip to England can be walking the footpaths. The narrow trails meander through lush green, flower-strewn fields, beside berry-laden hedgerows or shady groves bordering pastures, and sometimes right through private gardens. The rules are simple: Stick to the paths, and don't let your dog chase the cattle. Why do English farmers and landowners allow this invasion of their property and go so far as to build convenient stiles (a series of steps) over their fences and paint yellow arrows on signposts to encourage the pleasant pastime of footpath walking? These paths are ancient right-of-ways held by the people for hundreds of years, and by common law these footpaths must be kept open as long as they are used. A footpath unused for a year can be closed off by the landowner, the stile abandoned, the signpost removed. In order to preserve this national asset, there now exist in England numerous footpath societies who make it their business to walk footpaths to assure they remain open.

We like to think of your food recovery and maintenance program as a footpath adventure. Sometimes the path will be rocky—some of the hills are steep with sudden drops—but the view from the top is incredible. We provide here the map to make your journey successful. But any seasoned footpath walker will tell you, no matter how good your map from the tourist information office, you may lose the path or think you have. The trick is to look around at the scenery, recheck the map, and make a reasonable choice on your own if you can't find another walker to ask. Soon you're sure to see one of those reassuring yellow arrows on a fencepost.

This section of the book is your collection of yellow arrows to guide you along the footpaths to recovery and maintenance. Happy hiking!

PREPARING FOR YOUR WALK

The first step to any successful journey is solid preparation, some of which you did in the first section of this book: identifying why you eat compulsively, surveying your relationships to find patterns in your addictive behavior, learning how the addiction cycle works, and breaking through denial. Now we want you to focus specifically on preparing to diet, what we like to call addiction control (the subject of the next chapter). We often tell our patients that successful dieting is possible only if they can answer yes to the statements on our diet readiness inventory.

1. BE SURE YOU HAVE IDENTIFIED ALL YOUR ADDICTIONS

Most people who behave compulsively are polyaddicted. The compulsive overeater may also be a spendaholic or a rageaholic, although some compulsions may be in various stages of remission. Before setting out on the footpath marked diet, look back through your inventories. Have you answered every question as fully as you possibly can?

Do you now see patterns you missed the first time through? It's not necessary to find more than one problem, but it's very important to be certain you know exactly what you are dealing with, so spend some time reviewing.

Now you must be willing to abstain from your addiction or addictions. At first this sounds like a classic catch-22. You may be feeling like one patient who said, "Now, just a minute. You're telling me I can't recover until I stop this. But I can't stop until I'm recovered."

Most people who have achieved the degree of understanding you now have if you've worked every step of the book this far, can get their addictions into sufficient control to progress into the recovery stages. A few of our patients cannot. For those who cannot achieve temporary abstinence we advise hospitalization. Here at Minirth-Meier we have a special eating disorders hospital unit that is part of our total patient care. If you feel severely out of control, discuss such a possibility with your physician.

But most people are like Troy, an alcoholic, who began by offering us a deal: "I'll counsel with you for a year. At the end of the year, if you've helped me understand why I drink like this, I'll stop it."

We explained that unless he could stop drinking we could not move on to the rest of the recovery process, because the ongoing abuse would wash out any therapeutic progress. "If you continue abusing alcohol while you're in emotional counseling, you're not going to be able to integrate what's happening in therapy."

Troy was able to see the reasonableness of this approach. He was able to stay dry long enough (with only two lapses) so that he could reach a level of emotional recovery that made permanent abstinence feasible for him. This is equally true for the compulsive eater because of the mood-altering properties of food.

Always, you must keep in mind that the emotional issues and the food issues are so closely interwoven that working on one strand alone would be as impossible as trying to cut a shirt from a piece of fabric that had warp threads, but no woof.

2. BE SURE YOU HAVE BROKEN THROUGH DENIAL

The universal response to being told of a tragedy is, "No! That can't be true!" The human reaction is to think that if we don't admit it, it didn't happen. But denial is only valid as a defense mechanism to get one through the first terrible shock of grief.

As we saw in Chapter 4, denial must be broken before healing can begin. You must say, "I have a food addiction" as the first step to understanding and getting off the addiction cycle. To open the gate on denial is to open the gate on all the footpaths. You can't get to recovery if that first gate stays locked.

We often find our patients in one or a combination of the following seven areas of denial. In any of the areas there are two levels of denial. There is conscious denial where the patient says to himself, *I know the truth, but I won't admit it*. That patient will look the therapist right in the eye and lie about his feelings, but give himself away in many little ways. There is also unconscious denial. A patient in unconscious denial could pass a lie detector test. He is truly in a state of amnesia. When he says, "My past was normal and happy," he thinks he means it. When the amnesia is punctured with therapy, the memories will flood back and can be dealt with.

See if you identify with the most frequently heard statements for each area of denial, which are listed on pages 72–74. Many of these statements are what John Bradshaw calls "rational lies." At first they sound like healthy, rational statements, while in truth they are emotional lies, covering the need to go back and dig out pain.

One of the best ways to be absolutely certain that no vestiges of denial linger, sabotaging your progress, is to fully acknowledge your addiction in writing. Take a clean sheet of paper, even a piece of personalized stationery if you like, and write a letter to yourself. Tell yourself exactly what you now understand about your addiction, why you are addicted, and what you plan to do about it. Make a full acknowledgment: *I am food dependent. I want to surrender*

TYPICAL DENIAL STATEMENTS

In each category, place a check mark by the statements that you make. Then make a conscious effort to stop telling these lies.

1. DENIAL THAT WEIGHT AND BODY IMAGE ARE A PROBLEM

____"I can lose this weight anytime I want to. I just don't choose to diet."

____"I eat just like everyone else. My metabolism is just slow, and my family is large boned."

____"My weight doesn't bother me. People really don't notice—they judge me by what's on the inside."

____"My doctor says I have to lose this weight, but what do doctors know? If weight doesn't get me, it'll be cancer or pollution or falling under a bus. Better to go out eating a chocolate fudge sundae."

____"When I'm ready to lose this weight, I can buckle down and do it by willpower."

2. DENIAL OF FAMILY OF ORIGIN PAIN

____"The past is the past. I've forgotten what it was like growing up in my family."

____"Sure it was tough in my family. But I've buried that pain, and no one's going to make me dig it up." We call this attitude militant denial. The pain is buried, but it's like burying toxic chemicals. The canisters may be out of sight, but eventually they'll leak their poisonous contents back to the surface.

____"My parents did the best they knew how. I can't blame them for what I am now."

____"People tell me I need to tell my mother, 'No.' She calls me every day, but I enjoy the security. She's trying to help me lose weight. She lectures me every day and never complains about the long distance phone bills."

3. DENIAL OF CURRENT RELATIONSHIP PAIN

____"I love my wife. Sure we fight like cats and dogs—but doesn't everybody?" (Your denial mechanism will always try to tell you that the status quo is normal.)

____"I couldn't ask for anyone better than my husband. He works a lot and is gone a lot, but that's because he wants to provide so well. Our relationship doesn't affect my weight."

____"There's no connection between food issues and people relationships in my life."

____"I know I'm afraid to date and afraid to assert myself at work. But I keep telling myself that if I'd ever lose this weight, then things would start clicking for me." (This is the old cart-before-the-horse syndrome. The patient has things in reverse; relationships must be in order before food issues can be in control.)

____"My relationships at home and the office are a mess. But what has that got to do with the fact that all the different diets have never worked? I know that someday I'll find the right diet that works." (We call this magical thinking—the right formula will do it.)

4. DENIAL OF THE EXISTENCE OF LOVE HUNGER

____"I'm a happy person. I don't understand why you keep insisting that my emotional needs have gone unmet just because I carry this extra weight." (This is a signal to look for what we call smiling depression. Many unhappy people plaster on a smile bright enough that they almost fool themselves along with everyone else.)

____"I guess I've gotten just about as much love as I deserve. I didn't get much from Mom and Dad, but maybe that was my fault—I never seemed to be able to make them happy."

5. DENIAL OF ANGER

____"You tell me I eat out of anger. But how can I be angry at my husband? In fact, I have him on a pedestal. I don't feel I deserve his love, so how could I blame him?" (Anytime one partner is on a pedestal, we find anger because, like children on a seesaw, when one is up, the other has to be down.)

____"I'm not angry at my wife. We don't have much of a marriage. If you want to know the truth, we don't sleep together anymore, but I'm not angry." (Lack of physical or verbal intimacy always reflects anger.)

6. DENIAL THAT I DESERVE HELP

____"I've never felt pretty. It's hard to imagine that God wants me to have a body that's healthy and attractive."

____"Life has always been tough for me. I read and hear about people turning their lives around, but I just don't feel I deserve any of that." (Denial caused by such severe low self-esteem is one of the hardest gates to open to get onto a recovery footpath.)

7. DENIAL OF DENIAL

____"I know myself better than anyone else. I don't need outside help to beat this weight thing."

____"People should be able to solve their own problems. I don't believe in hanging dirty laundry out in public."

____"I'm not denying anything—there just isn't anything there."

this addiction. I will work to my utmost to achieve total recovery.
Sign this just as you would any letter to your best friend, and date it.

One patient of ours liked this idea so much that she even mailed the letter to herself. She reported that three days later when the letter arrived in her mailbox, she was able to read it from a fresh viewpoint and found this to be an immensely freeing experience.

ACKNOWLEDGE THE PROBLEM TO GOD AND OTHERS

Step five of the Overeaters Anonymous Twelve Step recovery program is admitting "to God, to ourselves, and to another human being the exact nature of our wrongs." Confessing to God is an important step in breaking out of denial. When we take our problems to God, we can then see them as He sees them, and this new perspective will help break the denial.

Then, when we have seen the problem from this new perspective, we must articulate it, must say something to God like, "God, this is the reality of where I am with this particular thing. I admit that it is wrong, and I admit that it is something I need to deal with."

The final step is to confess our faults to one another. James 5:16 urges us to confess our faults to one another and pray for one another, "that you may be healed." The ultimate result of this process is freedom and wisdom; God has promised that knowing the truth will make you free, and Psalm 51:6 says that God desires "truth in the inward parts, / And in the hidden part [He] will make [us] to know wisdom."

3. BE SURE YOU HAVE IDENTIFIED YOUR TRIGGER FOODS AND SITUATIONS

An essential step toward abstinence is to identify your trigger foods and situations. If you're not sure what your own triggers are, look back through your relationship survey to the section on your relationship with food. What repeating patterns do you find there? If the answers aren't apparent, try digging deeper. Take another sheet of paper and do some more nonstop writing. What food makes me feel happiest? What food relaxes me most? If I were packing a hamper for a week on a desert island, what foods would I put in it? What foods do I daydream about? What situations make me eat most? What situations do I dread and therefore eat to get myself through?

Your conscious mind may not know its own triggers, but your subconscious does. Give it a chance to tell you what you need to know. Remember Joey, whose selfish father used him as slave labor? Identifying the fact that seeing selfish fathers on TV or in real life triggered his binges was a major factor in Joey's recovery. Identifying your own triggers will do the same for you.

4. BE SURE YOU HAVE ENLISTED
YOUR FAMILY'S SUPPORT

One of the most common causes of diet failure is family sabotage: husbands who bring home a wife's favorite ice cream, children who beg for freshly-baked cookies, mothers who prepare the dieter's favorite fattening food. Know ahead that this may happen, and be armed with a counterplan. Stock your refrigerator with watermelon or low-fat yogurt to eat instead of ice cream. Buy the kids packaged cookies of a kind you don't like. Ask your spouse to prepare the recipes in this book for you.

Use subtlety in preparing your family to cooperate with your new regimen. Simply announcing, "There are going to be some changes made around here!" is threatening to your family— especially regarding something that has as many emotional ties as food has. Change your family's habits gently. Change your family's habits slowly. Change your family's habits quietly. Instead of sautéing the mushrooms in butter, use beef bouillon, and don't mention the health hazards of fried foods. Take the wrapper off the light margarine, and they'll never know the difference. Serve the recipes in this book, but don't tell them it's diet food.

One of our patients poured 2-percent milk into the whole milk container for two weeks. No one noticed. Then she switched to 1 percent. They still didn't notice. Most people can make simple habit changes in two months or less, and people will like any food that's well prepared, as long as they haven't been given information they consider negative: "This is diet food." "This is good for you." "You've just got to get used to this."

We see many patients who blame their compulsive eating on mothering. They say they're buying the chocolate creme cookies for the children, but they go home and eat half the package themselves. They say they're making the chocolate chip cookies "because I want to be a good mother," but they eat half the dough themselves. Or they don't eat it and then are miserable while the cookies are in the house. It's a rare person who can constantly have chocolate chip cookies in the jar and not feel a consuming desire to dip in every time they go past the cookie jar. So why put yourself through that? The family doesn't really need those sweets anyway. Sometimes it's appropriate to make chocolate chip cookies, but we don't need them in the house all the time.

DIET READINESS INVENTORY

BEFORE YOU WALK THE FOOTPATHS
TO RECOVERY . . .

1. Be sure you have identified all your addictions;

2. Be sure you have broken through denial;

3. Be sure you have identified your trigger foods and situations;

4. Be sure you have enlisted your family's support;

5. Be sure you are dieting for the right motives;

6. Be sure you set reasonable goals;

7. Be sure you understand the medical risks of overweight;

8. Be sure you have your doctor's approval to diet;

9. Be sure you understand why diets in the past haven't worked;

10. Be sure you truly want to be free.

5. *BE SURE YOU ARE DIETING*
     FOR THE RIGHT MOTIVES

Do not start a diet to win love or approval. Don't diet for your husband or your mother or your boyfriend. Be sure you are doing this for yourself, or you will subconsciously be angry at the person you are dieting for, and that suppressed anger will cause roller-coaster eating.

The healthy position from which to begin a diet is: "I am lovable and loved just as I am." Then you are free to lose weight for yourself.

A person may say, "Well, I'm not lovable now, but when I lose twenty pounds, I'll be lovable." Even if they're successful in losing the weight, however, the emotional dynamics haven't changed. If they didn't love themselves when they weighed 250 pounds, they won't trust themselves when they weigh 150 pounds. The childhood scars that drove them to eat to a weight of 250 pounds will still be there at a weight of 150 pounds.

When this happens, disillusionment sets in. Someone who has dieted from the wrong motives will wind up saying, "I thought I'd win love if I lost weight. I lost the weight, but I don't have the love. I might as well go back out and eat."

6. *BE SURE YOU HAVE SET REASONABLE GOALS*

While some surveys suggest that as many as 90 percent of Americans consider themselves overweight, only 25 percent are, in fact, significantly obese. Remember the cultural pressures we discussed in Chapter 2, and be sure you, with the help of your doctor, set dieting goals that are right for your body. Life insurance charts can be helpful as guidelines, but there are other factors to consider as well.

One of the latest theories in weight control studies is the "set-point" theory. According to this theory, every person has a genetic point at which his or her weight is the healthiest and easiest to maintain. In an ideal world we would all reach our set-point weight at adulthood and stay there. Unfortunately, we all know this isn't how life works. But finding your set point and staying there can make lifetime weight control much more comfortable than trying to look like your favorite movie star or sports figure.

The danger of the set-point theory, however, is that some people assume it means that if they've always been fat and their family has always been fat, that's the set point fate has decreed for them. Yes, you were born with a certain body type and bone structure, which means that there is a weight range within which you will function best. This does not mean, however, that you are predestined to be a certain weight.

In order to get an idea of the range around your set point, look back at your relationship survey of your body. What is your weight history: Up and down? A gradual weight gain? A sudden jump after an emotional trauma?

Now ask yourself: At what times in my life was I happiest? At what times did I function the best? At what times was I healthiest? What did I weigh at these times?

Another factor in setting realistic goals is to consider your percentage of body fat. Most doctors feel that 15 to 20 percent of a man's body weight should be fat; 20 to 27 percent for women. The popular "pinch an inch" test is based on attempts to determine percentage of body fat. Unfortunately, such a simple do-it-yourself test is not very accurate. To get an accurate reading of percentage of body fat, one needs to be measured in at least three places, usually the abdomen, upper arm, and thigh, with skinfold calipers. Doctors, health club therapists, and coaches are often trained to take such measurements.

Dr. Minirth gives his patients a simple formula to use as a guideline. "Females should weigh one hundred pounds, plus five pounds for every inch of height above five feet. For men, weight should be one hundred and six pounds plus six pounds for every inch above five feet." Again, this is not an absolute, but can be a helpful guideline.

You also need to have realistic goals regarding how fast you will lose. Ralph lost his weight in four weeks, far ahead of the others in his group. This gave him a satisfying sense of accomplishment but has made maintenance a greater challenge.

For most people dieting at home, a two-pound-a-week loss is a reasonable goal. You must understand, however, that it is perfectly normal to lose faster at the beginning of your diet, perhaps five pounds in the first week or two, then slow to only a one-pound drop the next week. For this reason, many doctors recommend you not weigh yourself every morning. A temporary plateau in weight loss can be devastating to a dieter's morale and precipitate a binge. Slow and gradual weight loss is most effective and most healthful because it allows your body to adjust to new levels.

7. BE SURE YOU UNDERSTAND THE MEDICAL RISKS OF OVERWEIGHT

In our discussion of right motives for dieting, we said to be sure you are dieting for yourself. The motive to have a long, healthy life is an excellent reason to diet, and understanding the medical risks of overweight can clarify that motive for you.

There are eight medical complications of severe overweight:

1. *Cardiovascular*

Overweight increases risk for heart attacks and heart failure. This can occur on the left side of the heart from having to pump blood through so much tissue or on the right side from an inability to lift the chest wall because of weight. Obese people don't oxygenate well because the blood vessels in the lungs squeeze down and the right side of the heart has trouble pumping. This also leads to strokes from high blood pressure.

2. *Cancer*

Obesity increases cancer risk, especially of the colon, breast, or uterus. This is primarily because of the increased estrogen production from fat tissue.

3. *Lipid Problems*

Increased triglycerides lead to pancreas and heart diseases. Increased cholesterol levels lead to heart disease and gall bladder problems.

4. *Type 2 Diabetes*

Eighty percent of those who suffer from adult-onset diabetes are overweight. The great majority of the sufferers of this disease could cure themselves by getting down to their ideal body weight, watching their diet, and exercising properly.

5. *Joint, Tendon, and Back Problems*

Such problems are far more common in heavy people. Knees, ankles, and back are especially vulnerable.

6. *Pregnancy Complications*

Overweight mothers are more prone to having large, difficult-to-deliver babies, gestational diabetes, blood pressure problems, and convulsions. Obesity presents a risk for both mother and child.

7. *Surgical Risks*

Obese patients are poor surgical candidates. They don't heal well, they are prone to infections, they are anesthetic risks, and they are more at risk from blood clots.

8. Aging
Because of these stresses on the body, overweight people do not age well.

8. BE SURE YOU HAVE YOUR DOCTOR'S APPROVAL TO DIET

A diet is a lifestyle change, and any lifestyle change—even a healthy one—will put stress on the body. Therefore, it's important that your doctor give you a physical examination before you begin dieting.

Risk factors to watch for include heart attack or stroke history, blood clotting history, liver or kidney disease, cancer not in remission, acute psychiatric disorder, type 1 diabetes. Being overweight puts patients with these disorders at a much higher risk than losing the weight would, but these patients should be monitored very closely.

9. BE SURE YOU UNDERSTAND WHY DIETS IN THE PAST HAVEN'T WORKED

In 1864, Dr. William Banting published the first diet book, *Letters on Corpulence*. A century later, dieting and the writing of diet books had become a major industry. The 1960s saw the flowering of quick weight loss, fad diets, such as those recommended by Drs. Stillman, Atkins, and Pritikin, or the Beverly Hills Diet. Such regimens touted eating only protein; or all protein and fat; or only bananas for one day, only green vegetables another. Indeed, people lost weight on such routines, but the effects were ephemeral because they did nothing to change people's eating habits, which has to be at the core of any long-term program.

About such diets, Dr. Sharon Sneed warns, "You need to be suspicious of any diet that talks about eating only foods of one food group because it's been proven time and time again that you need all these different foods for the nutrients they supply your body. You cannot replace those nutrients with a vitamin pill. No vitamin pill is the equivalent of a well-balanced diet."

Some of the popular diets and diet programs in the past have been unbalanced, unhealthy, or simply outrageous such as the Beverly Hills Diet that suggested: "Don't eat potatoes; they turn to vodka in your stomach." Many others, however, such as Weight Watchers, offer a sensible, reduced-calorie method of losing weight. Nothing before in the varied history of diets and dieting has offered the comprehensive, approaching-the-problem-from-all-angles program that we present here.

For the first time, you will not be walking a single, straight path that ignores the vital territory on both sides. Instead, you will be following a map where the paths continually cross and recross on the way to physical, emotional, and spiritual recovery.

10. BE SURE YOU TRULY WANT TO BE FREE

Lord Byron's "The Prisoner of Chillon" tells the story of François Bonnivard, a Swiss patriot who was imprisoned in a castle on Lake Geneva for six years. When men finally came to set him free, the prisoner found that he had "learn'd to love despair":

> These heavy walls to me had grown
> A hermitage—and all my own!
> And half I felt as they were come
> To tear me from a second home.
>   . . . . .
> In quiet we had learned to dwell—
> My very chains and I grew friends,
> So much a long communion tends
> To make us what we are—even I
> Regain'd my freedom with a sigh.
>   (ll. 377–80, 388–90)

In order to achieve long-term mastery over your weight, you must want it enough to be willing to break the emotional and spiritual bonds that you may have befriended.

When this is done, you will truly have gone on your last diet. World War I was called "The War to End All Wars." Unfortunately, that didn't prove to be the case. Our complete recovery plan, however, *can* be your diet to end dieting. No, you can't go out and gorge again when you've completed our ten footpaths—that would not be victory, but defeat. The victory will be that you will be able to control your desire, physically or emotionally, to gorge, and you will know how to respond successfully when relapse threatens. Then you will be able to live in peace and freedom with your body and your appetite.

6

PATH TWO: EATING FOR SUCCESS

SINCE BARBARA had neither any idea what kind of diet she wanted to go on nor any solid nutritional knowledge from which to choose healthful foods, the doctors recommended that she consult Dr. Sharon Sneed. So Barbara got a medical check-up from her regular physician, to be sure she had a clean bill of health to diet, and made an appointment with Dr. Sneed. While she waited in Dr. Sneed's reception room, Barbara thumbed through a stack of popular magazines. Every one of them featured a diet article. Some of the lines that caught her eye were:

- At any given time 20 percent of the U.S. population is taking part in a weight loss program. That's 1 in 5!
- More than 1 million people participate in weight loss groups each week.
- The diet industry generates at least $10 billion per year.
- The most typical member of a commercial weight loss program is a woman between 30 and 50 years of age who weighs 154 to 176 pounds.

Barbara wasn't sure whether that information was comforting or not. It was nice to know she wasn't alone, and it certainly seemed to emphasize the cultural aspect of the problem. But on the other hand, the problem was so widespread that she wondered if there really were a solution. She noticed, however, that none of the articles talked about the emotional, spiritual, and psychological aspects of the problem the doctors at the clinic had been emphasizing. They said that would make all the difference, and she hoped they were right. But for now she needed the nutritional and diet information with which she could get her addiction under control.

Dr. Sneed welcomed Barbara to her office. Smiling, Dr. Sneed said, "I've been in private counseling for seven years. There is a lot of important nutritional information coming out—information that could be life-changing to so many people, but when I began this practice, very little of it got to the general public. At that time there were a few rather unprofessional people out there publishing in the field, but no one said the things I felt really needed to be said.

"So I opened a private clinic. Primarily patients came to me for weight loss, but common ancillary problems were high blood pressure, high triglycerides, backaches, orthopedic problems. Since I've been in private counseling, I've probably seen three thousand patients with a variety of nutritional problems, and I work as a consultant with physicians."

Barbara was impressed, and even more so when she noticed Dr. Sneed's two published books on her desk. *OK*, Barbara decided, *I'll pay attention to this. Maybe her information really will work.*

Dr. Sneed's first words made Barbara feel as if the counselor knew what she'd been reading in the waiting room. "Because of the large numbers of people involved in dieting and because of past fad diets and other types of unsuccessful diets that people have placed themselves on unadvisedly, I'm afraid the term diet has become synonymous with self-deprivation. Like the joke, 'What's the worst four-letter-word you know?' and the answer is 'D-i-e-t.' I think we should adopt the English term *slimming*, because that sounds so much more positive than *dieting*. But the thing I most want to emphasize is that diet does not have to mean self-depravation. Diet simply means bringing your life under control, bringing your life into balance. Quitting bad habits and starting good habits does not have to be self-depriving. It means that you control your food choices and the portions of foods you eat. The food does not control you."

"That sounds good," Barbara said.

A HEALTHY DIET MEANS A HEALTHY YOU

Dr. Sneed went on to point out that good nutrition and fitness help you optimize your own best level of health. If you feel better, then you're going to be more motivated in every area of your life. A healthy diet will increase your life span, but even more important than lengthening your life, is raising the quality of your life. "The goal of my work is not just to help people live longer, but to live better," Dr. Sneed said.

Then she asked Barbara to think of the last time she picked up a fifty-pound bag of dog food. "Remember what an intolerable burden that seemed just trying to get it out of your car? Think of the fact that if you are fifty pounds overweight, you're carrying that around day in, day out. Think how much better you'll feel when you can leave that fifty-pound burden in the garage and not have to carry it around all the time."

The first thing Dr. Sneed gave Barbara was some general dietary information on what constitutes a healthy diet. She gave her a leaflet similar to our Illustration #1 (pages 86–88), which includes the dietary recommendations of the National Research Council and Nutrition Board. This chart shows basic good nutrition and what is often called "eating as preventive medicine" because a healthy diet is of great value in preventing cardiovascular disease, diabetes, stroke, and cancer, besides the aesthetic reasons for maintaining a slim body.*

In the current American diet, according to Dr. Sushma Palmer, director of the Food and Nutrition Board, fat provides about 37 percent of the total calories, including 13 percent of the calories from saturated fat. Carbohydrates typically provide 45.5 percent of the calories, but the average American eats daily only 2.5 servings of bread, cereal, and grains, and only 2.7 servings of fruits and vegetables.

Barbara could see she had her homework cut out for her. When she thought about it, the information all made sense and shouldn't be difficult to follow once she got used to it. For the moment, she knew she'd have to post the chart on her refrigerator and refer to it frequently. She looked up from the paper in her hand and nodded at Dr. Sneed. "OK. I'll try. It doesn't sound that bad."

"No, it's nothing bad at all. I promise my patients that when they get used to healthy food properly prepared, they'll be eating better than they ever have in their lives. Of course, they always look doubtful at first. It's usually about three weeks before I start getting rave reviews.

"Now, let's move from general good nutrition to focus on the way you'll need to eat to achieve your optimum body size. I call these my Twelve Quick-Hitting Rules to Losing and Maintaining Weight."

RULE #1: CALORIES DO COUNT

"It's important to imagine the *do* in all capitals: *DO*. Calories DO count. Even though we no longer totally focus on counting calo-

---

*For full information on preventive medicine, see Dr. Sneed's *PRIME TIME: A Complete Health Guide for Women 35 to 65*, Word Books (1989).

Illustration #1

WHAT IS A HEALTHY DIET?

#1 Reduce the total fat intake of your diet to less than 30% of the total calories. If you want to count grams of fat, then you may do this by referring to the food charts and fat intake suggestions in the appendix of this book. The fat content should be less than 30% of the total calories whether you are maintaining your weight or losing weight.

• Divide your fat intake equally among sources of saturated, poly-unsaturated, and monounsaturated fats.

Definitions

Cholesterol—Found mainly in products of animal origin, such as egg yolks (there is no cholesterol in egg whites), liver, brain, and other organ meats and meat fats. Cholesterol is also produced by the liver. To see the exact cholesterol content of selected foods, see Chart 3 in the appendix.

Saturated Fats—Considered the most dangerous of the three types of fats, saturated fats are carbon atoms saturated with hydrogen atoms. These fats raise levels of cholesterol in the body and are therefore restricted on low-cholesterol diets. They consist of whole milk dairy products, palm and coconut oils, nondairy substitutes (especially creamers), and hydrogenated oils and shortenings.

Polyunsaturated Fats—These have recently gained favor because they help to lower cholesterol. Vegetable oils such as corn, safflower, sunflower, soybean, etc., contain polyunsaturated fats.

Monounsaturated Fats—Considered the healthiest of the three types of fats, olive oil is the most widely known monounsaturate. Its consumption can help reduce serum levels of cholesterol.

Guidelines

• Substitute fish, chicken and turkey (no skin), lean meats, vegetable protein substitutes (i.e., beans, tofu), and nonfat dairy products for fatty meats, fried foods, and high-fat dairy products.

- Limit daily cholesterol intake to 150 mg per day or less.

- Be very careful to limit your use of oils (even polyunsaturated varieties), egg yolks, and other fatty foods.

Suggested Total Daily Fat Intake	
Calories Per Day	Suggested Grams of Fat in Diet Per Day* (maximum suggested amounts)
800	27
900	30
1000	33
1100	37
1200	40
1300	43
1400	47
1500	50
1600	53
1700	57
1800	60
1900	63
2000	67

*All types of fat have the same calorie content.

 #2 Eat five or more half-cup servings of vegetables and fruits per day.

- Green and yellow vegetables (which are not considered starches) contain large amounts of nutrients for very few calories. They should be a dietary staple.

• Even though fruits are a good choice, don't overdo them, especially juices. They are relatively calorie concentrated compared with low-calorie vegetables.

#3 Eat six or more servings per day of breads, cereals, or legumes, unless otherwise specified by weight loss regimen.

• Choose whole grains and unprocessed varieties whenever possible as these provide you with more fiber and micronutrients.

• Carbohydrate intake should represent at least 55% of your total calorie intake.

#4 Do not consume more than 3 to 6 ounces of high protein foods per day (i.e., meats, fish, eggs).

• Emphasize low-fat protein sources or vegetable alternates.

#5 Get regular physical activity in order to help maintain your normal body weight. Your overall calorie intake and therefore your diet will depend on your meeting this basic human need.

#6 Alcoholic beverages are not recommended.

#7 Limit your daily salt intake to no more than 4 grams per day of standard table salt. This can be easily accomplished in many cases by not adding salt at the table and by avoiding overtly salty foods. (A 4-gram salt diet is roughly equivalent to a 2-gram sodium diet.)

#8 Maintain an adequate calcium intake. Women need at least 1000 milligrams per day (1500 milligrams per day for postmenopausal women not taking estrogen). This is more than the suggested amount found in the Recommended Dietary Allowances (RDA). However, recent research indicates that those values must be increased to prevent bone resorption (osteoporosis).

ries as diets did twenty years ago, calories are still important, and they actually determine how much weight you are going to lose or gain during a period of time." Dr. Sneed showed Barbara a picture of a balance beam sitting on a triangle:

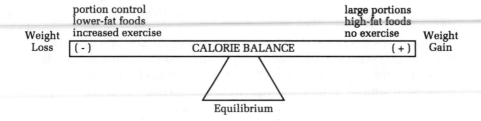

"This simple illustration shows how weight loss and weight gain comes down to an equation all revolving around calorie balance. If you eat larger portions of food, then you're going to have to put something else on the other side to counterbalance that. For example, if you eat large portions, then you've got to make up for it with either lower-fat foods or with increased exercise."

Dr. Sneed then gave Barbara a calorie counter similar to the one we include in the appendix of this book (see Chart 2, p. 292). "But you need to remember," she cautioned, "that not all calories are the same." The recommendation now from nutritionists is not that you just count the calories, but that you know where they're coming from. In general you should have at least 55 percent of your calories coming from carbohydrate, 30 percent from fat, and 15 percent from protein. If you choose to have a lower-fat diet, then the extra calories should come from carbohydrates. So you might then have a diet that's still 15 percent protein, but 20 percent fat and 65 percent carbohydrate.

RULE #2: FAT IS FATTENING

"Remember, Barbara," Dr. Sneed said, "the whole purpose of fat is to be a fuel source—a stored fuel source. So it just sits in our bodies—not requiring energy for maintenance—until it is needed. I equate fat needs to the big tanks of oil we see in petroleum-producing areas of Texas." She held out a chart with three boxes.

4 calories	4 calories	9 calories
1 gram protein	1 gram carbohydrates	1 gram fat

Each box represents how many calories one gram of that essential nutrient would be. You can see that the protein and the carbohydrate are four calories each for one gram, but the one gram of fat is nine calories. More than double the calories. Fat is concentrated energy for the human body, and it's a starvation protection. But in the United States, our problem isn't starvation; it's over-nutrition. Because of the rich foods we eat, we're experiencing an overabundance of stored fats.

And we don't really have to be on the currently popular national witch hunt for saturated fats. It's not just the saturated fats that are doing the harm; it's the overall high fat intake in the American diet. For example, *butter and the highly advertised polyunsaturated margarines have exactly the same calorie content.* They contain exactly the same grams of fat. The difference is that one is a polyunsaturated product and one is a saturated product with a little bit of cholesterol. If you are a normal, healthy person and don't have cardiovascular disease or high cholesterol levels (above 200 mg/dl, milligrams per deciliter), it doesn't really matter whether you have a teaspoon of butter or a teaspoon of margarine; the important thing is not to have two teaspoons of either product.

The more we're learning about how harmful fat is in our diet, the more we're able to do about problems that we once thought were permanent. Current research shows that you may even be able to reverse something as serious as coronary artery disease (to a certain extent) if you will get on one of these restrictive diets that only has 10 percent of the calories coming from fat.

There are three steps you can take to determine how many of your calories are coming from fat and to learn how to keep your diet to 30 percent or less fat.

1. Using Charts 1, 2, and 3 in the appendix (pp. 291–298) and food label information, you can calculate your daily intake of fat and calories. Then use this equation:

$$\frac{\text{\% fat eaten}}{\text{that day}} = \frac{\text{grams fat eaten/day} \times 900}{\text{total calories eaten/day}}$$

2. If you are eating packaged foods, read the labels and apply this equation:

$$\text{\% fat} = \frac{\text{grams fat/serving} \times 900}{\text{total calories/serving}}$$

This equation can actually be used in the grocery store. Take your calculator with you to determine what kind of frozen dinner you want, what kind of cheese you want, what kind of bread you want. This is one of the handiest weapons you can have for the battle to reduce fat. Remember, as long as you're consistently choosing things below 30 percent fat and making very minimal use of the almost 100 percent fat products like butter and oil, you'll probably be all right.

3. A third option is simply to attempt eliminating all fat from your diet. If you never eat any oil, butter, fried foods, or rich sauces, you will probably end up with a diet that's about 10 percent fat from fats occurring naturally in foods. This sounds like the easiest course, especially for anyone who may be "math-averse," but it means you never eat any fatty meats, cheeses, high-fat dairy products, or even packaged foods such as high-fat crackers, so you may find that a calculator is a wise investment.

Although this book is not about cholesterol, it is an important consideration in planning a healthy diet. You will note that most of our recipes are very low in cholesterol, using egg substitutes or egg whites. Cholesterol is not like the rest of fat; it is a different chemical compound from saturated or polyunsaturated fat. Foods can be low in fat and high in cholesterol. For example, an egg is not all that high in fat; however, it's very high in cholesterol. Cholesterol is the waxy substance that can build up on the inside of your arterial lining to cause atherosclerotic plaques. Especially if you're genetically predisposed, this can lead to hardening of the arteries and to coronary artery disease.

In general, adults need to have a cholesterol count below 1200 mg/dl. But don't be satisfied with merely knowing your cholesterol level. You also need to know what level your "good" cholesterol is, your HDL cholesterol. This good cholesterol protects you against heart disease. Your HDL cholesterol ratio should be 4.0 or below. Many Americans have a higher than 4.0 ratio, which reflects our overweight and rather sedentary population.

From our Percent Fat and Nutrient Content Table in the back (Chart 3, p. 296), you can see which foods have cholesterol and which don't, but in general, if you've got a cholesterol problem, you need to avoid egg yolks, organ meats (liver, brains, kidneys), fatty red meats, and saturated fats because an excess of saturated fat will turn into cholesterol in your body. Saturated fats include high-fat dairy products such as milk, butter, and cheese. It also includes hydrogenated products, tropical oils (coconut and palm oil), and nondairy creamers.

Remember, fat is fattening. It's the most concentrated source of calories you can consume. Many people simply do two things to lose weight: *eat fewer fats and exercise.* Fat is bad for your heart, bad for other physical problems, and bad for your weight-loss and weight-maintenance program.

RULE #3: FEAST ON FIBER

Dietary fiber consists primarily of 1) soluble fibers such as the pectins, oat bran, and the fibers found in many fruits, and 2) insoluble fibers such as celluloses, hemicelluloses, and those found in wheat bran and vegetable skins. Soluble fibers help reduce cholesterol by combining with the bile acids in the intestine. Bile acids are made out of cholesterol, and the soluble fibers combine with these bile acids to draw them out of your body, into the stool. This is the only way the body has of discarding cholesterol. If you include 5 grams of oat bran per day in your diet, you can lower your cholesterol level by 5 percent.

The insoluble fiber is primarily found in the outside hulls of wheat, rice, and vegetable skins. It goes through your digestive system virtually unaffected. The theory behind a high-fiber diet is that this fiber pushes the food through the digestive system faster, reducing the time for absorption of fat. And, of course, there's the fact that fiber fills your stomach and gives you a greater feeling of satiety. For optimum health your diet should contain 25 grams of crude fiber a day. This is almost impossible to achieve on a weight-loss diet unless you are careful to eat a high-fiber cereal every day or add a few heaping tablespoons of bran to some of your foods. Check the Nutritional Value of Cereals Chart in the back of the book (chart 4, p. 299) to see the nutritional value of the breakfast cereals you eat. Many people think they are eating a high-fiber cereal but will find from this chart that they have been misled. Shredded wheat, for example, contains only 3 grams of fiber. Dr. Sneed especially recommended Fiber One to Barbara. "It's my personal favorite because it's extremely high in fiber and extremely low in calories." Even people on liquid diets can blend half a cup of this cereal, which provides 13 grams of dietary fiber, into one of their drinks. This will help with any constipation problems they may have and add all the values of fiber to their diet as well.

RULE #4: CONTROL YOUR APPETITE

"Let me break that down for you into something more helpful, what I call my 'Super 8,'" Dr. Sneed said. "These are eight hints to help you control hunger":

1. Moderate exercise helps reduce appetite. I'm going to give you lots more information on exercise, so we'll just leave it at that for now.

2. A diet slightly higher in protein, such as one comprising 15

to 20 percent of your total caloric intake seems to help ease hunger pains because protein is digested more slowly. This should be high-quality, low-fat proteins such as skim milk, cottage cheese, fish, fowl, or other lean meats.

3. Eat a high-fiber diet because it expands in your stomach and helps decrease hunger pains.

4. Decrease sugar. Sugars seem to increase hunger because they raise blood insulin levels, which cause a drop in blood glucose levels about two hours after the sugar intake.

5. Eat frequently to stabilize blood glucose levels. You don't want your glucose levels to take sharp drops and then have to come back from that.

6. Don't overeat. If your body becomes accustomed to overeating for even one or two meals, the habit will form. One also tends to be more hungry after massive overeating than after moderate eating.

7. Drink hot liquids. Hot liquids seem to be more satisfying than cold liquids. If you are considering a liquid diet program, look for one with a hot soup alternative. Take advantage of low caffeine and caffeine-free hot drinks.

8. Avoid alcohol and caffeine. Both alcohol and caffeine are appetite stimulants and should be avoided during weight loss.

RULE #5: CONTROL YOUR PORTION SIZE

All anyone needs is one plate of food. One should not consume more than a cup of starch or of a lower-calorie vegetable at any one time and certainly not more than 4 ounces of meat in one meal. People need to become accustomed to the portion sizes with which they can maintain their weight. You have to be your own nutritionist.

Unless you have a special medical complication such as diabetes or heart disease, nothing in your diet has to be totally restricted once you reach maintenance. You can even have fudge brownies once in a while in an appropriate amount. Where most compulsive eaters go wrong is in their portion sizes. They eat too-large portions, especially of their binge foods.

RULE #6: TAKE SUPPLEMENTS WHILE LOSING WEIGHT

It is very difficult to get all of the nutrients your body requires when you are following a restricted diet. Choose a moderate vitamin/mineral supplement. There is no need for megadoses; they will not help you lose weight, and in some cases they can actually be harmful. "Look for a good basic vitamin that has a lot of extra things at 100 percent of the RDA level," Dr. Sneed told Barbara. In addition to that, she explained that many people like to take extra vitamin C supplements. There's probably nothing wrong with taking up to 250 milligrams per day of vitamin C. A few of the newest reports coming out show that vitamin C may have some marginal benefits in preventing disease and viral infection. These large doses have nothing to do with preventing scurvy, which is what the original vitamin C recommendations were based on.

With an increased emphasis on less beef and more fish and poultry in the diet, it's possible that mild mineral deficiencies may occur, especially iron, chromium, and zinc. Two minerals that women need to be especially careful to have in adequate supply are calcium and iron. A woman's vitamin/mineral supplement should contain 10 to 18 milligrams of iron, but no more than that. Check the Recommended Daily Dietary Chart in the appendix (Chart 15, p. 328) for a complete listing of the newest Recommended Dietary Allowances of the National Research Council.

RULE #7: BE SUPERMARKET-WISE

If you have the wrong ingredients in your kitchen, it's going to be very, very difficult to eat right. A healthy diet must start in the shopping cart.

Breads and Cereals. Buy whole grains whenever possible as they provide more fiber and usually more micronutrients. During weight loss the light breads which are 40 calories a slice can be very helpful in giving a feeling of satiety and providing two slices of bread for the same calories as one slice of another type of bread. The foods in the bread and cereal category are generally very low in fat and should not be avoided as many dietary myths have suggested in the past.

Meats. Fish that has not been fried and skinless chicken, prepared without frying, are usually the best choices. However, if you compare the dark meat of chicken to extra lean and trimmed round steak, there's very little difference in terms of cholesterol, fat content, or calories.

"Beef has gotten a bad reputation," Dr. Sneed said, "because people were choosing the wrong cuts of beef for many years. They were choosing fatty cuts, such as chuck roasts, arm roasts, rib eye steaks, T-bones, or porterhouse steaks. The ones you want to choose are anything named 'round,' such as ground round, round steak, eye of the round roast. Good choices also include sirloin and tenderloin. Tenderloin such as filet mignon—without the bacon, I'm afraid—is a good choice because this is a muscle that is naturally tender but is not usually marbled with fat. Also, veal is a good choice because it comes from a young, milk-fed animal, and its meat is not highly marbled. Even lean hams and lean pork roast can be very similar in cholesterol content to the dark meat of chicken without the skin. Don't let the bad choices other people have made keep you away from good food. And remember that no meat eaten in excessive quantity can be considered a good choice."

Dairy Products. "The one overall thing I want to say about dairy products is that too many doctors have said, 'avoid dairy products,' to people with high cholesterol or a weight problem. And that is the poorest advice I've ever heard," Dr. Sneed said. "In fact, there's nothing better for you than a glass of skimmed milk or nonfat yogurt. Adults need milk, especially adult women. Osteoporosis is a major killer of women in the United States because they're not getting enough calcium. The thing to avoid is the fat in milk. No one over the age of two should drink whole milk unless he or she is seriously underweight.

"Here is a favorite little chart of mine that can help you remember the fat and calorie content in milk."

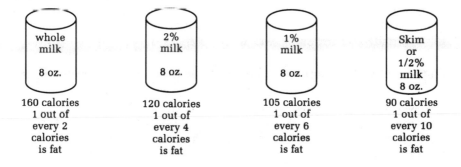

whole milk 8 oz.	2% milk 8 oz.	1% milk 8 oz.	Skim or 1/2% milk 8 oz.
160 calories 1 out of every 2 calories is fat	120 calories 1 out of every 4 calories is fat	105 calories 1 out of every 6 calories is fat	90 calories 1 out of every 10 calories is fat

You need to be very careful, however, when it comes to cheese. If you turn to the Foods and Fat Content Chart in the back of the book (p. 301) you'll see that cheese can be 70 percent fat or even upwards of 90 percent fat with the double cream varieties. Cheese has undeservedly gained a reputation as a healthful food when it is, in fact, extremely high in saturated fat. Although there are some lower-fat cheeses, including for example, Kraft light naturals, mozzarella (provolone is not a low-fat cheese), and some processed cheeses, cheese is not a good choice and should be used very sparingly. When using a cheddar cheese or any full-fat cheese, use a strong-flavored one and use less of it. Our low-fat recipes emphasize the use of cottage cheese and yogurt-cheese made from nonfat yogurt.

Fats and Oils. As has been mentioned, fats and oils have the same amount of fat and calories. Margarine is polyunsaturated; butter is saturated fat. If your cholesterol is down around 180 and your HDL/cholesterol ratio is less than 4.0, it really is all right to use butter. Some physiologists prefer butter because it's a natural product.

Of the monounsaturated oils, olive oil is the best one for helping to lower cholesterol levels, but all of the oils have the same amount of calories and can be used interchangeably. Again, the focus is the amount—use the least amount possible. Cooking sprays are very helpful here. These can be used to save calories in almost every area of your cooking, such as coating food you want to cook to a crispy texture like our recipe for Skinny French Fries or Buttery Popcorn. The sprays come in a buttery flavor, and there are also many good buttery flavor substitutes, which can be used on vegetables, potatoes, rice, and pastas (see our recipe section).

Dressings, Condiments, and Gravies. Once again Dr. Sneed spoke with great emphasis. "One should rarely indulge in a regular high-fat salad dressing or mayonnaise because it is just too high in calories and total fat content. For example, if you go to McDonald's and think you're going to make a wise selection by ordering the chicken salad and then top it with house dressing, you're adding 300 more calories to your salad. If you calculate how many grams of fat you had, you probably would have done better to order a hamburger. So always use a low-fat dressing. Choose a dressing that is 25 calories per tablespoon or less and use that light, cholesterol-free mayonnaise.

When in a restaurant, never choose anything but an au jus or a thin natural gravy. If you want a cream gravy or a thickened brown gravy, wait until you can make it at home from our low-fat, low-cal recipes.

Fruits and Vegetables. Choose produce that looks very fresh and has a lot of color. Dark green leafy lettuces and other greens are much better choices nutritionally than pale iceberg lettuce. You also want to look for things that are decay-free because decayed produce can actually put toxins into your body. Get a good vegetable brush and scrub your vegetables as well as possible, and then keep the skins on. The outside covering of most vegetables contains cellulose, one of the insoluble fibers that is helpful in pushing food through your intestine at a faster rate.

Processed and Packaged Foods. When you buy these, you need to be your own nutritionist. The main thing to watch out for is too many additives. When you buy packaged foods, read the label. Avoid too many artificial ingredients, and apply our rule of choosing only products with 30 percent or less fat.

Beverages. On a weight loss diet there is no room in the caloric allotment for alcoholic beverages since alcohol can stimulate your appetite. Fruit juices are not a good choice either because of their concentrated sugar content. Tea and coffee, especially the caffeine-free versions of these, are your best choices. Herbal teas are good. But best of all, drink water. Be sure you drink six to eight large glasses of clear liquids a day.

RULE #8: EAT AT HOME WHENEVER POSSIBLE

The latest statistics indicate that as many as 30 percent of the meals eaten in the United States are eaten outside the home. It is interesting to note that as eating out has escalated in this country, so has obesity. Restaurant food is generally more calorie concentrated than home-cooked food, because high-calorie products are easy to work with, are satisfying, and make the food taste good. If you eat at home, you can get more healthfully prepared food and can eat more of it for the same amount of calories.

RULE #9: MAKE WISE CHOICES WHEN YOU EAT OUT

When you eat out, you must stick to the same principles you would apply if you were eating at home. Don't give yourself carte blanche to have whatever you want. You still have to be on guard against hidden fats. Most people eat out at least once a week, and breaking your diet once a week will make weight loss impossible. Only the person who eats out six times or fewer a year will be able to relax the restraints in a restaurant.

Hints for healthful restaurant ordering:

- Help to choose the restaurant.
- Make up your mind what you need before you go into the restaurant.
- Be the first one at your table to order so that you're not influenced by anyone else.
- Don't order extras, such as alcoholic beverages, appetizers, or desserts.
- Avoid the complimentary extras on the table, such as tostada chips, bread, cheese, or spreads.
- Order the same types of food you would have cooked at home.
- Beware of hidden fats: fried foods, fatty meats, cheeses, sauces, mayonnaise.

Fast-food restaurants are so standardized that nutritional information on what they offer is readily available. Therefore we have included extensive tables in the appendix that tell you exactly the calorie content and cholesterol content. Check the Fast Food Chart (Chart 6, p. 303) before eating in one of these places.

RULE #10: BEAT THE ROLLER COASTER

If your weight has gone up and down like a roller coaster for your entire life, you need to rethink what you're doing. Many doctors believe it would be less stressful on your body simply to remain heavy than to have your weight go up, then drop by twenty or thirty pounds, and then zoom back up again. Recent research has indicated that each time you regain weight it becomes more difficult to lose that same thirty pounds. Something happens to the fat cells that makes them not want to let go of the fat so easily. Commit now to changing your lifestyle to one that produces slow, consistent weight loss.

RULE #11: CONTROL YOUR CUES

People receive many signals to eat that are entirely unconnected with nutritional needs. Walking through the front door can be a signal to eat for someone who has come home from a long, hard day of work even right after a late coffee break that included a cheese Danish.

Items in your cupboard can give rise to a temptation to eat. If you need to keep fattening ingredients, put them in the back of the pantry or on the bottom shelves or in the back of the refrigerator. Put only good choices out front.

Other temptations can arise from activities that encourage eating, such as watching television or reading, talking on the telephone, or riding in your car. Make a rule that when you eat you only eat.

Another danger time is preparing dinner or preparing snacks for other people. If you must continue preparing meals for others while trying to lose weight, do your meal preparations while your control isn't weakened by hunger and fatigue. Try preparing a casserole in the morning when you're not hungry. Then all you have to do is heat it up when the family comes home. If your children demand snacks throughout the day, fix them in the morning as well, and put them in a covered bowl dedicated strictly to the children. When they're hungry in the afternoon, they can come in and grab a little sandwich bag of carrot sticks, raisins, or ginger snaps. For more detailed suggestions, see "Behavior Modification and Cue Elimination" in the appendix (Chart 7, p. 311).

RULE #12: SALT IS OUT—SPICE IS IN

You should be eating about 3 grams of sodium or less per day. A simple rule for detection is: If it tastes salty, it probably is salty. Consult the High-Sodium Foods to Avoid Chart (Chart 8, p. 315) in the appendix and read through it so that you can readily identify and avoid salty foods.

Spice is in. Spices are easy to use, and well-spiced food does not require salt. Often you can also cut down on butter or other ingredients to be avoided by the deft use of spices. The traditional method of seasoning foods has been to sprinkle with salt and pepper and top with butter. You can continue using pepper, but learn new seasoning methods to eliminate the salt and butter. A healthful diet is not a bland diet. You can have all the herbs and spices you want. To help you enter the truly exciting culinary world of herbs and spices, see the Savory Herbs Chart in the appendix (Chart 9, p. 316).

EXERCISE

"Are you still with me?" Dr. Sneed smiled at Barbara.

"Oh, yes! I'm a bit overwhelmed. I mean it'll take me a while to get all this down—but I love it! It's so exciting to know what I really ought to be doing to lose weight and to be healthy and if I ever have a family to cook for. They ought to require this stuff in school. Everybody needs to know it!"

"Well, we've got another major thing to talk about, and that's exercise. We really need to include this in any discussion of diet because it's the other factor of the balance scale we talked about right at first when we agreed that the goal of a diet is to bring equilibrium into your life."

Barbara grimaced, "Do we have to? What's so important about exercise?"

WHY EXERCISE?

To lose weight and keep it off successfully, a regular exercise session of about thirty minutes a day is absolutely essential. Dr. Sneed explained that there are many reasons for this:

- Exercise builds muscle, or lean body mass. Muscle uses more calories than fat tissue and therefore helps you maintain your weight loss. (See the Calorie Values for 10 Minutes of Activity Chart 10, p. 317).
- Exercise improves body toning and body strength during a time in which the body is deprived of food sources of energy. (See the Benefits of Various Exercises Chart 11, p. 319).

- Exercise helps increase the body's metabolism. Very low calorie diets, those below 1,000 calories a day, make the body's metabolism decrease by as much as 45 percent. The body slows down so that it can function on such low caloric intakes. The body will also conserve fat in preparation for what it thinks may be a long period of starvation. This conservation of fat causes larger percentages of muscle to be burned and less weight to be lost on the diet. At this point many people abandon their diets because of lack of progress. Exercise and the greater muscle mass that develops from exercise both increase your basal metabolic rate and help offset these natural survival processes.
- Aerobic exercise strengthens the heart and lung muscles, thereby decreasing blood pressure.
- Recent research indicates that aerobic exercise lowers blood cholesterol, triglycerides, and glucose levels.
- Load-bearing exercise causes a decrease in calcium loss from bone mass. This is especially important for women.
- Consistent aerobic exercise increases your energy levels and gives you a more positive outlook. All forms of aerobic exercise will increase your productivity.
- Exercising thirty minutes a day will decrease your appetite.
- Consistent aerobic exercise will produce positive attitudes because it triggers endorphin secretions in your central nervous system.

WHAT IS AEROBIC EXERCISE?

"I hear the term *aerobic exercise* a lot, but I don't really know what it is," Barbara said. "Does that mean I have to buy a hot-pink suit and join a class at the 'Y'?"

Dr. Sneed laughed. "Not anything like that. But you have no idea how often I hear that question. I think 90 percent of my clients would abandon the whole thing if I told them they had to buy a purple and chartreuse jogging suit. Really, it's very simple."

Dr. Sneed explained that aerobic exercise is any exercise performed for at least twenty minutes at a steady, nonstop pace. The best examples include fast walking, jogging, swimming, biking, and aerobic dancing. The word *aerobic* refers to the presence of oxygen, and the principle is that aerobic exercise improves respiratory and circulatory function by increasing oxygen consumption.

"And that's really all there is to it? Just being active enough to keep your heart rate elevated?" Barbara asked.

"A wonderful summary, Barbara! That's the absolute heart of it."

Dr. Sneed then gave Barbara a chart of aerobic exercises (see pp. 103–104).

HOW MUCH SHOULD I EXERCISE?

"So how often do I have to do this?" Barbara asked.

"Maybe the question should be how fast you want to lose weight," Dr. Sneed answered. "To exercise your heart and lungs, most experts agree that you should exercise four times weekly. To use exercise as a tool for weight loss and maintenance, you'll need to work out thirty minutes every day."

Dr. Sneed then emphasized the most important point she was trying to make: "The more you exercise, the faster you will lose weight. To do this, you must find something you can grow to love. This means something that will fit into your schedule and your financial budget. I recommend fast walking or a combination of walking and jogging. But it's important to understand that if exercise has not been part of your life for some time, you may have to work up to thirty minutes per session. Don't get discouraged. Be patient with yourself."

We want to underscore Dr. Sneed's advice here because someone who has been out of shape and hasn't exercised for years may have to start with five minutes a day, and that's fine. That will be as big a victory for that person as a five-mile jog for someone else. If all you can do is walk to the end of your block and back on your first outing, that's fine—the key is to do it!

Also remember that everyone, before starting an exercise program, must see his or her physician. That especially applies to smokers and those with any kind of health complication, such as excessive weight, high blood pressure, heart disease, diabetes, hyperlipidemias (i.e., high serum cholesterol or high serum triglycerides), or orthopedic problems.

Another thing to remember is that casual exercise, such as belonging to a weekend softball team or playing a basketball game in your driveway a couple of times a week, is not an aerobic exercise program. That is increased activity, which is important for a healthy lifestyle, but it is not aerobic. Neither, unfortunately, is golf or tennis, because these games have intermittent periods of inactivity, which allow the heartrate to drop.

This chart shows how you can progressively build an exercise program to whatever level you believe, or your doctor advises, will be best for you. Start wherever you are—if it's five minutes a day, that's fine—then progress as you feel comfortable.

Progressive Exercise Program

Level	Duration	Frequency	Suggested Exercise
1	5 minutes	7 times/week	Walking
2	10 minutes	7 times/week	Walking
3	10 minutes	6 times/week	Fast walking or other aerobics
4	15 minutes	5 times/week	Fast walking or other aerobics
5	20 minutes	5 times/week	Fast walking or other aerobics
6	25 minutes	5 times/week	Aerobics, 20 minutes; Calisthenics, 5 minutes
7	30 minutes	4 times/week	Aerobics, 25 minutes; Calisthenics, 5 minutes
8	45–60 minutes	4 times/week	Aerobics, 30–40 minutes; Calisthenics and weight training, 15–20 minutes

Adapted from *Prime Time,* Sneed, Word 1979.

HOW HARD SHOULD I EXERCISE?

The only way to determine whether you're working hard enough is to monitor your heart rate two or three times during your workout. The following chart identifies the rate at which your heart should beat during aerobic exercise for your particular age group.

10-Second Exercising Pulse Rates

Age	Age-predicted Maximal Heart Rate (per 10 seconds)	***Training Sensitive Zone*** Lower Limit 70% Heart Rate (per 10 seconds)	***Training Sensitive Zone*** Upper Limit 90% Heart Rate (per 10 seconds)
15	35	24	31
20	33	23	30
25	32	23	29
30	32	22	28
35	31	21	28
40	30	21	27
45	29	20	26
50	28	19	25
55	27	19	24
60	26	18	23
65	25	17	22

Adapted from *Prime Time,* Sneed, Word 1979.

BASIC AEROBIC EXERCISES

Walking. Very popular but must push yourself for a full aerobic workout. Can take up to three times as long to get the same aerobic benefits as with jogging. It is very easy on the joints when compared to the added physical stress of running. Head for the hills as these can present increased cardiovascular challenges. Try to walk a mile in fourteen minutes or less.

Cycling. This exercise is less wear and tear on the joints than any other land-based sport. You must hit speeds of fifteen miles per hour or greater to have an effective workout. Though outdoor cycling is preferred, some of the stationary bikes also provide an excellent workout (i.e., Schwinn Air-Dyne, recumbent bikes).

Swimming. If you have problems with bone and joint aches and pains, then this is the exercise for you. You can either do laps as is traditional for an aquatic aerobic workout or you may attend an aquatic aerobic class in a local gym. These are similar in nature to other traditional aerobics classes, which include dancing, calisthenics, and floor exercises, except that they are done in the water. Again, this is an excellent choice for those with aches and pains. Make sure to check your heart rate as you would with a more typical walking program.

Jogging/Running. Be aware that this can put stress on your bones and joints, but you do get a complete aerobic workout faster than with walking. If you're trying to save time and can handle this form of activity physically, jogging/running may be for you. If you are thirty pounds over your ideal body weight do not attempt a steady jogging program until you have reduced your weight to this level. It is very important that you have an excellent, supportive running shoe and appropriate cool clothing to begin such a program. This can take the place of your walking program if you can work it in three to four times per week.

Aerobic Dancing. An excellent activity for improving your cardiovascular fitness, increasing lead body mass (LBM), and decreasing your weight. Forty-five- to sixty-minute workouts are usually advised. Look for the low-impact classes if you are having joint problems.

Circuit Training. Circuit training simply means that you are doing calisthenic-type or weight training (free weights of Nautilus-type machines) exercises in a thirty- to forty-five-minute circuit and that you are doing sixty seconds of aerobic exercise in between each exercise. This type of exercise has become popular at many health clubs and fitness studios as well as in many public parks that are equipped with stations for various exercises with a track to jog on between stations. Circuit training is best accomplished in a gym with specialized equipment designed to exercise specific muscle groups. However, you could design your own circuit program at home using familiar exercises such as sit-up crunches and push-ups, and lifting free weights.

Other Activities Which May Be Aerobic. Any sustained activity which keeps your heartbeat elevated for at least twenty minutes will achieve aerobic benefits for your body. These might include cross-country skiing, skating, racquetball, handball, and lawn mowing.

The easiest gauge of all is simply that if you're not sweating, you're probably not working hard enough. It takes thirty to forty minutes of sustained aerobic exercise for fat breakdown to equal the energy expenditure of your muscles. Therefore, you will use a higher percentage of fat when you exercise for longer periods of time.

Another thing to consider is your overall activity level. The biggest difference between normal weight and overweight people is often not how much they eat, but how active they are. Activity is not limited to formal exercise, but includes everything we do throughout the day. The more active a person is, the more calories he or she burns. Examples of ways to increase your general activity level are: taking the stairs instead of the elevator, parking at the back of the parking lot, standing while waiting instead of sitting, retrieving things for yourself rather than sending someone else, and doing housework or gardening with gusto.

This overall lifestyle exercise is vastly different from the exercise programs people attempted thirty years ago when they followed little stick figures doing spot exercises to reduce the size of their tummy or thighs. Research has shown that spot reducing exercises such as sit-ups, leglifts, and toe-touches do not reduce the amount of fat in a specific area. Many people still think that if they're gaining weight in their middle, they need to do sit-ups to reduce the size of the stomach. That has proven to be an inaccurate concept. What does reduce the size of the fat layer over one's stomach, in fact, is aerobic exercise.

Specific exercises will tone the muscles underneath the fat and are important for athletes in training programs. They have very little to do with actual weight loss, however.

Dr. Sneed says, "It's important to do your own work—your own housework, your own gardening, washing your own car. I find over and over again that busy people, such as salesmen who are on their feet all day, come to me and say, 'Surely you don't expect me to go home and walk another two to three miles.' And I tell them, 'Yes, I do.' If people are fatigued from their jobs to the point that they can't consider an aerobic exercise program, then they need to make a lifestyle change. Some people even need to make the decision to live on less money and free up enough time so that they can be healthy and enjoy life. People must not think of aerobic exercise as an option just because they're busy.

"It all goes back to the cultural factors we discussed earlier and explains why we have such a tremendous problem with obesity in the United States. We all grew up in this environment, but we don't have to stay locked in it. We can control our own lifestyles to make room for physical, emotional, and spiritual health."

7

PATH THREE: SAYING GOOD-BYE

ONE THING you must do when you set out on your pathway to recovery, just as you would when setting out on any journey, is to say good-bye. You must say good-bye to food dependency, good-bye to situation dependency, and good-bye to people dependency.

And you must be aware of the dual nature of the good-byes you will be saying. You will say good-bye to some kinds of food and your relationship to them and to the comfort food has brought you, which may be painful. You will also say good-bye to the pain the addiction has caused, and this is a very positive thing. You need to be aware, however, that as strange as it may sound at first, pain itself can be addictive. Even though you are undoubtedly saying right now, *Of course I want to say good-bye to pain,* subconsciously part of you will want to cling to this, like the Prisoner of Chillon who had become friends with his chains.

A number of years ago an earthquake in Mexico ripped an enormous hole in a prison wall. The prisoners ran out shouting to embrace the fresh air and sunshine of freedom. Within a few hours, however, most of them had come back, seeking out their old cells. No matter what its drawbacks, the prison represented security. You must say good-bye to food as a security blanket and the familiar pain caused by overeating.

SAY GOOD-BYE TO FOOD DEPENDENCY

Irene was probably the most intensely overweight patient Dr. Minirth had counseled. Of only average height, she weighed more than four hundred pounds! She had no overt memory of the source of the low self-esteem that had led to her addiction, yet through therapy, she was able to reach far enough back in her pain to discover that she had been sexually molested as a small child. For twenty-five years she had covered this pain and this shame with layer after layer of fat. When she was finally able to say good-bye to her pain, the chain was broken, and she was also able to say good-bye to her food dependency.

Food can play many roles in the life of a compulsive eater. Walk through this list and identify what food has been to you. As you realize a codependent relationship, say good-bye to it.

Is food a parent to you? Say good-bye to it.
Is food a god or an idol? Say good-bye to it.
Is food your best friend? Say good-bye to it.
Is food a plaything? Say good-bye to it.
Is food a source of sensuality? Say good-bye to it.
Is food a mood-altering drug to you? Say good-bye to it.

You will also have to say good-bye to specific foods and eating patterns:

Say good-bye to high-fat foods.
Say good-bye to overly large portions of food.
Say good-bye to gulping food.
Say good-bye to old cooking methods.
Say good-bye to some old recipes.

And say hello to the recipes in this book and our exchange diet.

Dr. Sneed introduced Barbara to this diet during Barbara's second appointment.

THE EXCHANGE DIET

"The specific diet I recommend," Dr. Sneed told Barbara, "is an exchange diet. Just as the name implies, all of the foods on each list—breads or vegetables or meats—are interchangeable. You can use any one of them to satisfy your calorie intake in that area. Let me give you a little background on the ideology. The exchange diet is based on the basic food groups. Its original use was for diabetics because it so carefully regulates exactly how much fat, protein, and carbohydrate you are getting. But then we found it was also one of the most effective tools for weight loss because it allows you to have just the right amounts of specific foods. Our program is different from the diabetic program, however, because there is not a sugar restriction, and there is more freedom in some of the other choices. You do need to be careful, though, not to underestimate the extras in your food, such as butter, mayonnaise, and sauces. These are separate exchanges."

Barbara looked confused, and Dr. Sneed laughed. "Sorry, I'm getting ahead of myself. I'll explain that in a minute. But the crux of the matter is that this program teaches you to eat properly. In our fast-paced American lifestyle we have people skipping meals and overdoing it later or making fast-food choices all the time. If you don't learn controlled eating of the right kinds of foods, you'll never be successful with your weight loss program."

Barbara nodded. "Right. That's what I'm here to learn."

"I really appreciate your open-minded attitude, Barbara. And from what I see of your lifestyle in your background material here," Dr. Sneed pointed to the sheet Barbara had filled out earlier, "I believe this program will be very easy for you to work—much easier than for many of my clients. Did you see the woman who left just before you came in?"

Barbara nodded. She remembered a tall, attractive woman, with black hair, probably in her early forties, about fifteen pounds overweight, in a striking red and black suit.

"That was Elaine. She's been overweight for ten years and can't get it to budge. She's a very successful real estate woman, but her lifestyle doesn't allow for any exercise or proper eating.

"And what does she do for her meals five or six days a week? She'll tell you she doesn't eat breakfast or lunch. But she has a couple of doughnuts in the office, then at midday she stops at a convenience store for something like a Coke and a package of little crackers with peanut butter—which actually contains more calories and fat than a hamburger. But she doesn't consider it a meal, so by the time she gets home late at night, she thinks she hasn't eaten all day and really indulges herself in a big dinner just before going to bed." Dr. Sneed shook her head. "This is a very, very typical lifestyle of patients I see. 'High-rollers syndrome' I call it. But I'm sure you'll do fine."

Dr. Sneed handed Barbara eight lists of foods like the ones beginning on page 320. "Now, the thing for you to understand is that the foods on each list are nutritionally alike. All of the things on each list are interchangeable, and that's the key word— interchangeable. For example, you might be allotted seven bread exchanges per day at your particular calorie level. This wouldn't necessarily mean that you need to eat seven slices of bread a day. You could exchange that bread with anything else on the list, so you might have three servings of potato and two servings of cereal and two servings of crackers, and all that would add up to your seven servings from that list for the day. It's really very simple, but just remember to watch out for butter or jam on your bread, because they are entirely different exchanges."

Dr. Sneed then outlined the five steps Barbara needed to follow to achieve success with the exchange diet.

1. Study the Food Lists

List #1 is the starch and bread list (Chart 12, p. 320). This includes all the grain products, breads, crackers, cookies, etc. Pasta, rice, tortillas, and pita bread are also here, as well as potatoes and a few of the starchier vegetables.

These foods should not be eaten to excess because they can cause you to gain weight. But neither can you eliminate them from a diet because they help prevent hunger, and they protect your lean body mass. (In order not to have muscle waste away during a diet you must have carbohydrate.) There are 70 calories per serving of these items, and we recommend you emphasize whole grain choices for higher fiber and better nutrition.

List #2 is all of the meats, including fish, poultry, eggs, and cheese (p. 321). Of course, the leanest, or nonfat variety should always be chosen. Fish and chicken are wise choices. There is no better choice for dieters than fish. The calorie content of all items on this list is 55–80 calories per exchange. In general, one exchange equals one ounce of a certain kind of meat. Remember, none of the meats should be fried and they must be prepared with no visible fat. Also, if you have a cholesterol problem, avoid egg yolks, liver, and fatty meats.

List #3 includes milk and milk products (p. 321). Remember we allow only ½ percent milk or skimmed milk products. Cheese appears here, although other lists might place it on the meat list. You don't get as much calcium per calorie in cheese as you do in milk or in nonfat yogurt. Also, there's more cholesterol in cheese products.

List #4 is the fruit and juices exchanges (p. 322). There are approximately 55 calories per serving of fruits. Notice that you need to watch your portion size here. For example, one-half of a very small banana is one serving—not half of a long, nine-inch banana. Whole fruits are much better than juices because they contain more vitamins, minerals, and fiber.

List #5 is the very low-calorie vegetables and free foods exchanges (p. 322). Everyone needs at least four servings from the vegetable exchange per day. These servings will range from 15 to 30 calories each. You may have to push yourself here a bit if you haven't been used to eating vegetables in the past. They're an absolute must for a healthy diet.

List #6 is condiments, spices, and beverages (p. 323); these may be used as much as you like. Go down the list and identify what you especially like so that you can zero in on it.

List #7 is fats (p. 324). Remember that foods don't necessarily taste better because of the fat; they taste better because of good cooking methods and the proper use of herbs and spices.

List #8 is the goodies exchange (p. 324), which may be used up to four times a week in place of one bread exchange. This is a list for people who simply can't live without a little sweet stuff every once in a while.

List #9 is the combination and fast food exchanges (p. 325). The foods on this list are not necessarily recommended as healthful foods, but they will help you learn how to make your own exchanges with combination foods.

2. Choose Your Calorie Level

Refer to our "Exchange Diet Allowances" chart below to choose the calorie level you should be eating. To lose weight most women will need to stay on 1,000 calories a day. Most men and very active women can lose weight on 1,200 calories a day. Then read down the column to see how many servings of the foods on each list you get per day. For example, if you look on the table under the 1,000 calorie level, you get four bread exchanges, four meat exchanges, two milk exchanges, three fruit exchanges, unlimited amounts of the low-calorie vegetables, and one fat exchange. That is your daily allotment for a twenty-four hour period.

Exchange Diet Allowances

	Calorie Level				
Food List	To Lose Weight		To Maintain Weight		
	1,000	1,200	1,500	1,800	2,000
#1—Bread/Starch	4	5	7	9	10
#2—Lean Meat	4	4	4	5	5
#3—Milk/Milk Products	2	2	3	3	3
#4—Fruits/Juices	2	3	4	5	6
#5—Vegetables/Free Food	—At least 4 or more exchanges per day—				
#6—Fats	1	2	3	5	6

NOTE: If you choose low-fat food items and employ the low-fat cooking methods recommended in other parts of this book, then you will achieve a diet in which the caloric distribution is approximately:

For Weight Loss		For Weight Maintenance
25%	Protein	15%
55%	Carbohydrate	60%
20%	Fat	25%

3. Design Your Menus

Before you begin designing your own menus, study the sample menus in Chapter 15 (p. 205), where you'll find nine days of menus at the 1,000 calorie level. You can follow these menus just as Dr. Sneed designed them, or there's an infinite combination of foods you can have if you prefer to design your own diet. We've provided a Daily Menu Planner for you to create your own menus. (See Chart 13 in the appendix, p. 326). Make several photocopies of your menu planner before marking on the one in the book so you can use it over and over.

When designing your own menus, be sure to distribute the calories throughout the entire day. Some people will lump their meals into one time period, like a four- or six-hour period from late afternoon through early evening. Spreading calories throughout the day will prevent fatigue and hunger and prevent the tendency to overeat at the next meal.

Most days you need the exact amount of food in each category of your exchange allowance list. Some days, however, you might go over a little in one area and under a little in another. That's OK. Our sample menus do that occasionally as well. Many of our menus are based on recipes in the back of the book. If they are, a page number will indicate where to find that dish. If you want to make a fast-food selection, or eat some other food that's not a recipe in our book, refer to the combination food list to see how to figure it.

4. Keep Accurate Records

This diet program absolutely will not work unless you write down everything you eat and then check with your exchange diet list to make sure the number of servings in each category is correct and that you're not exceeding the limits for that day. This is essential even for an expert in foods and nutrition because it's so hard to keep track of everything you've eaten in a day.

5. Try It—You'll Like It!

If you grew up learning poor eating habits, as most Americans did, if you believe there's only one way to fix meat and that's fried, if you believe sauces and gravies are a must on everything, give this new style of light eating a chance. "Some of my clients like it immediately," Dr. Sneed says, "but others just have to make themselves do it anyway. Especially people who became accustomed to what they liked during childhood and couldn't let go of the nurturing feelings they equated with food that meant love and acceptance. Even with my tough cases, though, it only took two or three months to change over to a whole new set of habits.

"So if it's not a case of *try it, you'll like it* for you, tell yourself, *try it, you'll like it eventually*. You may not like the taste of ½ percent milk right now, but eventually, after you give yourself no other alternative, you really will prefer it over the taste of whole milk. Patient after patient tells me that very same story," Dr. Sneed said.

As Barbara began using the exchange diet, Dr. Minirth and Dr. Hemfelt helped her to say her other good-byes: to situation dependency and to people dependency.

"You are now ready to start your trip diary," Dr. Hemfelt told her. "A looseleaf notebook will probably work best, so you can add and rearrange pages as you wish. Title it MY JOURNEY TO RECOVERY, date it, and proudly list yourself as author. In the front put your relationship surveys and the letter you wrote to yourself. Now, for this day of travel, list the good-byes you are saying and make a note of how you feel about taking this major step to recovery."

SAY GOOD-BYE TO SITUATION DEPENDENCY

As we have so often stressed in this book, we are working for total recovery. So at this point, if there are other dependencies in your life, any unhealthy obsession or fixation, even the milder, socially-acceptable compulsions such as keeping your house too clean or serving on ten church committees, this is the time to say good-bye to those behaviors as well.

If, however, you have identified a more serious problem such as alcoholism or drug dependency, this book alone will not solve those, and we advise you to seek medical help.

SAY GOOD-BYE TO RELATIONSHIP DEPENDENCY

We find codependent relationships in almost all cases of eating compulsion. A codependent relationship is one in which people are overly dependent on one another and often swing between extremes of dependence and independence. In our book *Love Is a Choice: Recovery for Codependent Relationships* (Thomas Nelson, 1989) we discuss fully the codependent personality and how to break free from this addiction. If you find the following definition of a codependent person at all describes you, we urge you to read *Love Is a Choice*. But for now, we will simply list some major aspects of the codependent personality:

- Codependents are addicted to people and things.
- Codependents suffer from love hunger.
- Codependents were abused, actively or passively, as children or are now in an abusive situation.
- Codependents believe something outside will make them feel OK inside.
- Codependents swing between extremes of dependence and independence in their relationships.
- Codependents are highly volatile in their moods.
- Codependents and their partners interchange roles of victim, victimizer, enabler, and rescuer in various situations in their relationship.
- Codependents have a compulsion to repeat an action, such as gorging.

Most codependents will show at least one other addiction besides their relationship addiction.

Although codependency can occur as a result of painful experiences later in life, such as death in the family or a traumatic illness, most codependency is caused by the pain of abuse early in life, which gets one onto the addiction cycle. Active abuse is usually relatively easy to identify. It is the direct transmission of pain from one person to another. For instance, a husband who fails in his job comes home and kicks the cat, yells at his son, and hits his wife.

Passive abuse, which is the most frequent cause of chronic overeating, is much harder to identify. Robert, a patient now in our eating disorders unit, was tremendously proud of his father—a two-star general, a true-to-life John Wayne. But in group therapy Robert admitted that it wasn't unusual for his dad to be gone nine months at a time, and Robert had swathed the pain of this abandonment in layers of fat.

We often ask our patients to think of one of those *occupied* signs you see on airline seats. Can you picture one of those on Mom or Dad's forehead? Were they so occupied with illness, cleanliness, career, or church work that you felt abandoned? And did you then assuage that abandonment with a Hershey bar?

It's also not difficult to define active sexual abuse. But one needs to understand that a total lack of hugging or caressing in the home can constitute passive sexual abuse, which makes the child feel unlovable. The three key ingredients every child must receive from his or her parents in order to prevent the love hunger that leads to codependency are time, attention, and affection. If it's too late for prevention, one must work for cure by saying good-bye to codependent relationships.

The person who wants to say good-bye to a codependent relationship must ask himself or herself: Am I willing to say good-bye to extremes in my relationship? Do I want to move toward balance? Am I willing to surrender rigid roles? The key to breaking free from codependency is achieving balance. The opposite of codependence is not independence, but healthy interdependence. Think of a teeter-totter. Dependence is on one end, independence on the other. If you are on either end, the teeter-totter is out of balance, and you are in a state of codependency. The central, balanced position is interdependence. Balanced, interdependent persons can be both dependent enough to allow trusting vulnerability and genuine intimacy in a relationship and yet at the same time be independent enough that they have their own emotional identity. They do not go up or down emotionally just because others go up and down.

ACHIEVING INTERDEPENDENCE IN MARRIAGE

If you are married, take your journal and do a marriage survey. Ask yourself:

1. How do we share control? Is one partner dictatorial? Is one partner always submissive?

2. How do we share time? For this you might make a pie chart of how you spend your time. Ask your spouse to do the same. Is your time reasonably divided between self, family, spouse, work, church, recreation? Or is one of these areas consuming an unreasonable proportion and squeezing out the others?

3. How do we share sexuality? Does either partner have the freedom to initiate sexuality? Are both partners comfortable in giving and receiving gratification?

4. How do we share money? Does one partner control all the money? Does one do all the spending? Does one make all decisions on major purchases?

5. How do we share spirituality? Does one partner always take the lead in family worship and spiritual matters? Does one partner dictate how the family will respond to religious matters?

Look back through your answers and look for distortions. Is your marriage relationship balanced or is one end or the other of the teeter-totter continually up in the air?

ACHIEVING INTERDEPENDENCE IN PARENT/CHILD RELATIONSHIPS

The normal progression of cutting the apron strings and leaving the nest, as the saying goes, follows a gentle pattern through the mid-thirties. Usually in the late teens to the early twenties residential separation occurs as the child goes away to college or takes a bachelor apartment or marries.

In the early to mid-twenties financial separation occurs as the child finishes college or advances in a job. Marriage, which usually occurs around this time, is the major step in achieving separation from the family of origin. The next most important is establishing oneself in a career, so that part of one's identity comes, not from being someone's son or daughter, but from being a teacher, a lawyer, a mechanic.

Each one of these steps, usually taken through the twenties, prepares us intellectually to be separate from our families of origin. But fully internalized, emotional separation doesn't usually occur until the early to mid-thirties. At that full achievement of adulthood, we should have completely said good-bye to Mom and Dad. We can stand on our own and not need Mom and Dad there to rescue us.

If both partners in a marriage do not achieve this, the marriage will often rupture at this point and one partner will "go home to Mama" or run off to a tropical island with a younger partner in a desperate attempt to recapture the safer time of adolescence. So saying good-bye to Mom and Dad is essential to a healthy marriage.

It is also essential to a healthy spiritual life. People who are clinging to their parents can't entirely embrace God as their Ultimate Father. Once we say good-bye to Mom and Dad, however, it is possible to say a full hello to God.

Ginger, Barbara's friend from the group therapy meeting, found the roots of her problem were in saying good-bye to her parents: "Mother's from an alcoholic family. She's the only one of five children that isn't an alcoholic, but she's addicted to food," she told Barbara after a group meeting one night. "Dad's a rageaholic, perfectionist, a black-and-white thinker who manipulates people with fear and intimidation. Mother manipulates with guilt. I love them dearly, but they are very unhappy people, and I have to release them. Those problems are their problems. I pray for them, but I have had to realize that it's not my job to change them or to fix them.

"I've learned to experience freedom. It hasn't been easy because they keep trying to call me back. I'm in a period now of allowing a long time between phone calls and between visits.

"This isn't easy because they live very close to me. But sometimes it turns out to be easier than I thought it would be. Ever since I can remember I've wanted a horse. I finally had an opportunity to buy a beauty at a really reasonable price. I'm thirty-five years old and earning my own money, but I was scared to death of what my folks would say when I bought a horse. I went ahead and did it, and you know what—they weren't upset at all.

"I've learned several techniques for letting go: I've learned it's OK *not* to feel guilty. I've realized that my parents are unhealthy people and that I have to protect myself from them. I've learned to set limits. If I'm in a conversation that's not going well, I simply say, in a very calm voice, 'I really didn't call for this abuse,' and hang up. Just the thought of doing that terrified me, but I've learned that it works.

"A big breakthrough was sharing this with my older brother. He said, 'Ginge, you've always taken that stuff too seriously. Tell Mom and Dad to back off. You know they love you; just let 'em get angry. They can't have their own way all the time.' And he's right. But I always wanted to *fix* everything. I guess that's something else I've had to say good-bye to—being a fixer."

Barbara nodded. Ginger had given her a lot to think about. Since her parents were dead she didn't have any physical good-byes to say. But she had a lot of emotional ones. Her father died in a hospital for alcoholics during her senior year in college, and her mother died of pneumonia less than a year later, so Barbara had been parentless for six years. But maybe she still needed to say good-bye to the pain of growing up with dysfunctional parents even though she thought she had said good-bye to them at their funerals.

ACHIEVING INTERDEPENDENCE IN WORK RELATIONSHIPS

A healthy work relationship with your boss, manager, or supervisor requires dealing with that person in the immediate situation, not projecting the shadow of one's parents onto this authority figure.

Richard came to us for help with his compulsive eating, not for career counseling. But when he surveyed his relationship with authority figures we found that although he was a charismatic, highly successful salesman, he had held fourteen jobs in almost as many years because of repeated clashes with sales managers.

"Yeah, I've really hit a string of lulus," he said. "I'm talking major jerks. Like my last boss here. He tried to cheat me out of my commission. When I got my check, I went straight to the vice president—I mean, nobody's gonna cut old Richard's commission in half and just call it an accounting error."

In going back through Richard's relationships with his family of origin, we discovered that he grew up with a dictatorial, rage-aholic mother and a passive, invalid father. When conflict arose in his job, Richard wasn't dealing with his manager, but with his mother. Richard, like anyone who grows up under an abusive authority figure, was suffering from love hunger. He believed that "You can't trust authority figures—they'll take advantage of you. They'll abuse you."

Richard had to do a lot of saying good-bye. He had to say good-bye to the illusion that "I've had bad luck with bosses—it's just circumstances."

He had to say good-bye to his denial of the pain of growing up with an abusive mother. And saying good-bye to this pain isn't easy, because once you admit the presence of pain, you *feel* it. Richard had to suffer the pain, which is the next stage of the recovery process; grieving out the pain. We'll walk that path in the next chapter.

8

PATH FOUR: GRIEVING OUT THE PAIN

ALTHOUGH RICHARD was an adult, he sat in our office and wept like a child. The first wave of pain was for growing up with a domineering mother. The sobs had barely lessened before he was washed with agony over having never known a true father. Finally Richard looked up, dabbing at his eyes. He opened his mouth to speak and broke down with the crashing of the third tidal wave, this one far stronger than the others, as he mourned the death of his father. This grief work, which should have been done years before, finally surfaced in a tearing pain that threatened to swamp Richard. And then, from the broken sentence fragments he shared with us, we could tell that all the pain was rolling over him in a confusion of memories and lost hopes—mother, father, the abandoned hope of finding a father figure in the workplace.

We knew better than to interfere. Richard was doing his own work, very likely the hardest work he would ever have to do in his life. We provided him with tissues, kept the room quiet, and when the sobs subsided, offered him a cold drink. Richard was as spent as a ship that had weathered a storm at sea, but now true healing could begin.

Doing a good job of saying your good-byes will bring you to experience a sense of loss of love in your past so that you can grieve out the pain. This is the hardest of the footpaths, but the most essential because opening yourself to excising pain is like having surgery. True healing can then start.

Dr. Paul Meier says the pain from love hunger creates an emotional pus wound that must be lanced with the needle of grief. Inside the victims of love hunger are both the vacuum, which they attempt to fill with food, and pain pockets, which continue to build pressure as people eat in a desperate attempt to stuff the pain down. If the boil isn't lanced with appropriate grief, the pressure can reach an explosive force as in the case of Adrian who had the bull-fight with the policeman.

If in doing your relationship surveys you have not found serious dysfunctions in your past or present, if your overeating is on a milder level and you do not have deep pockets of pain, you will still have a share of grief work to do. There is a natural grief in the regular transitions of life: the first child going off to school, graduations, weddings, and, of course, funerals. Even the "happy eater" must grieve over the loss of food as a friend. Food brought the "happy eater" a lot of pain, but it was always there when he turned to it. So he must grieve over that farewell.

If your pain is deep and the pressure is intense, however, your grief may come out in violent explosions. If this occurs, don't be frightened. Know that it is good. The pus erupting from the boil can now be replaced by healthy flesh.

You may need help to get through this most difficult of stages. Find a supportive fellowship group, such as Overeater's Anonymous. (We'll discuss possible groups in Chapter 12.)

Richard had made a major breakthrough in his recovery process when he began his grief work in our office, but we knew the real battle had just begun, so we advised him to join a supportive fellowship group. "Overeaters Anonymous meets just a mile up the road from here every Wednesday noon and every Friday evening," we said.

Richard's reaction was typical of one who has had trouble with authority figures. "Hey, I don't need any bimbo meetings where they announce your weight to the group and make you eat celery sitting in a Yoga position. I bet they've got more rules than Bluebell ice cream's got calories."

We urged him not to judge something he hadn't tried.

Richard looked doubtful. "Well, we'll see," he said.

Like Richard, Barbara also resisted entering the grief process. "That sounds awful. I'm already miserable and sad. Why should I work on becoming more miserable?"

"If you don't lance the boil, you'll be putting a bandage on a tumor," we told her.

"I guess I can see that. But maybe if I lost a little weight first, even just ten pounds, so I'm feeling better, then I could handle this grief stuff."

"Barbara," we tried again, "in our experience, many people who have been on multiple diets, trying over and over to lose the same twenty-five pounds, are attempting exactly what you suggest—attempting healing without cleansing first. Would you trust a dentist who filled your cavities without drilling out the decay first?"

She smiled. "OK, I get your point. But it *would* hurt less to skip the drill."

That evening Barbara sat in bed, her journal on her knees. At first the list of good-byes she had said made her angry. She felt cheated. She'd missed so much.

- A loving father. How different her life would have been if she'd had a nice, normal father like Gail, the most popular girl in her class.
- Fun-filled college life. She could have made so much more of her college years if she hadn't been so dependent on Calvin— if she could have seen how he was using her.
- Parties and pretty dresses. She missed a lot of social life because she was too fat.
- The fun and comfort of food. She knew she couldn't have that any more.
- Tom. They could have had such a good marriage.
- French fries. What would she do without french fries?
- A successful career. She could have gone to school to become an interior decorator if her life hadn't been so messed up.

It wasn't fair! She hit the bed with her fist, then choked on a sob. The page blurred before her as sadness replaced anger.

For the next three days Barbara lived on an emotional roller coaster. Now that she realized the full depth of her grief about her alcoholic father, her difficulty in relationships with men, her loss of career, and her food issues, she was overwhelmed. One morning she was mad and couldn't figure out where that anger was coming from. By the afternoon she was weeping. The next morning she woke up in denial again, telling herself everything would be all right if she just lost twenty-five pounds. And then the denial itself triggered anger over what her obesity had cost her, and she was back into the grief process.

Most of our patients share a similar experience. Once they are in the grieving process, the issues become blurry. They may begin thinking they are grieving their own marriage, then find the focus has switched to their parents' unhappy marriage, and then it blurs as to which is which. Patients will go through all the classic stages of grief.

1. SHOCK AND DENIAL

One enters this stage of grief immediately upon the occurrence of a trauma. Watch television news coverage of a plane wreck. The survivors are calm, quiet, often sitting huddled in blankets. They are in physical and emotional shock. They may make comments like, "I don't believe it." "That couldn't have happened." This protective, God-given defense mechanism is essential to human survival and enables people to live through disaster.

The shock and denial period should be relatively brief, allowing the person to progress through the more difficult stages to healing. The majority of food-addicted people we see, however, have been frozen in shock and denial for years. This has happened for two reasons: Emotionally, they have simply denied their feelings and refused to go on with the normal process; physically, they have tranquilized their feelings with food, just as a drug dependent person would have done.

This was the case with Bob Green, the patient who was too big to fit into Dr. Hemfelt's wingback chair. The grief process in his life was so arrested, so thoroughly tranquilized with food and alcohol that even when he lost his son, daughter-in-law, and infant grandchild in a car wreck, he could not grieve for them.

Melissa was another patient with an eating disorder fed by arrested grief. She had been her father's best friend until he died suddenly of a heart attack when she was twelve. Her mother would not allow her to grieve. "Your father is in heaven. This was God's will. It's wicked to grieve."

For thirteen years this message had played in her head until she married a much older man in an attempt to replace her father. When she discovered her husband couldn't replace her father, she began overeating as an escape and finally entered counseling for severe depression.

If you have been frozen in shock for many years, it may take some time to thaw out your emotions. Continue looking back through your relationship surveys, saying your good-byes, and keeping track of your feelings in your journal. It's OK if this comes slowly. Give yourself time to discover and experience what you haven't been feeling.

To get out of the shock and denial stage, we ask our patients to make a list of the losses the addiction has cost them, just as Barbara did. Some like to do this in a shopping list form, but one of the most effective ways to get a complete spilling out of the items held in your subconscious mind is to use the technique of webbing:

Take a clean sheet of paper. In the center write the word LOSSES and circle it. Draw a short line out from that and write the first loss that comes to your mind, such as *activities*. Circle that and around it write all the activities you would have liked to participate in but couldn't because you were overweight. Draw lines between the words to connect them. When you've listed all the activities you've lost out on, choose another word such as *relationships*, write this word out from your core word, *losses*, and make a web of your losses around that.

Don't edit yourself on anything you want to write down. The favorite key chain you lost during a binge in a fast-food restaurant is as valid an item as the job promotion you lost because your boss believed the myth that fat people are inefficient. Think about every aspect of your life: social, physical, emotional, spiritual. Continue webbing as long as you can—until your paper looks as if it's covered with a giant spider's web.

Once patients see their losses all in one place in black and white, they experience the spontaneous flow of grief. Unfortunately patients sometimes play a version of the shell game with their grief. They will look at one loss, then cover that with a shell before uncovering another loss. In order to recover completely you need to leave each loss out in the open so that you can see the whole picture. All through adolescence and early adulthood, Richard had denied the pain of growing up with a tyrant of a mother and had sabotaged his body with food and his career with anger in extended denial. We encouraged him to continue the healing process that had begun in our office as he made a web of his losses. It looked something like the facing page.

2. ANGER

When the shock and denial thaw and the lancing needle reaches the pocket of pain, anger will erupt. Nearly every compulsive overeater is angry, either at self or at others. In most cases, patients are blind to their own bitterness. They will say calmly, "No, I'm not angry at all."

There are three forms of anger. Anger directed outward, we call conventional anger, which leads patients to shake their fists at God, hit their spouses, or yell at their bosses. Anger directed inward, we call depression. This will take a quieter form as the griever deals with his own anger at himself. Then there is projected anger. Some people project the anger they feel for themselves and their addiction

RICHARD'S WEBBING

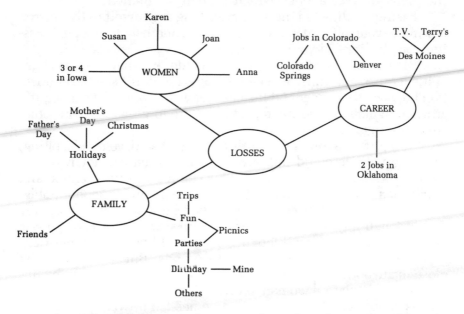

onto those around them. They may deny that the real problem is discontent caused by low self-esteem or anger over one's addiction, and say, "If only my spouse would pay more attention to me, I wouldn't be mad at him, and then I'd quit eating." Also, there is legitimate anger—a normal, healthy reaction to circumstances and relationships, which people may express through eating if they don't know how to express it in a healthy way.

Whether the anger is inward or outward, legitimate or projected, it must come out. The healthiest way is verbal. If you are carrying anger at a living person near to you, you may be able to go to them and say, "I need to express how I feel about this." The more clearly you can state your feelings and the reasons for them, the better. For some people, simply writing in the journal will be sufficient.

In therapy we often use role-playing. We put two chairs in the middle of the room. The patient sits on one chair and visualizes the recipient of the anger sitting on the other. The patient then expresses all the old hurts and angers. There is more freedom to express strong emotions in a role-playing situation than if the person were actually there. If the anger needs to be expressed physically, we sometimes give the patient a Nerf bat or suggest making one out of newspapers and using it to give full expression to their rage.

If your angers are old and the person is deceased or has moved away, the role-playing technique can be very effective, or some people prefer to write a letter, which is often not mailed.

For angers directed inward, try talking to yourself in the mirror, talking to yourself as if you were sitting in another chair, or expressing your feelings in your journal.

Richard had been angry most of his life. He knew he was angry at his mother, but until he began therapy, he didn't see the connection between this anger and his belligerent, "I won't take any guff" attitude, which caused his repeated failure to get along with other authority figures.

As a further expression of this anger, he had developed a biting, sarcastic wit. He could put anyone or any situation down with a stinging, Don Rickles-style joke. This could win him attention and laughs at a party, but made sustained relationships uncomfortable.

A third type of armor his anger had built was the Humphrey Bogart tough-guy image he assumed with women. Because he was smooth-talking, and good-looking in spite of his overweight, Richard never had any trouble getting girlfriends. But his "I don't get close to anybody" attitude on dates made lasting relationships impossible. Whenever a woman left him, Richard got very depressed. But he simply could not admit that he needed a woman in his life until it was too late. Then the Humphrey Bogart image would crumble. Anna was the worst of all. When she left he became almost suicidal. In the week after she left he sent her seven dozen roses. "I couldn't believe it when I counted them up. I don't know what came over me," he told us later.

The shield of anger Richard carried against his mother had to be pierced before he could lower the shield he carried against other women.

3. BARGAINING

After the emotionally consuming stage of anger one often experiences a letdown or a sense of being drained. In this period of calm after the storm, it is normal for people to try to bargain their way out of the situation, which we call magical thinking. We often see this in cancer victims who try to bargain with the chemotherapist for a longer session or in parents of terminally ill children who try to make deals with God: "If you let Joey live, I'll build a chapel on the mission field." Food addicts will often try to bargain their way out of their addiction by finding a magic diet. "If I follow this diet, my problems will go away."

When you find yourself in this stage, know that it is normal, and take comfort in the fact that reaching this stage is evidence that you are making progress. But resist the urge to give in to magical thinking. Give up the idea that God is Aladdin's lamp. We cannot earn our way into grace, either physically (by eating only grapefruit) or spiritually (by bargaining God into healing our addictions).

Bulimics or anorexics especially indulge in magical thinking when they think, "If I can get thin enough, I'll be lovable." An example of how little such ideas are rooted in reality was the beautiful, successful singer, Karen Carpenter, who died of anorexia because she didn't feel lovable.

Your self-worth must not be founded on anything conditional. Your worth as a human being must be founded on the fact that you are a child of God, created in His image, and saved by His grace, which is freely given to you in love. With this solid self-concept one can find the courage to move ahead into real grief.

Richard found that even winning in a bargaining situation doesn't bring success. When he received a commission check that was half what he thought it should be, he didn't discuss it with his boss or go to the accounting department to see if it was merely a mathematical error. He went directly to the head of the company and bargained for his rights. "Well, I guess I more demanded than bargained," he admitted. "Yeah, I got the money all right. I won the battle over the commission, but I lost the war with relationships. Going over my boss's head burned my bridges with that company."

4. TRUE GRIEF (SADNESS)

Ralph, our roller-coaster eater, had the unusual experience of doing his grief work after his weight was lost. To the outside world, it looked as if Ralph's battle was won. He was trim and handsome in a well-cut new suit. But inside, he knew he was just starting his battle. Maintenance was where he had always failed before. Was it twelve times? Fourteen times? He couldn't even remember. But because he had lost his weight on sheer perfectionistic willpower and not walked the paths of recovery, he was thin, but not victorious.

Ralph found he had to grieve two paths of pain, as most of our patients do. First there was the original pain that started him on the addiction cycle as a child. the pain of having an alcoholic father and a mentally ill mother. As part of facing his pain he visited his mother in a mental hospital in New Mexico. This was his first visit in many years, and the first time he saw her in complete honesty, facing the fact that she did not know who he was, that she would never be able to live normally in the outside world, and that he had never had a mother and never would. When he returned to group therapy and shared this, there was not a dry eye in the room as we joined Ralph in doing his grief work over his original pain.

After this group session, Ralph was able to go on and grieve his losses from his pain. His webbing held no surprises for him. He knew he had lost confidence in himself. He knew he had lost assurance of success, almost hope of success. Again, he brought this insight to group therapy. "I'm scared to death," he said. "I'm so sad over my lack of confidence in myself and in the future. It's a terrible thing to begin every day with fear." Again, the group wept with Ralph, and the tears were cathartic.

Weeping is the most honest expression of true grief. Sometimes people say, "Crying never solved anything." That's not true. Tears bring cleansing, as if they were physically washing the emotional wounds. We often find that this is far harder for our male patients than for women. Boys in our society have been told from infancy, "Men don't cry. Be a big boy." They have been denied this healing release. It is often like trying to get an emotional response from Mr. Spock on *Star Trek* when we try to help our male patients through their grief work. But it can be done. Even if one's emotions have been held in check for years and seemingly programmed into oblivion, they are still there, just as God created them, waiting to do their healing work for you.

One must feel grief over the addiction itself and over the losses that were by-products of that addiction: relationships, experiences, career advances. When the full impact of the loss strikes, there is often a flood of tears. We may spend two or three days simply nurturing our patients as they go through this stage and keeping them safe while they let the sadness flow out.

On the other hand, it is equally normal to find that your grief comes in small pockets. One may spend a morning in tears, then feel no more deep sadness for several hours or days until another wound surfaces and the loss must be grieved.

It is also important to understand that one may have to recycle through the stages several times. Often patients will conclude a period of grief and feel they are ready for acceptance when a new wave of anger hits them. "I must have done something wrong," they tell us. This is the perfectly normal process as layers of scar tissue are peeled away, one at a time.

We often tell patients to think of peeling the layers off an onion as they try to get to the core of their pain. They must peel through layers of anger, depression, and sadness. Often, as Barbara found, one must continue to peel as sadness will be followed by more anger and depression, and the cycle will repeat until all the pain is grieved away.

You also need to be aware that it is possible to get stuck in one of the stages, such as anger or depression. We have seen patients panic and fear they are going crazy or that they'll be depressed for the rest of their lives when this happens. Again, know that this can happen as a part of the normal process; then take steps to move yourself along.

We use a technique called "flipping the coin." Anger and sadness are two sides of the same coin. If you are stuck in anger, if you find yourself being grouchy and disagreeable all the time, look for the sadness on the other side of your anger. Give it a chance to surface. We have talked several times about stuffing down anger with food. You could now possibly be stuffing down sadness with anger.

Or, if you seem to be stuck in sadness or depression, try getting mad. Roll up a newspaper and take a swat at whatever you're feeling sad about. At first you may have to imagine you are in the stage you want to move to, but soon the coin will flip and you'll be on your way.

Even though Richard broke into his grief cycle with a flood of tears, he still had more periods of sadness to experience. One night in group therapy another member told about seeing his father through the final stages of cancer. "I picked him up to carry him from the chair to his bed, and I felt as if I were cradling a wounded bird."

Tears began streaming down Richard's face. Through hearing another's story, he could vicariously grieve for his own father's death. The wisecracking Humphrey Bogart became an openly bawling little boy as tender grief flooded out.

5. ACCEPTANCE, FORGIVENESS, AND RESOLUTION

The ultimate goal of all your grief work is to achieve the three-faceted, precious gem of peace. We begin with acceptance as the first facet because acceptance can be an act of the will. A person can say, "This is an unfair situation. This is a painful situation. But I will accept this." From such a decision, one works on to achieve true emotional and spiritual forgiveness. And finally comes the sparkle of resolution: An inner knowledge that this issue is laid to rest: *I am at peace.*

ACCEPTANCE

A favorite prayer of many recovery patients is the Serenity Prayer of Reinhold Niebuhr: "God, grant me the serenity to accept the things I cannot change, courage to change the things I can, and wisdom to know the difference." One must choose to accept the acts

of one's past life. They cannot be changed. To deny, forget, or minimize these facts would be harmful. Accepting facts for what they
are and then moving on with your life is acceptance.

John Bradshaw's challenge to his recovery audiences is, "Can
you look back on your one and only, God-given life and say, 'It
needed to be that way'?" If you are still regretting or fighting with
the facts of the past, you have not reached acceptance. If you can see
that you had to go through it all to become the person you are, then
you can be at peace.

It is not unusual to hear someone say at an OA meeting, "Hi,
I'm John. I'm a grateful recovering overeater." When one considers
the pain of the recovery process, this can sound like a strange statement. But one can soon sense a genuine gratitude in the testimonies
of recovered people as they tell how even the painful experiences
brought them to a new life and helped them become better persons.
"I had to go through that," they say, "to find God and to develop
healthy relationships in my life. Now I can look back in peace."

The Big Book of Alcoholics Anonymous stresses the importance of daily acceptance. It urges readers to accept any person,
place, thing, or situation that is disturbing them as "being exactly
the way it is supposed to be at this moment. Nothing," they say,
"absolutely nothing happens in God's world by mistake. . . . I need
to concentrate not so much on what needs to be changed in the
world as on what needs to be changed in me and in my attitudes."
There are many paradoxes in recovery, and this is one of them: I can
only change things after I have accepted them.

FORGIVENESS

At this point we always warn our patients, "Now don't do the
Texas Two-Step in your grief work." This fancy piece of footwork
looks nice, but it involves jumping from denial directly to forgiveness, thus skipping several beats of the music in its execution. You
must not skip any of the steps in your grief work. This is especially
likely for Christians who look down the list, see forgiveness there,
and say, "Well, of course, it's my duty to forgive. Certainly I forgive
my alcoholic father."

This Two-Step is well-intentioned, but it short-circuits the
God-given grief process and leaves the love hunger intact. Intellectual and spiritual forgiveness are important, but you must work
through all the stages to achieve emotional forgiveness. You must
feel the pain, feel the anger, weep for the losses; then you can forgive with your mind, spirit, and heart.

The patient of ours who declared, "I can forgive, but I can't
forget!" was stuck in anger and had not moved on into sadness and

grief; therefore he had not achieved heart forgiveness and could not find resolution, which must be the end result of the grief process.

We use the term "forgiving and forgetting" a lot, but actually forgiveness is not the same thing as forgetting. In fact, our brains simply will not allow us to forget certain things, since the events are ingrained in the biochemical pathways of the brain. Often, when we talk about forgiving and forgetting, we're really practicing a form of denial.

The concept of forgiveness is based on a word in the Bible that means "to send away." The Old Testament concept of forgiveness was acted out in a ceremony the Hebrews called "the ceremony of the scapegoat." Priests placed their hands on the head of a goat, figuratively conferring all the sins of the people onto the animal. Then they led the goat into the wilderness where it could never be found.

Forgiveness is being able to accept the grievance as something that has happened and then to go on from there. When George Santayana said, "Those who cannot remember the past are condemned to repeat it," he was speaking of the history of the world, but the principle is equally true for the history of an individual. If we make peace with our mistakes, we can learn from them and go on to a better life.

There are two kinds of forgiveness: active forgiveness and receptive forgiveness. Active forgiveness is forgiving others and forgiving myself. Receptive forgiveness is accepting forgiveness from others whom we have injured and from God. The Twelve Steps of OA and AA and other such programs emphasize the importance of forgiveness in their steps eight and nine, which direct their members to make a list of all the persons they have harmed and then to make amends whenever possible. This is active forgiveness, taking steps to seek it, then opening yourself to accept the forgiveness and to accept the situation.

As the first step toward reaching the peace that follows true forgiveness, you need to make a forgiveness inventory in your journal. Make three lists: others you need to forgive for hurting you; things you need to forgive yourself for; and others whose forgiveness you need to seek.

Forgiving Others

When we direct patients to make a list of all those whom they need to forgive for pain caused in the past, the response is often, "But, that's like making a list of people I blame for my problem. I don't want to blame anyone else." While that's an admirable attitude, we need to realize, as John Bradshaw says, "No one is to blame; everyone is responsible." This is not a question of placing blame; it is a question of trying to uncover what has happened. You must know who you need to forgive before you can do it.

Richard, who had done such an excellent job expressing grief and sadness in the early stages of his grief work, suddenly found a difficulty with forgiveness, so he went in to discuss it with Dr. Meier: "Oh, I know whom I need to forgive—no problem there. My mother was a tartar, and my father was a wimp. I've faced it, and I've cried over it. But that doesn't change the facts. So how do I forgive?"

Dr. Meier leaned back in his chair. "Remember, Richard, forgiveness is not excusing, or tolerating, or justifying, which are ways that we frequently try to cope with having been wronged. Nor is it minimizing the pain. Forgiveness is an act of the will, just as happiness is a choice. We choose to forgive others because God forgives us for our sins."

Richard thought for a moment, and then nodded. "Yeah, that makes sense. But some people just don't forgive. How come?"

"Pain," Dr. Meier said. "It hurts too badly. Pride, too. We don't want to lower ourselves to the level of that person. And third, vengeance. We feel the justifiable need to even the score.

"Failure to forgive is holding a grudge, and that is one of the most harmful things we can do." Dr. Meier opened his Bible and held it out to Richard. "You'll see there in Romans 12:17–21 an extended passage in which Paul warns against holding grudges. Go ahead—read it aloud."

Richard cleared his throat and read. "'Repay no one evil for evil. Have regard for good things in the sight of all men. If it is possible, as much as depends on you, live peaceably with all men. Beloved, do not avenge yourselves, but rather give place to wrath; for it is written, "Vengeance is Mine, I will repay," says the Lord.'" Richard looked up. "Man, that's direct."

"That's right," the doctor said. "Forgiveness is not getting even. Another thing you need to understand is that forgiveness is not conditioned on 'if you do so-and-so' or 'if you never again do so-and-so.' This is a part of what Jesus was getting at when He suggested we forgive seventy times seven."

"It's a long process, huh?" Richard said.

Dr. Meier nodded. "Forgiveness often comes slowly. Yet the more insight we have into other people's motives for harming us, the more we are able to forgive. Of course, the ultimate example is Jesus, hanging on the cross. He said, 'Father, forgive them; they know not what they do.' He had insight into their ignorance of what had happened. Frequently a person can experience forgiveness or choose to forgive when he understands the other person's motives. For instance, maybe that person was so afraid he'd lose his job that he had to lie about what happened, making you look bad, rather than tell the truth. Once you realize this, you can almost feel sorry for him."

Richard gave a wry smile. "Well, maybe I could now. In the past I'd have had my vengeance by smashing him one."

"Yes, and you may still have those impulses now, but you'll have the understanding to deal with them in a healthy way. Now, one more thing I want us to look at is the fact that often we don't forgive because we think we've already forgiven."

This time the book Dr. Meier wanted was on his shelf, so he crossed the room and returned with it, flipping pages. "Ah, here it is—I thought I could find the passage. This is Charles Stanley's book *Forgiveness*. He says, 'Sometime in your past you may have acknowledged that you were wronged. You may have admitted that you needed to forgive others. You may have even prayed a prayer in which you said the words, "I forgive _____ _____ _____." You may have meant it with all your heart, yet there is emotional and verbal evidence that something is still gnawing at you on the inside. If you're still uncomfortable around the people who wronged you . . . chances are you have not completely dealt with the situation.'*

"I like to talk about a person's gut forgiveness, as opposed to his mental forgiveness. Dr. Stanley uses the example of when a person has had an affair. Frequently the wronged spouse will choose to forgive with the head right away, but it will take the gut months to catch up with the head."

Richard looked puzzled. "So if saying, 'I forgive you,' isn't enough, how can you tell when you've forgiven?"

"An excellent question!" The doctor smiled. "If the bitterness is gone, if you can accept the person, if fellowship has been restored, if you can choose to do good to those persons who were your enemies and love them, then probably you have forgiven."

Richard sighed. "Yeah. That sounds good. Well, I can see that I haven't forgiven yet, but I've made progress. At least, now I want to forgive."

Forgiving Yourself

Judy was a perfectionist who grew up in a somewhat Victorian Christian home. In spite of their legalistic tendencies, however, she got along fine with both Mom and Dad, earned good grades, went

---

*Charles Stanley, *Forgiveness* (Oliver Nelson, 1987), 117.

off to a highly regarded Christian college, and achieved good grades there. In her third year she developed a pattern of going too far sexually in her relationships with boys.

Judy should have admitted her mistake, confessed it to the Lord, grieved out the pain, received His forgiveness, forgiven herself, and gone on with life. But because she was perfectionistic—a black-and-white thinker—she didn't believe she deserved forgiveness. She decided that God couldn't use her; she was worthless. To protect herself from that ever happening again, she put on a lot of weight and kept it on. She never married and became attracted to abusive men.

When she came to our clinic she was living with a man who was borderline mentally retarded. She had bruises on her arms from his beating her when she wanted to read her Bible. Finally her family persuaded her to come into our hospital for treatment for the depression that had lasted for fifteen years.

Unfortunately, this is not a happy story because as soon as Judy began gaining insight into her problem, she left counseling and went back to her boyfriend. She felt such an overwhelming need to suffer abuse for that one mistake that she could not seek forgiveness.

Do not let yourself get stuck in punishing yourself for things you need to forgive yourself for. Remember our "flipping the coin" technique (p. 127) and push yourself into anger or into sadness as a preliminary to forgiveness if you are not yet ready to forgive yourself.

Seeking Others' Forgiveness

You will need to think through all your relationships and look back through your relationship survey when making your list of all those you have harmed in the past by your compulsive behavior. For example, a mother who was overweight for many years may have to ask forgiveness from her children because her overweight kept her from playing with them, prevented sharing many of their activities, and often embarrassed them. A father might need to ask his family's forgiveness for money he spent on binge food that could have gone for family needs. One may need to seek a spouse's forgiveness for failures in physical and emotional intimacy. If you don't know how you have harmed those close to you, ask them to tell you.

Seeking God's Forgiveness

Human power alone is not sufficient to reach full forgiveness. There is an element of forgiveness that is divine. It cannot be reached without God. The last residue of grief is often a shame so deep, as it was in Judy's case, that it makes the person believe, "I am bad. There is something innately defective about me beyond the original sin that is common to mankind." The Twelve Steps of Alcoholics Anonymous deal with this problem by directing those working with them to "Make a searching and fearless moral inventory" of themselves, admit their wrongs to God and another human being, and ask God to remove their shortcomings. We ask you to do this too.

In Psalm 103:3 David says that God is a forgiving God, and David articulates his comfort in that in Psalm 32:1, "Blessed is [the person] whose transgression is forgiven." David, writing that out of intense guilt feelings over his sin with Bathsheba and her husband Uriah, was able to express the release that he felt in forgiveness. The Lord's Prayer reminds us of the dual responsibility: 1) to experience God's forgiveness but then, 2) to extend forgiveness to others.

The old saying that "at the foot of the cross all ground is level" is especially applicable here because in the sight of God no one is less lovable than anyone else; no one is any harder for God to forgive than anyone else. The foot of the cross is the only place where anyone and everyone can reach the "peace that passes understanding."

When Richard came to the point of needing to forgive his parents, he got stuck. "I can't do it. I don't want to forgive," he told us.

We told Richard that if he had found himself at this barrier early in his recovery process we would say it was because he hadn't said his good-byes, worked through his anger, or reached true sadness. Richard, however, had taken all the preliminary steps to forgiveness. So we told Richard he needed to find the spiritual dimension in his forgiveness. "Surrender this to God," we said. "Tell God, 'I don't think I can do this. I don't even want to do it. I turn it over to you.' Pray this prayer every day for a week. It's perfectly true that in your own human power you can't forgive. Ask God to make you willing to be willing."

RESOLUTION

Resolution is the opposite of resentment. Resentment is unresolved anger that continues to boil away inside, creating pressure until it can erupt in an abscess. Resolution is the sense of health, cleanliness, and peace that comes from knowing that the issue has been put to rest. The problem has been solved, and I can go on from here with confidence.

If you have worked your way along the footpath of grief carefully and completely, you have been through the nadir of the healing process. This catharsis should leave you feeling clean and fresh, but a little empty. That is normal, because you have created a new vacuum in the space that was formerly filled with emotional pus.

This, however, is not like the vacuum created by love hunger, which will suck anything into itself in a desperate attempt for filling. You can fill this space creatively with new experiences and healthful relationships, which we will explore on our next footpath.

Richard found this to be true as God did answer his prayer to lead him into forgiveness. From there he reached resolution, and he is now making real progress in his food compulsivity and his career. He has a new job and told us that for the first time he's not focusing on paychecks but on relationships. And he's made a commitment to put down roots. When he looked at his webbing, he realized that everytime he'd changed jobs he had also moved to a new city or state. "I realized that changing geography didn't change anything inside me. I'm going to stay in the old place but be a new me."

CHAPTER

9

PATH FIVE: EXPLORING NEW VISTAS

YOU HAVE been through the depths of grieving out your pain. Now it's time to choose a footpath that heads upward to new views and new experiences. Upward and onward to victory.

MAKING PEACE WITH YOUR BODY IMAGE

We have noted earlier how people with eating disorders do not see themselves at all as others see them. But the distortion needn't be as severe as the patient who couldn't recognize her own snapshots in the family album or the three-hundred-pound patient who said, "Yeah, I need to lose a few pounds." Due to the push-pull, crazy-making messages of our culture, few Americans have an accurate image of their bodies. The *Los Angeles Times* recently reported that 75 percent of the women interviewed in a survey thought themselves fat, even though only 25 percent were actually obese by medical standards.

Whatever our image distortion, we can all agree with Robert Burns' conclusion after observing a louse on a lady's hat in church:

> O wad some Pow'r the giftie gie us
> To see oursels as others see us!

And even if we started out with a realistic assessment of our body's size and shape, we need to be aware that there's usually a twenty-one-day delay between body change and the ability to revisualize oneself. Others may be telling you you look great, your scales may be reporting a weight loss, your clothes may be fitting loosely, but you still see the old image in your mirror.

A friend of ours spent a summer in Europe. During that time she walked miles every day, often in uncomfortable climates. She ran very low on money, so she ate only two small meals a day. When she got home and discovered she had lost twenty pounds, she was flabbergasted. "Well, I saw that my face looked kind of thin in the mirror, but I thought I was just tired. And I knew my clothes were baggy, but I thought the fabric had stretched!"

Plastic surgeons have learned this phenomenon of delayed reaction and will often ask their patients to get psychiatric consultations before and immediately following the plastic surgery; they have discovered that when they take the bandages off, the patients still look the same to themselves. Dr. Maxwell Malts, a noted plastic surgeon, reported that even after he showed patients before-and-after photographs, many would still rage at him, "You quack! Why didn't you fix my nose? I'm going to sue!"

Know that this visualization lag is a normal part of the process and be patient with your brain and your eyes; they'll catch up with the rest of your body.

No matter what your mirror or family snapshots may be telling you right now, you tell yourself: *I can have a body I like. I can like the body I have.*

MAKING NEW DECISIONS

Now that your internal slate has been wiped clean of the old pains and fears that you may have carried for years, you need to program in new decisions about who you are and what you want your life to be. Ginger, who loves to encourage others, says, "There's a lot of power in a decision if you can just make it and believe you've made it. Get out of denial and make a decision." Take your journal and make a list of new decisions you want to reach. Look over your list of forgivenesses to help you see new directions you want your life to take.

NEW DECISIONS ABOUT YOURSELF

If the pain that created your love hunger and got you on the addiction cycle came from your childhood, you have spent many years of your adult life carrying a wounded child within you. Now you will need to make new decisions regarding the child within you. As the poet Wordsworth said, "The child is father of the man," and the adult cannot be healthy if the child from whom he grew (and who remains within) is still in pain. You may need to make the decision: *I will be a good parent to the child within me.*

It is not unusual for patients to withhold permission for themselves to heal. If you feel any reluctance inside yourself to accept full healing, make the decisions: *I deserve to be healthy. God wants me to be healthy. I can be healthy.*

How have you always viewed yourself? If you have not seen yourself as healthy, confident, and successful, you need to make new decisions in these areas: *I deserve to feel good. I am confident of my abilities. I can be successful.*

You need to decide that you are a lovable person: loved by God, loved by your family, loved by your friends, loved by yourself.

The first step to seeing yourself as a lovable person and accepting the love of others is accepting God's love. If you have trouble truly believing that God loves you unconditionally, give Him a chance to tell you so. Get out your Bible and read of God's love. In the Old Testament the book of Hosea shows the love of God played out in human terms, as Hosea marries the beautiful but unfaithful Gomer and, because of his love for her, seeks her restoration to his home again and again, in spite of her repeated infidelities.

If you feel unworthy of God's love, read Romans 5:8 and insert your own name: "God demonstrates His own love toward _____, in that while _____ was still a sinner, Christ died for _____."

Then read the words of John 3:16, again inserting your own name: "For God so loved _____ that He gave His only begotten Son that _____ might believe in Him and _____ might not perish, but have everlasting life." Repeat this morning and evening for a week to give your subconscious mind time to internalize it. Most people have heard all their lives that Jesus died for the sins of the world, but the life-changing experience comes when you realize that if you had been the only person in the world, He would have died just for you.

And remember, God's love is offered freely to all; we don't have to do anything to earn it in the sense of being good enough. But we do have to receive it. We must open ourselves to receive the flow of love and forgiveness God offers as a gift.

You need to decide that you are a useful person: useful to God with a special place in His scheme of the universe, useful to your family and friends with a unique ability to meet their needs, useful to yourself with the ability to meet your own needs.

NEW DECISIONS ABOUT FOOD

Your new decisions about food will need to reflect your new understandings about what food is. Decide: Food is a source of nutrition, not a drug. Eating is a source of sustenance, not a recreation.

I eat only when I'm hungry; I stop eating when I'm satisfied. I have plenty of time to eat, so I never need to gulp my food.

Especially if you have a history of going on and off diets, you'll need to make new decisions about dieting such as, *Dieting is giving good things to my body, not keeping goodies from it. My diet is my friend.*

Make new decisions about the role you will let food play in your life from now on. Dr. Frank Minirth uses himself and his twelve-year-old daughter, Renée, as an example of people who restrict food to a very limited role in their lives. "Because we're both diabetic and have to watch our diets carefully, it would be easy to get obsessive about this," he says. "But we've determined to enrich our lives beyond food. We love anything outdoorsy: camping, swimming, hiking, horseback riding. Renée is a talented artist and loves to sketch. We all love to read and share items from our reading with each other. Sharing spiritually is a great enrichment to our lives. We like to sing old hymns as a family and share Bible verses or spiritual insights while we're sitting around the table. Having such stimulating things to think about just doesn't leave time to worry much about food."

NEW DECISIONS ABOUT RELATIONSHIPS

Most compulsive overeaters have been so obsessed by food and diets they've had little time in their lives for building relationships with people. Now is the time to decide that you will enlarge your relationships, perhaps letting people into your life for the first time in years.

To build bridges over which you can reach other people and they can reach you, you will need to make such decisions as, *I want other people in my life. I can trust other people. I have forgiven the people who betrayed me in the past. I can make wise choices about friends.*

Right now, Ginger is in the process of walking this footpath. Making wise decisions about relationships was impossible for her in the past when she was trapped in a codependent relationship with her parents. Now that she has said good-bye to trying to fix their illnesses, set limits on the amount she will allow them to invade her life, and grieved over their unhappiness and her own, she is taking the first tentative steps to building lasting relationships.

"This isn't easy—not easy at all," she says. "I made such a mess of things before, it's really hard to trust myself to do it right this time, even though I realize I'm working from a whole new set of motivations.

"Right after college, I was married for four years to an extremely violent man. I was scared to death of him. I got out of the marriage and moved out of the frying pan and into the fire—back home with my parents.

"It didn't take me long to see that I was caught in the triangle between my parents and to realize this was not a good place to be. I finished my master's degree, got a job, and moved out on my own. I was single for about three years; then I got married again. Now I realize I was saying to Lee 'Rescue me, rescue me.' It was a totally inappropriate marriage and didn't last long.

"Now I'm dating a fellow from New Zealand. I'm not sure I'd consider him a candidate for marriage, but his views on weight are certainly refreshing. We had been going together for weeks, with me worrying all the time about whether I was thin enough, when one evening I wouldn't let him come over because I'd overeaten and felt fat. When I finally confessed this to him, he just laughed. 'You silly thing,' he said. 'What is this big deal you Americans have about weight? I don't get it.'

"The major decision I've made about my relationships is that I don't have to be friends with or to marry another codependent person. My therapist explained to me that a codependent is emotionally a half person, and the codependent has a built-in radar that will lead him or her to other half persons in an attempt to make a whole person.

"But codependency doesn't add, it divides. Two half people don't make a whole person, they make a quarter person, because your sicknesses multiply each other. I have decided I am a whole person, and, if I marry, I will marry a whole person. And, if we have children, we'll have healthy, whole children."

In making new decisions about your relationships, ask yourself:

- What do I want to put in place of the problems in my parent/child relationships?
- What do I want to put in place of the problems in my friendships?
- What do I want to put in place of the problems in my marriage?

In a marriage relationship, we at Minirth-Meier always try to counsel with both partners at this point. Each one must answer the questions:

- What needs do I have that I want my partner to fill?

- What am I willing to give to my partner?
- Does one partner need more time or attention from the other?
- Does one partner need to give more authority to the other?
- Does one want more sexuality in the relationship?

Barbara looked back in her journal at the good-byes she had said and on the page across from it made a corresponding list of new decisions she was determined to say hello to. This is part of her list:

Good-bye to french fries.	I eat only healthy food.
Good-bye to gulping food.	I always eat in a relaxed, civilized manner.
Good-bye to binging to feed my love hunger.	I fill my life with more rewarding things than food.
Good-bye to isolating myself.	I deserve to have lots of friends.
Good-bye to hating my father.	I am free from the pain of my childhood.
Good-bye to forming relationships with people who use and abandon me.	I deserve relationships with people who will nurture me.
Good-bye to relying on Tom to fix me.	I can be happy and healthy.
Good-bye to a job I hate.	I can use the artistic talent I was born with.
Good-bye to blaming God for my past.	I accept God's love.

It's important for patients to realize that they may not receive all they ask for in a new relationship or in revitalizing an old one, but probably some of their needs will be met. The real key here is giving yourself permission to acknowledge your needs. Let yourself express verbally what you want to receive and what you want to give.

In a marriage in which one spouse has been a compulsive eater, there is usually some degree of sexual dysfunction. If your attitude toward sex is basically healthy, but perhaps you've lost sexual interest in your partner because weight has made sex inconvenient, you will only need to make decisions of a minor tune-up nature: *I will be more loving to my spouse. I will be more accepting of my spouse's advances.*

If you have never viewed sexuality as a God-given privilege to make the utmost of your marriage, then your decisions will need a major overhaul, and you must start with the basics: *Sex is God-given. I have permission to be sexual.*

NEW DECISIONS ABOUT WHO GOD IS

Because we are children of God, created in the image of our Creator, it is necessary to have a valid concept of God in order to have a valid concept of ourselves. Unfortunately many people, like our patient Bill who had been raised by a perfectionistic, rageaholic father and therefore saw God as an angry, punishing father, have a distorted image of God. They need to decide: *God is my Heavenly Father, waiting to embrace me. God loves me. God accepts me. God understands all my problems and is waiting to help me with them.*

Bill had projected his negative images of his earthly father onto God. In order to reverse these projections so that he could see God as a loving heavenly Father, we told Bill to write out a personality profile in his journal, describing exactly what he would want in an earthly father.

Bill came back with a sketch of a father who was caring, compassionate, loving. "But he's not soppy," Bill added. "He guides me, instructs, and disciplines me lovingly but firmly."

"That's great, Bill," we said. "The man you describe would be an exemplary father. Now take those same characteristics and write a description of your heavenly Father."

This was a breakthrough for Bill, and it can be for you, too. We have found the results are almost always in line with Scripture: My God is all-powerful, my God is merciful and just, my God values and encourages me.

To help you get started, read again the story of the prodigal son in Luke 15:11–32. Focus on the father as he welcomes, forgives, embraces, and accepts the wayward son. And read the parable of the lost sheep, Luke 15:3–7. Notice the good shepherd, caring, seeking, risking all to find the lost lamb and bring it back to the fold.

LEARNING POSITIVE SELF-TALK

As you look at your list of new decisions, you should be feeling pleased about the new directions your life is going to take. You may even be excited about all those positive decisions. But you may realize, *Saying I'm going to decide this is one thing; believing it is another.* The key to establishing this new belief system is repetition. If you've been hearing negative messages about yourself—from your-self or from others—for years, it's going to take time to program in a new message.

It's also important that you understand the narrow line between denial and positive self-talk. One must not use positive self-talk un-til he's broken through denial and grieved out the pain, or he will make the situation worse by burying the problem deeper. Patients often ask us, "Now which is it? Am I to face the pain or look for the positive?" And our answer is, "Both." You must know whether the glass is half empty or half full. Grieve for the emptiness; then be positive about the fullness.

We sometimes call this the Mr. Magoo syndrome. The terribly nearsighted Mr. Magoo can step off a sidewalk into a mud puddle and say, "Ah, I must be on the Riviera. The sand between my toes feels so-o-o good." You need to admit you aren't on the Riviera, but still feel the nice sand wherever you are.

COPING WITH THE NEGATIVE FLOODTIDE

Sometimes one positive message will trigger a flood of negative messages until, as Dr. Hemfelt puts it, "You feel like you're trying to hold up an avalanche with a toothpick."

If you encounter a flood of negative messages on your way to believing your new messages, understand that's perfectly normal and don't be swept away by the flood. Go ahead and let your mind express the negative thoughts, but don't dwell on them. Just tell your arguing mind, *Thank you for expressing your opinion, but I disagree.* Then go ahead and listen to your positive messages.

Sometimes in therapy we even have patients change chairs for the positive and negative messages. You might want to try this tech-nique at home, just be sure you spend lots more time in the positive chair than in the negative one.

Talking to yourself in the mirror as if to another person can help too. Let the negative messages come from that foreign being in the mirror; then you answer back *out loud* with the truth. The old messages will fight, sometimes sounding like a chorus in a Greek play trying to shout you down. But be reassured: the reason they are kicking and screaming so hard is that they know they are dying. This is their last desperate attempt to stay around. The new, stronger you can outlast them.

In his book *The Lies We Believe*, Dr. Chris Thurman has two other suggestions we want to share with you for dealing with the negative lies your mind will tell you. Dr. Thurman sometimes tells patients to write down the negative thoughts that occur to them dur-ing the day. He suggests that at the end of the day, you write a positive statement under each negative one. You can then use these positive statements on your self-talk tape during the next day.

Dr. Thurman calls another technique "thought stopping." When a negative thought strikes you, give yourself fifteen to thirty seconds to think about it; then make a loud noise such as clapping your hands, shouting "Stop!" or setting a timer. After a few times of doing this, you will be able to divert negative thoughts more quietly.

PROGRAMMING IN THE POSITIVE

Now you are going to make a positive self-talk audiocassette tape, which you will use at least once a day for two to six weeks to restructure your thought process from the destructive negativism that has been your normal pattern to the constructive positivism that will set the tone for the fully recovered you.

1. Writing

Look over the list of new decisions in your journal. Examine the positive statements you have written under negative thoughts that occurred to you. Look carefully at the following list of positive self-talk statements we have compiled, and choose the twenty-five to thirty-five statements you most want to describe your life.

The more specific the self-talk statements, the more helpful they will be. Name your specific trigger food as Barbara did when she wrote, "I can live a long happy life without eating fudge." Or be very specific in referring to a new step you want to take in your relationships as Ginger did when she wrote, "I deserve to be in relationships with men who are willing to commit to me."

Look back through the good-byes you've said to be sure you've given yourself something positive to fill the space left by every good-bye. If you don't, old negative messages will refill the space you've purged out with grief.

This is a 'no holds barred' assignment. There is no way you can overdo your work on this section. We are focusing on exploring new vistas, so be sure that you have climbed the highest mountain around for the clearest view you can find. Once you've seen where you want to be from the broad overview, take time to move in closely and examine your special places in minute detail. You are setting the scene for the rest of your life, so do it carefully, do it in detail, do it prayerfully.

2. Recording

When you are satisfied with your written list, you are ready to record it onto a cassette tape. Begin by recording a minute or two of a favorite piece of music that you find soothing and relaxing. Then,

POSITIVE SELF-TALK STATEMENTS

1. I eat only when I'm hungry.

2. I give my body the most nutritious food I can.

3. I stop eating when I'm satisfied.

4. I always chew my food thoroughly.

5. I take plenty of time to eat.

6. I easily resist social pressure to eat.

7. I easily resist my trigger foods.

8. I can resist trigger situations.

9. I never eat in secret.

10. I am a lovable person.

11. I am a useful person.

12. I enjoy feeling good.

13. I enjoy looking good.

14. I enjoy taking good care of myself.

15. I deserve to live.

16. I want people in my life.

17. I can enjoy healthy relationships.

18. My spouse is my best friend.

19. I deserve to succeed in my career.

20. I can reach the top.

21. I deserve to be healthy.

22. I deserve to be sexual.

23. My diet is my ally.

24. My diet is a choice I am making.

25. My diet is a gift I'm giving myself.

26. My body is my friend.

27. My body is a living expression of myself.

28. My body is a gift from God.

29. My body is something I have control over.

30. Sex is good as God created it to be.

31. I am happy to be the gender God created me to be.

32. The child within me is a precious being.

33. The child within me deserves love.

34. The child within me deserves nurturing.

35. God loves me.

36. God forgives me.

37. I accept His forgiveness.

38. God guides me.

39. God gives me strength to enact my new decisions.

stop the music, and, in a clear, affirmative voice, read your first statement. Pause one beat. Read it again. Pause, and read it again until you have recorded the statement four times. Continue with the rest of your list, and end with a few more minutes of music.

3. Listening

Once you begin using your tape, remember: self-talk will work only with long and frequent repetition, and it will not work as a band-aid. When directed to this healing footpath, many patients have told us, "I tried that already. I ordered a whole set of thirty-five-dollar self-help tapes, and they didn't do a thing for me."

We find that in cases of reported failures, either the patient failed to do the proper repetitions (listening to the tapes two or three times in his car on the way home from work, then giving up), or he had failed to clear out space for the new messages by doing his grief work first. Positive messages can be recorded only if the old negative ones have been erased.

Although many people like to listen to their tapes in their cars (and this is an efficient use of time), your most effective programming will occur when you're fully relaxed. That's one reason for recording some soothing music first. For optimum results choose a time when you're alone, adjust light and temperature levels to your preference, sit in a comfortable chair or lie down, and close your eyes.

Try not to analyze the messages or to argue with them. Simply let them sink into your subconscious mind. If you still find negative thoughts recurring, turn off your tape, and write down the negative thought. Then put a positive one under it. Once you've got that negative message off your mind, you're ready to go on with your tape.

Take time to do this exercise fully every day for two weeks, and also play the tape as often as you want in your car or while cleaning the house or getting ready for bed. Continue playing the tape at least once a day for up to six weeks until you find yourself fully in agreement with all the statements and no negative thoughts interrupt.

VISUALIZING YOUR SUCCESS

While you are playing your self-talk tape or anytime you think about the future, imagine yourself where you want to be. Form a picture in your mind of the happy, slim, free you wearing a new suit, enjoying the company of a new companion, accepting a new challenge at work.

Especially when you know you have to face a difficult situation (such as attending a banquet where your trigger food will be served, seeing an old acquaintance with whom you have had a traumatic relationship, giving a public speech), prepare for it by visualizing yourself in every step of the situation. How will you look? How will you stand? Sit? What will you wear? See yourself smiling. What will you say? Picture yourself enjoying small portions of everything on the menu except your trigger food. Picture yourself shaking hands confidently with your old acquaintance. Picture yourself accepting applause for your speech.

When you find yourself in the real situation, it will seem easy because you've done it all before.

And as you simultaneously travel your diet footpath, picture yourself slim and confident. Patients who have lost tens, sometimes hundreds, of pounds have reported they did not feel as if they were losing part of themselves. They felt they were finding themselves. Michelangelo is supposed to have said after sculpting the David from a huge block of Carrara marble, "I just chipped away the bits that weren't David." Picture how you will look when you have chipped away the bits that aren't you, and then enter your new life.

10

PATH SIX: TRUSTING NEW DIRECTIONS

"I'VE DECIDED I do want more people in my life," Barbara Jamison told us. "I want to be more trusting. But where do I go now? I've been hurt so many times in the past, I'm just not sure I can trust anyone."

This was a very normal reaction. Almost all of our patients feel this way at this point in their recovery. So we did the same thing for Barbara that we do for the others: we gave her a specific assignment. "We want you to start by trusting a very small, very safe group. We want you to start by trusting us and your therapy group. Tomorrow when you come in for group therapy, we want you to share something you've never shared with anyone before."

The look of fear on Barbara's face told us that she knew what she needed to share. And that it wouldn't be easy.

The next day Barbara took a seat in the most shadowed corner of the room, but didn't resist when we asked her to come forward and share. She sat with her hands folded on her lap, staring steadily at them. "I was always a very good girl. I never meant to go too far with Calvin. He didn't exactly rape me. I don't know . . . it just happened. Then he left me. He probably felt guilty too. I don't know."

The fact that none of us shamed her or told her she was a bad person for this long-ago mistake was very reassuring to her. Someone in the group asked her if she'd asked God's forgiveness for this, and she said she had. When they asked, "Well, have you forgiven yourself?" she wasn't sure at first.

Then she smiled. "Yes, I think maybe I have. Now." She paused. "Yeah. I have."

Barbara had taken all the steps: she had said good-bye to the pain of her guilt over this experience, she had grieved for it, and she had decided to move on with her life. But the abstract decision was not enough. She had to take an action to reinforce the decision.

This important step of launching out and trusting people can be taken with any support group or person: a trusted friend or family member, an Overeaters Anonymous group, a pastor. But whomever you choose, we can't overemphasize how essential it is that you take this overt action. You could instruct someone for twenty years on how to swim—teach the hydrodynamics of it, show movies on how the muscles coordinate—but until the student actually gets in the water and has firsthand experience of the act of swimming, he'll never learn to swim. Until you jump in the water and take the risk of trusting someone, you'll never learn to trust.

Take the list of new decisions you made in following footpath #5, the decisions you are now listening to on your self-talk tape, and on a sheet of paper directly across from this list, write down a step of trust you can take to put this decision into action. Some of the steps may be small ones; some others will look so audacious it will scare you to see them written down on paper; but you must attach an action to every decision you have made.

If you decided you deserve to be healthy, perhaps your step will be to join a support group. If you decided you will give yourself plenty of time to eat, perhaps now you need to ask your boss for a longer lunch hour or set your alarm earlier so that you can eat a satisfying, unhurried breakfast. If you decided you want to achieve a better relationship with your roommate, perhaps the first step will be apologizing for the bad attitude you've had.

TAKING HEALTHY RISKS

There are three major components to achieving change in your life: decision, action, and feeling. Often our patients will chase those three around mentally, trying to decide which should come first in a chicken-or-the-egg dilemma: When I feel like it, then I'll take the action; I'll try the action, then I'll decide if I want to stay with it; I can't make a decision until I feel like it.

Affecting change in your life has to be a mind over matter affair. You must make a decision and take the action on faith; the feeling will follow sometime later. If you wait until you "feel like it," you could be waiting into the twenty-first century.

It may even take more than one step before the feelings will come. You may be like the Air Force Academy cadet who made the decision he wanted to learn to skydive. On his first jump, he counted and pulled the cord just as he'd been taught, but he didn't open his eyes until the chute opened. On the second jump he managed to get his eyes open. On the third jump he landed with a shout, "I love it!" and went on to win honors in the Wings of Blue skydiving team. You've made your decision; now close your eyes and step out of the plane.

The slogan that goes, "You can't think your way into better acting, but you can act your way into better feeling," is true because with feelings, there is a delayed reaction.

We call this risk taking, however, because occasionally you may take a misstep. Remember, though, that these are healthy risks, ones that you can afford to take a chance on—not like the risk of obesity which is certain to shorten your life. If, however, you find you have taken a step that resulted in a turned ankle, realize that even this can have its positive aspect. As you sit there with an ice pack on your sprained ankle, you will see that one small failure wasn't the end of the world. One misstep didn't spell disaster. Put a wrapping on your sprain and go out and try another risk. This is growth.

Be certain that you are taking healthy risks in all the areas in which you made new decisions in pathway #5: yourself, food, relationships, God. Concerning those scary feelings that say don't take a chance, keep telling yourself, as those who attend self-help groups are taught: "Feelings are not facts." Some of our patients put that on a card to carry in their pocket.

ENRICHING YOUR LIFE BY TRUSTING FOOD

For Barbara, food had been both a security blanket and an enemy. It was something she couldn't live without and yet seemingly the cause of all her troubles. Now she had made the decision that food could be an ally, and she was following Dr. Sneed's exchange diet. Intellectually she knew she could trust food not to betray her. Yet emotionally, this was harder. It was so hard to trust food that instead of going to the grocery store, which she considered the ultimate confrontation with food, she went to a movie. She chose *Indiana Jones and the Last Crusade* because a really fast-paced adventure movie could take her mind off food. Following Indiana Jones on his search for the ark of the covenant was great because she had loved stories of King Arthur since early childhood.

But in the final scene when Indiana had to step off the precipice to what looked like certain death, her mind was jerked back to her problem with food. Could she take a step of faith like that? Could she step out into the void and trust food as Indiana trusted his father's directions? She was so gripped by the image of the bridge springing up under Indiana's feet that she couldn't concentrate on the end of the movie.

As soon as she got home, she called Ginger. "I don't know what to do. I've got to take the first step, but I don't know if I can."

It was a wonderful relief to talk with someone who really understood, as Ginger agreed. "Boy, do I know how you feel! The hardest thing I ever did was go to a welcome-back-to-school party after I'd started my diet. I knew all the other teachers would be eating nachos piled high with guacamole and sour cream, and I wasn't sure I could survive. If I hadn't known my principal would be watching for me, I'd probably have skipped it. But you know what? Celery sticks are really very good. And I never would have noticed the bowl of cottage cheese dip if I hadn't been dieting.

"Remember Ralph?" Ginger asked Barbara. "I think you heard him speak at a support group meeting? . . . Yeah, the blond one. He said once that when he joined Alcoholics Anonymous they told him he'd have to learn to trust the absence of alcohol. He thought he could never go to another business meeting if he didn't drink. When his boss said he had to go, he discovered that there were lots of people there who didn't drink at all, and one whole section of the bar was stocked with soft drinks—diet soft drinks, even.

"Listen, Barb, you need to trust that you can go to a party and have fun without eating—or with eating very sparingly."

Barbara hung up and pulled the note out of her wastebasket that had been shoved under her door that morning. The management was throwing a party around the pool for their apartment house. She smoothed out the wrinkles to read the bottom. "Bring your favorite cassette tape and a plate of snacks."

Celery sticks and cottage cheese dip? she thought. *Well, this might be a chance to try out Dr. Sneed's recipe for baked tortilla chips with salsa. That didn't sound too bad.* And she could always flee back to her room if it got overwhelming. Besides, she wouldn't look too out of place wearing a caftan to a pool party.

She even decided to buy a tape of the sound track of *Indiana Jones and the Last Crusade* to take as her musical contribution. No one else need know the step she was taking was as difficult as Indiana's.

The next evening the weather was perfect and the tiki torches around the pool flickered in a gentle breeze when Barbara, forcing a bright smile, joined her fellow residents. Fortunately the girl from across the hall was one of the first people she saw because Barbara knew hardly anyone else in the whole complex.

"Hi, Barbara. Come meet Mary Sue," her neighbor called.

An hour later, Barbara finally decided to visit the refreshment table for some of the great-looking fruit kabobs she saw other people eating. In all that time she had been laughing and talking and thoroughly enjoying meeting the people who lived near her. At that moment the man running the stereo system put on her Indiana Jones tape. She realized the bridge had sprung up under her feet, and she hadn't even noticed it. She had had fun at a party without eating. She didn't need food for courage. She had had a much better time focusing on people than she would have had focusing on food, and she was much freer to talk and laugh and move about when she wasn't hindered by food in her hands or mouth.

So first, like Barbara, you must learn to trust the absence of food in your life. Then, especially if you have been on a liquid diet or a highly regimented low-calorie diet, you must learn to trust the presence of food. As you near your optimum weight and move toward the maintenance part of your recovery, you will begin what we call at the clinic "refeeding," learning to make wise food choices. This is a very frightening time for many patients. Many people are black or white eaters. They can starve themselves, or they can gorge themselves, but the thought of eating in the gray areas where they must make wise, controlled choices, is frightening. Decide you can do it. You can make food choices that are healthy for you. You can eat sparingly and not plunge back into gorging again. Take the first step by choosing a celery canapé.

Enjoy your new food experiences. Enjoy savoring the flavors of your new low-fat, high-fiber food selections. Have fun experimenting with the new recipes in this book and other low-calorie ones that you may find in magazines or get from friends. Try adapting your old family favorites to this new low-fat, low-sugar, high-flavor, high-satisfaction method of cooking. Enjoy exploring new restaurants or ordering from the "lite" side of the menu in old favorites.

But most of all, enjoy congratulating yourself as you exercise your new control over food. The sense of power that comes from controlling one's own eating can be a real thrill. As you go from day to day regulating your food, realizing that you no longer have to binge, this in itself is a new experience. Like the alcoholic in AA who discovers, "Hey, I went thirty days, then sixty days, and now I've been dry for six months! It's amazing! Before this I told myself I couldn't stop drinking. Now I find I'm having these fantastic new experiences of honoring the new decisions I've made."

Some of our patients find it fun and helpful to reward themselves with a new scarf or a new necktie or something every month or six weeks they've stayed on their diet. If you like the idea of marking your anniversaries this way, by all means do so, but the realization of your own power is really the best reward of all.

ENRICHING YOUR LIFE BY TRUSTING EXPERIENCES BEYOND FOOD

Most binge eaters have been so focused on food that it consumes all their experiences. They cut out everyone and everything else in their lives. Now is the time to start getting the balance back in your life: meeting new people; revitalizing old relationships; growing in your career; taking up hobbies, sports, intellectual and spiritual pursuits.

Joanne was an extremely overweight perpetual student. She had earned her master's degree in psychology and was working on her doctorate. As she ended nine years' work toward this degree, however, her professors had to confront her with the fact that if she didn't finish up, they would have to drop her from the program. The problem was that Joanne was terrified of new experiences. She was so overweight that she felt there was nothing else she could do but study. She knew that although she was a brilliant woman, she would never be hired by a psychiatric clinic or be able to win the confidence of her clients in a private practice.

Look again at the pie chart in Chapter 7 of how you spend your time. Is that still an accurate assessment of your life? If not, do a new one. What areas do you see that need broadening? Are there some items that need to be there but aren't? For example, have you made time for daily exercise yet? Is Sunday the only day you give any time to God, or do you have a daily devotional and Bible study time? What about relaxation—spending time talking to your spouse, reading a novel? Are the things you spend time on satisfying, or do you need to make some changes?

In looking at her pie chart, Barbara, too, saw that the thinnest areas in her life were people and career. The time she spent checking out at K-Mart was not a career. Only using her God-given artistic talent would count as a satisfying career. Barbara knew her skills were rusty and her confidence shaky. To rebuild both, she decided the best step would be to take a design course at the community college just a few miles from her home. She sat staring at her telephone. She'd made the decision. Now she had to take action. She drew a deep breath and called the registrar to request a college catalog and registration form.

The next area was even harder, but having done the easier one first gave her courage. She hadn't talked to Tom since she began this whole world-shaking process of recovery. She didn't really know what chance their marriage had to survive, but she knew she wanted it to. If he would talk to her and maybe agree to counseling with the doctors at the clinic, surely they could make it.

EXPLORING NEW EXPERIENCES WITH PEOPLE

Calling Tom was the hardest step Barbara had ever had to take. *Thank goodness I tried trusting food first,* she thought. That had seemed so hard at the time, but now she realized it was nothing in comparison with calling her estranged husband. The bridge had been there when she stepped off the precipice by going to a party. Surely it would be here now.

She picked up the phone and dialed the number of his office. She prayed that he wouldn't be there. Salesmen spend so little time in their offices. With luck she could put this off for days.

He was in. "Tom, this is Barbara. I—er, how are you?"

He didn't sound any more confident than she did. "I'm OK. How are you?"

This "How are you? I am fine" business could go on forever. She took a deep breath and plunged. "Tom, I've called to tell you I'm different. I've made a lot of changes in my life, and . . ." Here she ran out of breath. ". . . and . . . Tom, could we meet and talk about this in person?"

Tom agreed to come over that evening after work. Well, the bridge had been a pretty shaky one, but at least she hadn't fallen off the precipice.

Although Tom was the most important person Barbara wanted in her life, he wasn't the only person in the world, and there was no sense sitting around waiting and worrying about this evening. She called Mary Sue, whom she had met at the party. "Hi, this is Barbara upstairs. I just made some iced tea. Wanta come up and help me drink it?"

Once you have made the decision to allow people into your life and have taken the first step of trusting someone near you, new and renewed friendships are possible. Most of our patients, however, find that they, like Barbara, must put a little effort into making this happen. The best place to start is with your journal. Look back at your relationship survey. What old friends and family members have you lost touch with? What ruptured relationships would you like to have healed? Now think about your everyday life. Picture the people around you at work, at church, in your diet club. Does the girl at the desk next to yours in the office look nice? Have you ever said more than hello to her? What about that new couple at church who may be feeling more lonely than you are?

Although calling an old friend or new acquaintance and saying, "Come over for a cup of tea," or, "Let's go to a movie together," may be the best thing to do, consider another possibility. Think about reviving the art of letter writing as one of your communication skills for building bridges back to people. Social letter writing was considered a fine art in the eighteenth and nineteenth centuries, but is almost a lost skill today.

Conversation, another fine art of gentler ages, is also a dying skill, particularly for overeaters who have been isolating themselves for a long time. They often report feeling like teenagers on a first date when they try to strike up a conversation at a party. There are several easy ways to overcome this: First, remember that the best talker is a good listener. Ask people about themselves and then *listen*. They'll think you're brilliant. Second, you should be interested in a variety of things. Read the newspapor and watch the TV news so that you can discuss current events; develop an unusual hobby that you can tell others about. Third, be willing to do a little homework. Our friend who unknowingly lost twenty pounds on a trip to Europe had occasion to take tea with a descendant of Charles II. "I hadn't been there very long," she said, "when I realized this lady had memorized my itinerary and my most recent letters so she could talk to me about my interests. I couldn't help wondering how many American talk show hosts (who get paid to know about their guests) would have had that kind of courtesy for their guests."

EXPLORING NEW CAREER POSSIBILITIES

Are you ready to start your career like Barbara, or are you ready to take on new responsibility or accept a promotion? You may be feeling a wonderful new confidence in yourself and in your life.

But you may be like Ralph, who found this a very difficult step to take. In spite of his employer's absolute confidence in him, Ralph had so little confidence in himself that he would go on an eating binge every time a promotion loomed. Now, in the maintenance stage of his recovery, Ralph was working on building his trust in himself.

Ralph's first step was to acknowledge his fear to his support group. His second step came that very night when he was able to listen to their affirmative comments to him without argument. He may not have emotionally believed them, but intellectually he heard them. A third step came when Ralph could report back to his group, "I still have fears at work, but I can accept that I do deserve the job. Even if I'm scared, I'm doing good work."

His most recent triumph came when he accepted an offered promotion without letting it throw him into a binge. In his new position he evaluates other workers, so he has now been able to accept his boss's evaluation of his work and to accept the responsibility of becoming an authority figure himself.

Most people, no matter how calm and successful they look, feel insecure at times. If you have failed in the past because you allowed old doubts to sabotage your success, realize that the situation is different now because you've grieved out your pain. Take the first step, hold steady, and wait for the feelings of confidence to catch up with you. Remember, you can only be as successful as you allow yourself to be.

EXPLORING RECREATION AND HOBBIES

In exploring the possibilities for recreation and hobbies in the new, richer life your recovery is leading you into, you might want to do a daydream survey. What have you always wanted to do but been held back from because of your size or other fears? If you could be any sports figure, living or dead, who would it be? If you could succeed in any field of the arts, which one would you choose? If you really had unlimited time and money, what would you do? Where would you go?

Sorry, we can't tell you, "Well, so go on out and do it." But these answers will be clues to the new interests that will be satisfying to you. If you've always dreamed of being Babe Ruth, check your community recreation calendar to find a baseball team you can play on, call the local Little League and see if they need T-ball coaches, buy a season ticket to your local team's games, or subscribe to a sports or health magazine. If you've always dreamed of playing with the Cleveland Orchestra, call a local music store to inquire about private teachers or group lessons such as Yamaha or Suzuki that often offer adult courses, or make a list of your favorite composers and favorite symphonies, and then start building your collection of tapes or CDs. Or explore the listening possibilities on your public radio station and tape your favorite programs if they come on while you're at work, or buy a season ticket to a concert series. The possibilities are limitless. Let your imagination soar, but don't stop with imagination; do something to make at least a small part of your dream come true.

Where have you always wanted to go? Australia? Tibet? The Hebrides? Contact a travel agent and start collecting material. Go to your library and ask for travel books. Start a savings fund with the money you are no longer spending on food.

Or, instead of asking yourself "What have I always wanted to do?" ask "What have I always hated or feared doing because of my size or fear of failure?" Now that you are on your way to recovery, even these activities will be possible to you. They might become something you want to take up voluntarily, such as skiing or something that you will now be able to do if circumstances demand it, such as flying.

And finally, look at the things you already do and ask yourself how you can expand your old interests. If you've always loved reading, ask your librarian to recommend a new author or a new genre. Join a book discussion group. Consider writing book reviews for your church or club newsletter.

One evening Barbara and Ginger were sitting together in their support group when Ralph shared about new directions he was taking to enrich his life. "One of the best things about getting my weight down is having all this new energy. So that's what I'm working on now—trying to find healthy things to do with my time. Of course, exercise is the key to keeping weight off. I watch what I eat, too, but I exercise to burn off what I do eat. Racquetball is my favorite. It's good because it's a year-round thing, but it's not aerobic, and I think the ideal would be aerobic exercise."

Barbara was puzzled. Dr. Sneed had listed racquetball as an aerobic exercise. She raised her hand. "Do you mean you don't sit around and take your pulse after you play racquetball?"

Ralph smiled. "Right. We don't check pulse rates, and there's too much stopping and starting. It has to be continuous to be aerobic. Well, let's face it—it would be aerobic if you had two very good players. But you don't really get that luxury every time you go out to play. I just play whoever's there, and they may not be at my level."

He paused and looked down. "Sorry if that sounds conceited. I do play a lot, so my skill is pretty good. But I'll be really honest here. It's a valuable lesson in self-esteem. If you won all the time, or if you lost all the time, it could be hard on your ego either way. It's a fine line. So I'm working at just trying to have fun with the game, playing it for health, and not necessarily to win. That's a benefit of exercise you won't find on any calorie-burning chart."

SPECIAL TRUST AREAS FOR RECOVERING OVEREATERS

At the clinic we help thousands of people recovering from every known addiction to learn to trust again. In the course of this we have discovered that there are three areas of trusting that are unique to those recovering from compulsive overeating:

1. It's necessary to begin trusting that it's all right to be sexual after your weight loss. Many dieters are shocked to discover that sexuality is suddenly a part of their lives. While their fat pad pro-

tected them from such considerations, they gave very little thought to the whole issue. Suddenly, they find themselves attracting attention from the opposite sex and feeling a responding interest themselves. This is usually unsettling at first. If your self-talk doesn't include the decision, "I deserve to be sexual," add it now, along with, "I can trust my own body," and "I can accept sexual interest from my spouse." Choose a first step to put these decisions into practice. Maybe buying a new nightgown or swim suit?

2. You can trust your new physical image. We talked about the time lag between physical change and mental perception. But that lag will catch up. When it does, you will see a new you in the mirror. Your eyes aren't playing tricks on you. That is the new you. Decide to trust it. Take steps to enjoy it. Buy a new suit or a new dress. Walk with new confidence.

3. And now you can trust compliments. This is an area that can be difficult for anyone. Children must be taught to say thank you without ducking their heads. A person in any area of life may unexpectedly find himself shying away from a compliment with the almost superstitious thought, *But what if I slip up next time?* This is hardest of all for overeaters, who have spent years deflecting sarcastic fat jokes and filtering out deserved compliments because of low self-esteem. Assign yourself the exercise of accepting compliments instead of minimizing them—no matter what you are being complimented on. If this is especially hard for you, try a little role-playing: Aloud, say, "That's a pretty dress." (Do not say, "I got it on sale.") Look at yourself in the mirror. Smile. Say, "Thank you, I'm glad you like it."

Say, "You did a great job on that report." Reply, "Thank you, I appreciate the encouragement." (Not, "It was really a team effort; I don't deserve the credit.")

Friends of ours who spent six months in France said one of the hardest things for them to get used to was the French response to compliments. One never accepts a compliment in France. The proper response, is "Oh, no, no, no!" In America, however, that is not a sign of humble good manners, but of insecurity and asking for repeated compliments. Unless you are planning an extended trip to the continent, learn to trust the compliments you receive and say a simple, straightforward, "Thank you."

EXPLORING A NEW RELATIONSHIP WITH GOD

This will be a good time to find a church home. Pray for guidance on this important decision, ask trusted friends for recommendations, and give yourself time to visit several churches more than once to find the group that truly meets your spiritual needs. Look for a church that is Bible-centered, where Jesus Christ is honored, and where you feel welcomed warmly. Then look for a small group within the church where you can receive special nurturing: a Sunday school class, Bible study group, ladies' fellowship, men's fellowship, or small support group.

And look for ways to make your daily devotional time more meaningful. We are often told to have a special time each day that we spend alone with God. But we don't so often hear of the importance of having a special *place*. And yet many of our patients have found this to be the key to a growing devotional life. One told us: "I always had this romantic notion of taking my Bible out to read under the willow tree or of sitting by the fire in the winter. Trouble was, I never got myself out to the willow tree, and by the time I had the fire built the kids were home from school. I finally put my Bible and study book by the big chair in my bedroom, and I go there the minute the kids leave for school. It has made all the difference."

Explore new devotional materials too: various translations of the Bible, a good study Bible, prayer books, daily devotional readings, great hymns of the faith and modern Christian music, poetry and other writings by modern writers and by Christians of the past such as Wesley or C. S. Lewis. One favorite, especially among male patients, is Oswald Chambers' *My Utmost for His Highest.*

It may be of special interest to you to find some of the devotional books that have been written specifically for recovering patients. Many people have found the Hazelden Meditation series to be helpful.*

As you explore every possibility along this footpath of enrichment, take Christ, who "increased in wisdom and stature and in favor with God and man" as your model and as your guide.

---

*To receive a catalog of Hazelden's devotional material, write to: Educational Materials, Pleasant Valley Road, P.O. Box 176, Center City, Minnesota 55012–0176, and ask for Recovery Resource, a catalog of inspiration and information in the Twelve Step Tradition.

11

PATH SEVEN: CHOOSING NEW GUIDES

THIS IS the footpath we most often call "reparenting." Reparenting is a normal process for all people, whether you left home in the regular course of events or have only recently left home emotionally. The nurturing role normally played by parents must be replaced in two ways. You need to learn how to walk alone, nurturing yourself, and you need to learn how to choose companions who will nurture you.

BEING A GOOD PARENT TO YOURSELF

Although reparenting is for everyone, it is harder for the person from a dysfunctional home because he lacks the necessary role models. If your parents didn't teach you how to be a good parent, you must learn what good parents do and how to do it for yourself. We take time to mention here only four major areas in which you will need to learn self-parenting.

GOOD PARENTS BUILD CONFIDENCE

You must build your own self-confidence. You've been doing this through using positive self-talk. You've been building confidence in taking the first steps to put your new decisions into action. As you continue to succeed with your diet, your confidence will grow. Yet be very careful not to slip into old roles. At some point in parenting our own children, we all eventually do some of the things we said we'd never do as our parents did them to us: "I told myself I'd never use that tone of voice on my children." "I said I'd never call my children that name." "I said I'd never use that excuse."

Especially, be sure you never use shame on yourself. The last thing you need is shame or condemnation, especially if you should slip into relapse on your diet. The self-nurturing person says, "I blew it. But I see where I made my mistake. I'll do better next time."

Don't ever tell yourself you are a bad or a weak person. Look back over your journal and see how far you've come. See how long you've stayed with your diet. See all the work you've been doing on relationships and career improvement. Only a very courageous, dedicated person could have made it this far. You can make it to total recovery.

GOOD PARENTS DISCIPLINE

Good parents discipline consistently and lovingly in a manner that will teach their children good habits and how to discern right from wrong. If you grew up in a family where discipline was too harsh and rigid or, at the other extreme, too permissive or nonexistent, you will not know how to discipline yourself. We've dis covered that many compulsive overeaters are too rigid with their self-discipline.

Whichever side of the discipline dilemma you find yourself on, find a fellow dieting person and establish mutual accountability. This could be an Overeaters Anonymous sponsor, someone from your group therapy, or any friend who is also on a diet. At first you will probably want to touch base with this person daily, at least by phone. Let your fellow dieter know how the diet is coming, how you feel, what exercise you plan for that day, what you plan to eat. Verbalizing it to another person is a way to make the commitment real.

But most importantly, give that person permission to confront you. If you need to spend more time exercising by adding more distance to your daily walk or if you're letting too many refined carbohydrates slip back into your diet, your partner needs to tell you so. Don't choose anyone who will shame you or yell at you, which is a very real risk if your parents did that to you, but someone who will point these things out to you in love.

Parents give love and warmth and security, but true love is not a mindless acceptance of anything the other person does. True love is being willing to confront honestly when it's for the good of the beloved.

GOOD PARENTS NURTURE WITH FOOD AND SHELTER

In going on your diet and following our nutrition tips, you are learning to nurture yourself with healthy food. Just the knowledge that you're doing good things for your body is comforting. Congratulate yourself on becoming a good parent in this area.

Parents also provide a home and clothing. Look around at your room, apartment, or house. Is it a *home?* A warm environment where people can grow physically, emotionally, and spiritually? Or does it resemble a motel room with no reflection of the owner's personality? Barbara had denied herself this important area of nurturance because she was trying to block out her hurt over giving up her dream to become an interior decorator. When she took the first step of rebuilding this part of her life, she applied many of the techniques she learned in her design class to her own apartment and found that a beautiful, creative environment could nurture her better than french fries ever did.

Take stock of your wardrobe. The closer you get to your ideal body size, the more pride you'll take in your appearance and the more important it will be to dress to exhibit your new success. Find someone to help you learn what colors and styles are best for you. Have your favorite suits retailored. Get rid of the shirts and ties you always hated anyway and treat yourself to some new ones in sizes that fit and colors you like.

Ralph said that redoing his wardrobe motivated him in his recovery program. "When I lost enough weight that just tightening my belt wouldn't make my pants fit, I decided to commit to retailoring. Since I'd been such a yo-yo, I had clothes of every size in my closet. Yet I determined I'd never wear those big ones again. I got rid of the really huge stuff—no tailor could cope with that, and I hated it anyway—but some of my just-fifteen-pounds-overweight suits were really nice. I have an Italian one, sort of a blue shadow stripe, that was almost worth weighing extra to be able to wear. So I got my whole closet to one size—my permanent size."

GOOD PARENTS NURTURE BY PROVIDING SEXUAL ROLE MODELS

There is probably no area of human experience and human functioning around which people have more false guilt and unnecessary shame than sexuality. Because true intimacy requires complete vulnerability, this can be a frightening, mysterious region for anyone, but far more difficult for someone from a dysfunctional home.

We all spend our first two decades of life in an intense sex education class: our parents' marriage. If we've learned good, healthy approaches to sexuality from our parent-teachers, developing our own sexuality will not be too difficult. But if our first teachers were not adequate, we must find healthy role models for this area of our lives.

Christine probably had the most creative approach to this of anyone we've counseled. Through the earlier stages of her recovery Christine gave herself permission to be sexual and made the decision to build healthy relationships with men. But in trying to find a first step to take she realized she had no idea how to go about this. She didn't know what a healthy relationship was like, how it felt, and what one did. So she decided to leave her singles class at church where there were no role models to answer these questions for her.

She asked several people to direct her to the most family-oriented class in her church. Then she went to the class and told them, "I want to watch you. I grew up without any role models for a good marriage. I want to be part of this class and see what good marriages look like." The hard part of self-nurturing is not digging out the dysfunctions; by this stage in your recovery journey you've undoubtedly identified and dealt with most of these. The challenge is to fill the void with healthy models.

In the past your fat may have been a buffer against having to deal with questions of intimacy. Often in group therapy we ask two patients to stand up, and we tell them to imagine that they both have huge feather-pillows strapped around the front of them. "Now come together and give each other hugs," we say. This is always a time for considerable levity as the two attempt to maneuver themselves into a position where they can put their arms around each other.

If you are married, you will, of course, want to achieve mutually satisfying sexual intimacy with your spouse, but an even higher level is emotional intimacy. One can perform the sex act mechanically, but true emotional intimacy requires a complete openness that comes from confidence built by healthy nurturing.

Dr. Hemfelt talked with Barbara and Tom about achieving this ultimate relationship in their marriage. "Can you honestly talk about your feelings to each other? Emotional intimacy is a two-way street. You need to be able to express your own feelings, and you need to be able to accept another's expression. Work for free emotional exchange in your relationship."

Barbara nodded, but she was looking at the doctor rather than at Tom. The doctor continued, "Mutual trust is also an essential element of emotional intimacy. We sometimes have our hospital patients go on a trust walk. One is blindfolded, and another leads him or her through the hospital—along corridors, up and down stairs, out on balconies. Barbara, Tom, I want each of you to close your eyes right now and imagine being the blindfolded partner on a trust walk with the other one. Think what it would feel like. Would you trust your spouse to guide you fairly? Which is harder, upstairs or downstairs? OK, you're coming to the cafeteria. If your guide says, 'Open your mouth,' would you trust him to give you a bite of something good for you? Remember, it's all on faith; you can't see a thing on your own. Think about that."

Barbara and Tom opened their eyes, blinking. Barbara laughed, "I loved the strawberry, Tom, but you forgot to take the stem off."

Tom grinned. "Couldn't you have found something more original to give me than a cracker? It was awful dry."

Dr. Hemfelt's eyes sparkled. "Excellent! I can see you got into the spirit of that. Now I want each of you to think of your own emotional life. Can you be transparent and vulnerable to each other and yet set boundaries? This is a matter of balance. You need to be entirely open to each other to express and receive feelings, as we said earlier, but you also need to be able to say, 'I need some time alone.' Tom, if you invite Barbara to go for a walk in the park with you and she's feeling pressured, she needs to be able to say, 'I need some time alone.'"

Barbara interrupted, "I might someday, but for now, I can't imagine wanting time *away* from Tom."

"Well, that's fine," the doctor said. "It's not the staying away that's important; it's the freedom to express how you really feel that matters. Now, a good way to judge emotional intimacy in your marriage is by the amount of touching you do. Do you still hold hands like when you were dating? Do you sit curled up together to watch TV? Do you snuggle in bed in a warm intimacy that has nothing to do with the sex act? These are good indications of emotional intimacy.

"And there's one final thing I want to stress. Praying together is one of the best ways to achieve emotional intimacy in your marriage and will lead to the highest plane of all: spiritual intimacy."

ALLOWING OTHERS TO NURTURE YOU

If you have said good-bye to the hurts of growing up without nurturing parents and have grieved your loss, you are now ready to find other people who can be loving parent figures to you. Your surrogate parent will need to become part of the total picture of your life because in a sense this person will be working in two time frames. Your surrogate parent will be filling in emotional and intellectual gaps left from your childhood, and at the same time he or she will need to give contemporary nurturance by holding your hand through recovery. An Overeaters Anonymous sponsor, a therapist or psychologist, or your pastor can be good temporary surrogate parents to help you walk through this reparenting process.

But you will also want to begin building emotional relationships to a larger circle of people who nurture you. People with codependency tendencies are likely to have chosen people whom they can take care of or control. That kind of one-sided relationship is not what we are working for here. The healthy interdependent relationship will be warm, comfortable, and mutually nurturing. So as you look for surrogate parents, be sure to pick a genuinely nurturing person or persons. Watch out for the old codependent radar that wants to repeat old ways. Tell yourself, "I *can* make a wise choice."

Now that you are about two-thirds of the way through your diet, it's time to get the focus of your life off food and back onto interpersonal relationships. To help you do this, do another relationship survey. But this time, make it a contemporary survey, focusing not on your past, but on the present and what you hope to achieve for the future.

Although it may be tempting simply to read through this shorter survey form and answer the questions in your head, it's important that you take the time and effort to write out full answers in your journal, giving truthful expression to what you think and allowing time for ideas from your subconscious mind to surface. An idea put into writing is a much stronger commitment.

1. Survey your friendships. Ask yourself: Do I have good friendships? Am I allowing people to feed me emotionally? If I do not have nurturing people around me, what can I do to seek them out?

2. Survey your relationship with yourself. Am I taking good care of myself physically? Am I being a good parent to myself? Am I nurturing myself emotionally and spiritually?

3. Inventory your family relationships. This is not, as in your original relationships survey, a reference to your family of origin, but to the family you are now living in. How are my relationships with my spouse or roommate? How do I relate to my children?

4. Inventory your relationship with God. Am I seeing God as a loving, caring heavenly Father? Do I feel myself growing closer to God? Am I learning to trust God as my daily guide?

A relationship is like a bank account. If I'm constantly giving—writing checks all the time—with nothing flowing back in to refill me emotionally, then I'm going to go emotionally bankrupt. That's what we call burnout, depression, or love hunger. One must work to build nurturing relationships that will keep the emotional bank account solvent.

DISCOVERING YOUR OWN CAPACITY
TO NURTURE OTHERS

When Polly finally achieved recovery from her multiple addictions, she and her husband threw themselves wholeheartedly into their plans to start a family. They would have two, maybe three, children. Since money was no problem, they began immediately decorating the nursery and collecting the best in educational toys. But Polly didn't get pregnant. They went in for genetic counseling. She had surgery on her fallopian tubes. They went out of state for *in vitro* fertilization. They spent thousands of dollars, and Polly endured some extremely painful medical procedures in a desperate attempt to have the children they dreamed of. Nothing worked.

So they adopted a child. Ironically, as so often happens, Polly then became pregnant. And ten months after delivering that child, she became pregnant again. Suddenly, Polly found herself the mother of three children under five years of age. It was the fulfillment of all her dreams except for one thing—Polly didn't know how to be a mother. The daughter of an alcoholic father and a cold, distant mother, Polly had never been nurtured herself, so she didn't know how to nurture others. She now goes weekly to a child psychologist, takes a parenting class, and has a nanny to help teach her how to feed her own children emotionally.

The need to be nurtured is one of the most basic human needs. In turn, the need to nurture others is equally basic. The preoccupation childless couples often exhibit with cats or dogs is an example of this need to nurture. Once you have become a good parent to yourself and have found others to feed you in this way, the next step is to give away what you have received. Become a good, nurturing friend to others. And remember to apply the healthy principles you've been learning: be accepting and supportive, not shaming or overly critical; be open and available; don't ignore yourself, and don't ignore others.

When we counsel with yuppie couples who have chosen not to have children, our response is, "Well, if you've honestly considered your life from all angles, that's a valid decision. But you must now decide what you are going to parent instead of your own children." People without their own children need someone to take care of: other people's children, senior adults, hurting people. Explore volunteer groups in your community or church that need help, such as Big Brother programs or Boy or Girl Scout programs.

If you already have children, this is the time to revitalize your own parenting style. You may not have been abusive, but if you're recovering from a compulsion, the chances are that you've been so caught up in your own problems that you now need to give your children more attention.

And always remember that you are at high risk of repeating your parents' abuse on yourself and on your children. It's generally recognized today that child abusers were themselves abused children. But the problem needn't be that severe. Were you raised by a supercritical parent? Your tendency will be to become self-perfectionistic and then to overcriticize your own children. The cycle must be broken. You can break out of it now with new, conscious decisions and actions about how you're going to parent yourself and then how you're going to parent others.

RELYING ON GOD AS THE ULTIMATE PARENT

God, who made us, knows us better than we know ourselves and can therefore do a better job of nurturing us than anyone else if we open ourselves to Him. Walking the road to recovery can be very frightening at times, especially when we realize that we have truly left home and that we must become our own parents. But we never need to walk any of these pathways alone.

Barbara had come a long way from the "I suppose there's some sort of God out there somewhere, but I don't need His rules interfering with my life" attitude of her earlier days. She realized now that the anger and rebellion she had projected onto God had really been her anger at an alcoholic father and anger at men who had used her and abandoned her. She now understood that the legalism she encountered in college had been distorted man-made rules, not the personality of an all-knowing, all-loving Father who had created her and wanted to guide her with His love.

And she had begun a daily quiet time with her favorite devotional book; she liked the way it was all in the first person—as if God were talking directly to her, and when He said something about "the two of you," she took it to apply to herself and Tom. She had been going to church for some time, and last Sunday Tom went with her. Since she could name progress from so many directions, why did she still feel an emptiness here? Why did she feel so tired of the struggle?

She laid down her journal and picked up her Bible. She had been working through the book of Matthew, and today she was at chapter 11, verse 28, "Come to Me, all you who labor and are heavy laden, and I will give you rest." That was what she wanted, rest from the old hurts, rest from the struggle of doing all this on her own, rest from fear of the future. And now as she thought about it, she saw the missing step. All her spiritual growth had been intellectual. She knew the loving Father had sacrificed His Son to provide abundant life, but she hadn't really personalized it—made it a heart experience. She had been doing everything she was told to do, but she hadn't turned anything over to God. It was still like back in college—trying to follow all the rules in her own strength. She needed Him to carry her burden for her. She needed Him to be her ultimate parent. "Yes, Lord, I come. I need your love and help. I need you to be the father I never had."

Barbara didn't know how long she sat there, just feeling warm and at peace. But when she got up it was with a new assurance. The future was secure because she had a heavenly Father to guide her.

CHAPTER

12

PATH EIGHT: JOINING A FOOTPATH SOCIETY

CHILDREN IN extremely dysfunctional homes will sometimes be removed by the state and put into a foster home where they can receive the nurturing they need. On our previous footpath we focused on reparenting—learning to parent yourself and finding one or two special people to be your surrogate parents. Now you are ready to move on to an extended family. We like to think of this as joining a footpath society because it is like the footpath societies in England, whose members walk the pathways together to keep them open for everyone.

BE ACCOUNTABLE

Early in Ralph's struggle to recover from his many addictions, he discovered that without the help of fellow walkers, the paths of wellness would not be open to him. Because he attacked his addictions in life-threatening order, Ralph first joined Alcoholics Anonymous to help him deal with his drug and alcohol dependency. As soon as he discovered the codependent nature of his problem and its roots in his father's alcoholism, he joined Adult Children of Alcoholics (ACOA). He has now been drug and alcohol free for three years, but he continues to attend these groups and has accepted a service position in his local A A chapter.

Besides the nutritional education classes which are part of his diet program, Ralph also consults with us and attends our group therapy sessions, the group you heard him speak to in the first chapter. Very few people would commit so intensely to recovery, and happily, most people don't require the intense support required by someone with Ralph's multiple addictions.

But Ralph is enthusiastic about the results. "I thoroughly plugged in to my new extended family. I'd never had a family and I'd been looking for one all my life. I didn't find it in the Marines; I didn't find it in the motorcycle gang; I didn't find it in my unhealthy marriage. But in these self-help groups I found a truly supporting fellowship where I was accepted just the way I was. No one ever condemned me for anything I had done or anything I said. They always understood. But when I asked for help, even confrontation, I got it.

"I told them I wanted to be accountable. I told them exactly how I was planning to control my weight. I said, 'I'm going to be seeing you weekly; I'll try to report to you each time. If I don't, I want you to ask me how it's going. And I want you to confront me if you see me going back into the old pattern again.'

"If I feel myself slipping off my diet, I need to be able to turn to you and say, 'I don't need shame or judgment or condemnation, but I've got to tell you what's happening with my food program right now. I know you can't make me stay on it, but you can make me accountable. I want to come in here every week and tell you what's going on in my life.'

"And what can I say? I did it and they did it and it worked." Then he paused and almost blushed to the accompaniment of his shy smile. "And I met Sally at OA. You know, I never could let myself get close to one person before. Anytime I'd date one woman I quickly had to start seeing at least two more as a protection against emotional intimacy. But with Sally it's different. She's the only one I need."

In choosing support groups, we recommend a mixed portfolio, as your investment counselor might. First, you will need a specific food support group. This group might have a weekly weigh-in and might talk a lot about weight and food. This group will be primarily educational and may have a prescribed diet. Then we recommend a group that is aimed primarily at emotional support. A general therapy group, a small group at your church, OA or Adult Children of Alcoholics (ACOA) could fill this function. This group will focus on spiritual and emotional dynamics. Then, when you feel ready to expand, you may want a group that is purely recreational, such as a hobby club. A group that stresses physical activity such as an aerobics club or golfing group will fulfill two functions: providing social support and helping you with your exercise program.

Ralph wanted his support group to make him accountable. They did, and it worked. But the ultimate accountability is not being accountable to a group, but being accountable to yourself. In a support group, no one will confront you or interrogate you, unless you've specifically given someone permission to do so. They will give you role models of openness and honesty, however. Meeting after meeting, you'll hear people talking frankly about where their food program is working and where it isn't working. Eventually this model will take hold, and you'll find yourself wanting to share with the group and wanting to make yourself accountable to a group that can be honest without condemnation.

BE WILLING TO COMMIT

Betty Jo was a busy, intelligent mother of three, who was making progress in her recovery program, but we could not convince her to join a support group. Every time we brought the subject up, she would counter with her legitimately busy schedule; full-time job, part-time class, time-and-a-half family. Last spring she finished her study course, her daughter married, and one son moved to another town to take a job. When she sent her younger son off to summer camp, we said, "All right, Betty Jo. You now have no valid excuse. Join a self-help group."

She looked at us for a good five seconds. "You're right. I don't have any excuse. But you know, I've never given myself permission to join a support group. I guess I've never given myself permission to recover fully." Betty Jo had to get out her well-worn footpath map and go back over some of the old ground again before she could allow herself to commit to a support group.

We hear all the excuses: It takes too much time; it's too much trouble; I'd have to drive too far; I'm too tired after work; it's too expensive; I'd have to have a babysitter; it's boring . . . .

Ginger was like that for many years. "I went to the Weight Watchers support group. They focused on what you can do to take care of yourself in situations that will be difficult for your diet, how to handle holidays, things like that. It was very educational, but no help on family issues. It was very good for what it did, but a person needs something else too.

"Without my therapy group I'd be on Weight Watchers for the rest of my life—strictly the Weight Watchers diet—too afraid to have chocolate pie, even once a year, because that would mean violating the program, and I'd be afraid of getting out of control—and if I got out of control who'd know what would happen! I never would let myself stick to a maintenance program. I'd lose my twenty pounds and be so excited about it I'd go out and blow it.

"So I finally let my therapist talk me into going to a self-help meeting. I found it was very, very helpful. There were times when I would listen to these people talk and I would think, *This is boring. What am I doing here?* But then later that week I would find myself applying something I heard someone talking about in a meeting, and I realized it works. You're learning coping tools at those meetings, and they really work."

BE PART OF THE GROUP

Barbara's phone call to Tom had been successful beyond her wildest dreams. Yes, he still cared about her. Yes, he was willing to try again. Yes, with some reluctance, he was counseling with the folks at Minirth-Meier. Now her life was really on track. She could accomplish anything! Until Tom actually moved back home.

When the first flush of excitement—he complimented her new appearance, he admired the changes she'd made in the decor—was over, he wanted his old chair back in his accustomed corner. Then he returned to his old workaholic patterns, and Barbara found herself alone in her room while Tom worked. She didn't understand what was happening until she caught herself moving toward the door with the idea of going out for french fries.

The bedroom door wasn't locked for protection, as it had been in her childhood. Tom was working quietly over a file of papers, not guzzling a bottle of whiskey. But her feelings of fear, isolation, and abandonment were the same as those she had experienced as a child. And her emotional reaction of turning to food for nurturing was the same.

Yet her intellectual reaction wasn't the same because this time she had walked the footpaths of recovery. She understood what was happening. And she knew she needed more help. The next morning she looked in the business white pages of her telephone book and got in touch with ACOA. People there were walking the same footpath she was walking and could help her find her way.

Even a person who is in a very loving family relationship will need the fellowship of walkers who have been over the same paths they have been. Too often a spouse who means to be helpful, but doesn't understand, will offer either denial or condemnation to a dieter who tries to share a problem. In a mistaken idea that if you deny it, it'll go away, they may say, "No, you're not slipping. You're doing fine!" Or, in an attempt to shame you back on the track, they may say, "You'd better get back with it. You don't want to blow it this time!"

Even if a loving marriage is meeting your other emotional

needs, at this stage of your recovery you will need a fellowship group that will neither deny your pain nor judge it harshly. People in your immediate family are in one sense too close to your problem because of living with you and in another sense, too removed from it because they haven't experienced the same addiction.

Barbara reported to us her almost inexpressible relief on walking into the ACOA room. "Everyone in this room has been down the same path I have. All the shame and guilt—the sense of being a freak—lifted immediately," she told us. Many adult children of dysfunctional families will say that after suffering for years under the burden of "terminal uniqueness," suddenly they found themselves in a room with twenty other people who could say, "Me too," to every one of their experiences.

BE LOVED

Almost any self-help group, and certainly all the Twelve Step groups such as AA, ACOA, OA work on the same organizational principles: there are no formal memberships, no fees or dues, no prescribed diet. Attendees don't give their full names. When some patients hear this, especially those accustomed to more rigid thinking, they ask, "How can anything so loose work?"

It works because unconditional love works. Legalism does not. Doctors with years of experience in the recovery field will often say something like, "When you boil down all that happens in recovery, the fundamental principle is that people can be loved back into emotional health." To have that happen, the patient must be surrounded by loving people.

Barbara, who had faithfully attended the group therapy sessions at the clinic, was surprised by the informal atmosphere of the ACOA meeting she attended. And she was even more surprised to find Ginger there. "I didn't know you had an alcoholic parent," she said, taking a seat next to her friend.

"I didn't," Ginger replied. "My father was a rageaholic, but it comes from the same thing. He could get into a rage without having to get drunk first. Adrenalin is a much stronger drug than alcohol."

"Maybe my situation was better," Barbara said with a rueful smile. "At least I had more warning. It would take Dad a while to drink his way into one of his storms, so I could be out the window before it got too bad." The meeting started, so she dropped her voice to a whisper. "But do these meetings work?"

Ginger nodded. "They work, all right. First thing they teach you is that you're a perfectly lovable person with a food problem, not some kind of freak. The next thing you learn is that things you can't do on your own you can do together. The hardest thing I ever had to do was come to this group and admit I'd messed up. But then I found out that other people had too. That helped me deal with the guilt and shame. Then you all say, 'OK, we goofed, but here's what we're going to do, and we'll do it together.' I can't tell you how many times it's kept me from total relapse."

Then their attention turned to the front. One of the group was introducing his recovered alcoholic father. "This is Dad's birthday. He's celebrating four years of sobriety, so I asked him and his AA sponsor to come to our meeting so we could celebrate together."

Strains of "Happy Birthday to You" and enthusiastic applause greeted the gray-haired guest who shared a bit about his recovery through AA and then introduced his own guest, a bearded, thirty-year-old man. "This is Gordon, my AA sponsor. And I want to tell you that Gordon saved my life. He taught me what a family is like. Can you believe I was forty-nine years old, the father of three children, and I didn't know what a family was supposed to be? Gordon taught me. He has been a source of support and nurturance and discipline. Gordon taught me unconditional love." Gordon stood, and the two men embraced.

Unconditional love is the quality we tell our patients to look for first when choosing a sponsor. Unconditional love loves even when the beloved needs to be disciplined, needs to be challenged, needs to be told, "No."

Choose a sponsor who will be neither too harsh nor too permissive. One who will say to you, "Stop and think about this. Do you really want to eat that candy bar? And if you do, are you willing to jog an extra hour this evening to work it off?"

Many self-help groups are referred to as Twelve-Step programs, because they emphasize following the twelve steps to recovery first formulated by Alcoholics Anonymous in 1939. If you live in a small or rural area where there are no self-help groups specifically for compulsive eaters, we recommend you go to the open meetings of your nearest AA group and apply their techniques of controlling alcohol addiction to your food addiction.

Although there are numerous Twelve-Step organizations, the ones most focused in areas that will be helpful to compulsive overeaters are: OA, Overeaters Anonymous; Al-Anon, for spouses, families, friends, and coworkers of alcoholics; ACOA, Adult Children of Alcoholics, a newer, more specialized group growing out of Al-Anon, which our patients from any type of dysfunctional family find very helpful; EA, Emotions Anonymous; and CODA, Codependents Anonymous. There are also Twelve-Step programs with a specifically Christian emphasis, such as Overcomers Outreach (2290 W. Whittier Blvd., Suite D, La Habra, CA 90631), and Overcomers: Victory over Addiction Through Christ (Overcomers Center, 4905 N. 96th St., Omaha, NE 68134).

If you choose a Twelve-Step program, do not confuse their Twelve Steps with our Ten Footpaths. The Twelve Steps can be integrated with our ten. The Twelve Steps do not fully substitute for the more comprehensive footpath.

Your church and small groups within your church should provide excellent sources of support both emotionally and spiritually. Many churches now even offer self-help programs for a variety of needs, and many have exercise fellowships you will enjoy. Look around at what other churches in your community offer as well as your own because finding support group help in another church will in most cases imply no membership change and can enlarge your support fellowship.

Since the family is the ultimate small group and we have seen the importance of reparenting, you may need to allow another family to "adopt" you, making you part of their circle for picnics, Thanksgiving dinner, and birthday parties, as well as for less formal occasions. Many churches and clubs have organized programs for families to "adopt" college students, singles, and the elderly, or such an arrangement can arise spontaneously if you are open to it. Ultimately, your own enhanced family relationships should be your richest source of support. Continue to work out any symptoms of codependency that might arise and lovingly urge members of your family who might need it to take part in such groups as CODA or ACOA.

Finally, once you have found help through support groups, you are ready to reach out to others. In this way you will be able to reinforce much of your new learning by passing it on to others and aid your own recovery by getting the focus of your life off yourself and onto others.

SUCCESSES OF SUPPORT

Barbara reported her enthusiasm over her first ACOA meeting to us and then sat back in her chair with a perplexed look. "So I had a great evening, and yet I keep wondering—I mean, I've got a new job that's a really major commitment, and here Tom and I are trying to work things out, and there are still only twenty-four hours in a day. And even if I decide it's worth it, how can I be sure I've got the right group when there are so many to choose from?"

Barbara's dilemma was typical of many of our patients. Perhaps you, too, are having similar doubts. We have compiled a list of twelve functions a good support group should fulfill. Understanding what a group can do should help you see the importance of making room for it in your busy life and will also provide a checklist for you to evaluate any group you may be considering. Probably no one group will fulfill all twelve purposes, and that is why we recommend finding at least three groups to find support for food issues specifically, emotional support, and recreational enrichment.

1. Support groups provide an antidote to shame as they offer unconditional love. Barbara had already experienced the most important function of a support group when she lost her feeling of "terminal uniqueness."

2. A support group fellowship breaks isolation. This is important because people caught in an addiction have been isolating themselves, either physically by staying alone or emotionally by feeling alone in a crowd. The awareness of her need to break out of isolation when Tom returned to his work was what drove Barbara to her meeting. There, finding Ginger and others who shared her experiences broke her isolation.

3. A self-help group provides on-going encouragement. Alfred Adler, one of the founders of modern psychiatry, broke with Sigmund Freud over this issue of encouragement. Most people are not really sick, Adler maintained; they are just discouraged. Alfred Adler saw encouragement as the key to psychotherapy.

4. A support fellowship will provide a true substitute family. The story of the recovered alcoholic and his sponsor, Gordon, was only one of the family stories Barbara heard that night. In fact, she was even beginning to think of Ginger in the role of the sister she never had.

5. A support group provides accountability. As Ginger warned Barbara, having to face the music and tell a whole room full of people you've goofed is incredibly hard. But the support for recovery that follows can make it all worthwhile.

6. Fellowship and support groups provide a church in the broadest sense of meeting Christ's definition that "where two or three are gathered together in My name, I am there in the midst of them."* Sometimes the success of such group dynamics baffles even therapists, who will say, "We don't know why a group works, but it does."

7. Support groups provide practical help and information. Although people attending Overeaters Anonymous are directed to have a personal food plan, the organization prescribes no set diet. At every meeting one will hear others testify to what has worked

---

*Matthew 18:20.

for them and share such tips as how to handle a sudden craving at 3 A.M.

8. Support groups provide vicarious insight. Even one who chooses to sit back and not participate actively in a group meeting will be drawn into the feelings and experiences of others. This is in perfect accord with Romans 12:15, which admonishes us to "rejoice with those who rejoice, and weep with those who weep." As we walk through the grief process with another, we can find ourselves mourning our own losses. Or, as we share another's joys, we are propelled into counting our own blessings.

9. Self-help groups provide new positive rituals. Much of eating is ritualistic. Barbara's turning to french fries whenever her father drank began as a nurturing need, but soon became a ritual. She ate when her father drank, whether or not she was feeling a need for nurturing at that moment. Such old rituals which lead one to overeat compulsively are negative. Going to meetings and participating in group activities can also be ritualistic. But these are positive rituals as they teach healing steps and crowd out old, negative rituals.

10. Self-help groups provide a constant reminder that food is not the issue. One fighting his or her way alone to gain mastery over food and diet can drown in food issues. Group meetings constantly force one to look beyond food. Although OA meetings provide specific, helpful diet tips, one usually hears far more about emotions and relationships, which are at the heart of the issue. It wasn't until Barbara was home in bed that night after the meeting that she realized she had heard nothing at all about eating at the ACOA meeting, and yet the compulsion to binge which caused her to attend the meeting had completely dissipated.

11. Support fellowships provide a continuing forum for the grief process. Grief work, as we saw on path #4, is the core of the healing process. Because life is a continual process of changes and many of them are unpleasant, normal grief work is something we cannot put entirely behind us, if we are to be fully and healthfully human. Hearing grief expressed will trigger one's own grief process and continue healing, just as the death of a pet or a friend's moving away will require new grief work.

12. Support groups remind one to put people in place of food. Love hunger tries to replace people with food. All along our journey to recovery we have been working to develop new habits to reverse that old order. If one is lonely, bored, depressed—situations which in an earlier day would certainly have led to compulsive overeating—the member of a fellowship group can easily find someone to talk to or to do something with rather than reaching for food.

THE TWELVE STEPS
Adapted for Compulsive Overeaters

Step One

We admitted we were powerless over our food compulsion—that our lives had become unmanageable.

Step Two

Came to believe that a Power greater than ourselves could restore us to sanity.

Step Three

Made a decision to turn our will and our lives over to the care of God, as we understood Him.

Step Four

Made a searching and fearless moral inventory of ourselves.

Step Five

Admitted to God, to ourselves, and to another human being the exact nature of our wrongs.

Step Six

Were entirely ready to have God remove all these defects of character.

Step Seven
Humbly asked Him to remove our shortcomings.

Step Eight
Made a list of all persons we had harmed and became willing to make amends to them all.

Step Nine
Made direct amends to such people wherever possible, except when to do so would injure them or others.

Step Ten
Continued to take personal inventory and when we were wrong, promptly admitted it.

Step Eleven
Sought through prayer and meditation to improve our conscious contact with God, praying only for knowledge of His will for us and the power to carry that out.

Step Twelve
Having had a spiritual awakening as the result of these steps, we tried to carry this message to other overeaters, and to practice these principles in all our affairs.

Our friend who recently returned from a month of walking English footpaths said, "It was one of the loveliest experiences of my life, but I would never have made it on my own. Even a light pack can get dreadfully heavy without someone to relieve you occasionally. And even as carefully as I packed, I forgot some things I had to borrow. And no matter how beautiful it is, no matter how much you love wildflowers and baby lambs, sometimes you get *so* tired, you need to have someone along who can make you laugh. And then there's the matter of map reading. I have no sense of direction. If our group hadn't had a good navigator, I'd still be wandering around somewhere over there, too lost even to ask directions."

There was one other companion Barbara longed to have share her footpath walk. Tom had reluctantly agreed to see the doctors at the clinic "because it might help her," but he had acknowledged no willingness to make any changes himself. In spite of her husband's reluctance, however, Barbara entered the counseling session with high hopes. Because the doctors had helped her so much, surely they could straighten Tom out, too, and then everything would be fine. Yet some sessions seemed to revive old contentions, rather than move toward complete recovery.

"If you had any idea how hard I work!" Tom ground out the words in a rigidly controlled voice. "If you could just get your mind off this diet thing long enough to think about my job . . ."

"That just isn't it," Barbara flung back at him. "*Your* work, *your* job. Did you ever consider that maybe if you spent a little more time with me I might not have such a hard time with my diet?"

"Now, look, if you're going to blame me . . ."

"Just a minute," Dr. Hemfelt interrupted. "I can see that you both have valid concerns here. But let's try turning this conversation around. Instead of pointing your fingers at each other, let's talk about what you can each do to contribute to your relationship so you'll be pulling in the same direction."

It was quiet in the office for a moment. Finally Barbara sighed. "All right. I can see that I shouldn't be concentrating on fixing Tom. I should concentrate on fixing me. And I know my recovery doesn't hinge on what Tom does." She turned to Tom. "That sales meeting you want me to go to Thursday—I'll go to a noon meeting of ACOA so I can go with you that night."

Tom's stiffly squared shoulders relaxed. "Okay, that's great. About my Saturday afternoon golf game with the doctors—I was thinking maybe I could start giving you lessons on Saturday mornings. When you get good enough you can join us—when the doctors bring their wives, that is."

Barbara and Tom exchanged cautious smiles.

CHAPTER
13

PATH NINE: MAINTAINING YOUR VICTORY

YOU'VE STAYED on the path. You've experienced the high. You've seen the view from the top. But most mountain climbers will tell you that the return is the most dangerous part of the journey. You are now ready to return to normal. That does not mean returning to the old ways—that would be to tumble down the slope. It means returning gently and securely to the normal life you always thought you could have. Barbara expressed that goal for all dieters when she said, "It is really a dream to think that I could ever get to an appropriate weight that I was happy with and stay there. I cannot fathom what that would be like."

RECYCLING YOUR STEPS

Did you ever play "Pass the Parcel" at a birthday party? You sit in a circle and pass a gaily wrapped package around the ring while music plays. When the music stops, the one holding the parcel peels off a layer of wrapping to find a prize and a forfeit—such as standing in the middle of the circle and singing a silly song. After the forfeit is fulfilled, the prize—a fancy pencil, for instance—is the winner's to keep. Then the parcel continues on around the ring until the music stops again and someone peels off another layer.

Sometimes you will feel as if you're playing "Pass the Parcel" as you follow the footpath of maintenance because there will be many times when you will feel the need to peel yet another layer off your obsessive-compulsive behavior, and you realize you have to go back and recycle through the steps you've already taken.

You may be near the end of your diet (your weight is in pretty good control) and suddenly, now that the weight issue is not front and center, you find yourself thinking a bit more about the family in which you grew up, and you realize, *Hey, I need to go back and rewalk paths three and four. I need to say good-bye to Mom and Dad, I need to do some more grief work.* Grief is the key to making room for healing and also the key to continued wellness. As old, unresolved issues surface, you will need to grieve them through to forgiveness and resolution, and you will need to grieve new pain. Vent your daily frustrations and fears; don't let them build up. The need to cycle back through the steps of the grief process may arise from something as minor as a traffic jam on the freeway or something as major as a death in the family.

Path #8, joining a support group, is another one that will likely need special attention as you may find you have to push yourself to maintain healthy fellowship. At the time of greatest pain, patients reach out for fellowship, but the complacency that comes with success leads to slacking off. If you suddenly feel a bit relapse prone, if you see that your attendance at support group meetings is slacking off, push yourself a little. In order to keep tabs on this important area of your life, do a new relationship survey periodically.

Understand that this repeated need to peel off the layers is not retreat or failure. Instead it's securing the victory you've already won. Once you've worked out the forfeit, you'll get to keep the prize in the parcel.

COMMITTING TO DAILY MAINTENANCE

Sometimes the early stages of recovery are the easy ones. Although the road ahead is long, there is the excitement of setting out on a journey to buoy one, and there will be persistent support from therapist, sponsor, or another guide. But we always suffer a letdown at the end of a trip, and a sense of panic can set in when we suddenly find ourselves ready to go back into the real world.

The degree of intensity with which one needs to work at daily maintenance varies with the personality of each patient and the severity of the addiction. But all recovering people need to incorporate these seven checkpoints into their daily routine, as surely as airline maintenance crews have to accomplish all the items on their list of preflight aircraft checks:

1. Take time for daily prayer and devotional reading. Be sure you specifically surrender your food issues for that day and explicitly mention concerns such as a luncheon or party you may be planning to attend. When Barbara debated with us about this point, we told her, "Right now, when you're entering maintenance, keep your

prayer simple, like a child talking to a loving father. You'll have plenty of time to wrestle with theological issues when you're fully recovered."

2. Maintain contact with one support person outside your family that you can call on a daily basis. This is not someone who can fix you as if you were broken, but merely someone you can fellowship with for a few minutes—talk about the weather or the fortunes of your favorite baseball team if you feel no need to discuss food issues.

3. Be sure that your daily or weekly schedule contains group fellowship time such as a self-help group or Bible study group.

4. Be certain your schedule calls for daily physical activity.

5. If you are really struggling, do a daily relationship survey. Every evening look back over your day and ask yourself: Have I had good fellowship? Is there someone to whom I've expressed my thoughts and feelings? Have I reached out to help someone else?

6. Have a structured plan for each day (unless you are too obsessive-compulsive and need to let up here), especially if you struggle with depression or are in an unstructured line of work that requires self-direction such as homemaking or any self-employed work. Take control of your day. Make certain that life isn't an accident that happens to you.

Barbara found that organizing her time was easy in the early hours of her day. She was excited about finishing her classwork, so she awoke with the alarm and jumped into the shower, her mind filled with interesting wall arrangements or drapery designs she could present to her professor. The trouble came at 6 P.M., when she returned home an hour earlier than Tom. Her first impulse, which she usually followed, was to fling off her shoes and flop onto the sofa. Her next impulse, which she had to fight off, was to dash to the refrigerator. By the time Tom came home tired and hungry, Barbara knew she should have some kind of nutritious dinner organized, but by then she was either too hungry to cook or had given in to the urge to snack and therefore wasn't hungry and couldn't stand the thought of cooking.

She discussed this problem with Sharon Sneed. Dr. Sneed recommended that Barbara plan a snack which she would eat just before beginning the drive home or as soon as she arrived. "Something hot will be satisfying and soothing after a hard day. Try a cup of chicken soup or tea with skimmed milk in it. Then add something filling like a piece of whole wheat bread or a whole meal cracker. If that's not enough, you could include a small serving of nonfat yogurt."

Since the drive home from school was always nerve-wracking,

Barbara decided to make a cup of strong tea in the lunchroom. When Tom came home that night to the smells of grilled chicken breasts with raspberry sauce (see p. 264), his end-of-the-day frown lifted to a smile. "What'd you do? Stay home from school?"

Barbara waved her wooden spoon at him. "Nope, finished my window design notebook and did a paper on furniture restoration. Then I had a cup of tea and a couple of crackers—and here I am."

Barbara's whole day had gone extremely well, but when Tom offered to set the table, the shock was almost too much for her.

7. Be sure you have a food plan for your day. If you are following a structured diet, look it over. If not, make your own careful, healthy choices. We always discuss these choices with our patients.

CHOOSING YOUR FOOD WISELY

Your body as well as your mind has been going through an education process in walking these pathways to recovery. Animals are born with God-given instincts to know what is good for them. You do not see fat animals in the wild. Only animals that have been man-fed on foods too high in fats or sugars will have to be put on diets. Many nutritionists believe that the same would be true for humans if we did not offer our children foods high in sugar and salt from infancy and our society did not blast "Eat, eat, eat!" messages at them several hours a day on TV. Yet even if your natural healthy instincts have been corrupted by years of improper eating, the knowledge your body was born with is still buried there.

Now that your life and your appetites are back in balance, you can get in touch with the real messages your body sends you. You can trust your body to tell you when it's really hungry. Learn to eat *only* when you are truly hungry. No matter what the clock says. No matter what the rest of your family is doing. One mother of four who practices this told us, "Sure, I have to feed my family on schedule—even if it is the pits having to cook when I'm not hungry. But I do it because I understand how important it is to nurture them. And I sit down with them, and we all talk about what we did that day. But if I'm not hungry—and I usually am not at that time—I take a few bites of meat and vegetables and drink a cup of tea with low-fat milk in it. Now that I've learned to eat only when I'm hungry, I think it would make me sick to force-feed myself just because my husband and children are hungry."

Some nutritionists who believe in the "uncorrupted nature" theory of eating claim that young children left completely free to choose what they want to eat would, over a period of time, select perfectly balanced diets for themselves. Whether or not this is true (and it's almost impossible to prove scientifically), it is true that once you get your trigger foods in control, your body will tell you whether it wants a juicy red apple or a crisp piece of whole wheat toast. It will take you a while to establish these lines of communication. First, it requires time and quiet for thought. People who are forced into making hasty decisions in busy restaurants with the waiters standing over them will almost always choose unwisely.

When you feel true hunger, think about the selections you've made that day from the basic food groups. What has been missing in your diet today? Do you need another selection from the fruit and vegetable group? Were your protein portions smaller than usual? Think about the healthy food you've already stocked your kitchen with, visualize yourself eating it. What makes you feel truly satisfied?

Of course, you can't always make your food choices on this "warm fuzzy" basis. You have to market ahead, you have to pack lunches ahead, and even then your planning may be thrown off because you eat at a friend's house.

Train your palate to go for the satisfaction of high-flavor ingredients rather than high-fat foods. Learn the delight of eating your fish with English malt vinegar rather than smothering it in greasy tartar sauce. Enhance the flavor of your turkey sandwich with Dijon mustard instead of slathering on mayonnaise. Or discover how good plain, low-fat yogurt tastes on a baked potato, and you'll never be tempted by sour cream again. One theory is that we eat for flavor and that when the craving for flavor is satisfied our appetites will be satisfied. Since fat is the least flavorful of the food groups, it's no wonder one has to overeat fatty foods to feel satisfied.

GENTLE EATING

Give yourself time to achieve satisfaction with your food. Practice gentle eating, one of the best techniques for cutting down on your food intake and maintaining your weight loss. Dr. Sneed says, "You know, Europeans think we're really crass, the way we bolt a meal in twenty minutes. In Europe they take time to enjoy their meals, even if it means closing the shop or library for an hour or so at midday or leaving the office earlier in the evening. After lunch, which may be a very simple meal, but eaten with a linen napkin and a flower on the table, they will often linger over a cup of coffee or go for a stroll with a friend before returning to work refreshed. I'm afraid we deserve the ulcers we've given ourselves."

One of our patients found that gentle eating was such an important key to her maintenance program that she arranged with her employer to take an hour and a half lunch, making the time up by skipping morning and afternoon coffee breaks which she didn't need anyway. In the morning she packaged her food in plastic containers, but she included a flowered pottery plate and silver knife, fork, and spoon in her lunch basket. "If I spend twice as long eating half as much food, I feel twice as satisfied," she said with a laugh. "I don't know—you'll have to figure it out. I never was very good at math."

Many of our gentle eating tips come from Amy Vanderbilt and Miss Manners, not from any diet book, and they work equally well for health and for culture:

Set the table in an aesthetically pleasing manner.
Enjoy relaxing music in the background at mealtime.
Take small portions.
Take small bites.
Lay your fork down between each bite.
Chew each mouthful of food thoroughly.
Never talk with your mouth full.
Wipe your mouth with your napkin before taking a drink.
Take time for pleasant conversation with everyone at the table.
Avoid controversy at the table.

Remember that it takes twenty-one minutes for the brain to receive the "not hungry" message after food has reached the stomach. In order to give yourself time to determine whether or not you've eaten enough, try the continental practice of eating your salad after the main course, or end the meal with fruit and cheese.

While you are developing your gentle eating habits, you might want to employ some techniques such as eating with your left hand or with chopsticks to force slower eating, or eating off a salad plate to make your smaller portions appear larger. After a few weeks, your new habit will be established, and such artificial tricks will be unnecessary.

STAYING ACTIVE

The two sides of the maintenance coin are: slow down your eating; speed up the rest of your life. Staying physically active can be as important as your diet in maintaining your weight. Besides the specific exercise program you have incorporated into your daily agenda, make it a habit to be more physically active in every way. Climb the stairs rather than taking the elevator at the office. Choose a space at the back of the parking lot at the shopping mall. Move fast to increase your activity level in whatever you are doing.

You have committed to a lifestyle change in this journey to total wellness. Moving more, moving faster, and enjoying life more are essential ingredients in this lifestyle. And remember, eating doesn't count as a physical activity!

LEARNING TO RELAX

But we are working with a many-sided coin here because the flip side of exercise is relaxation. You will now need to learn new techniques for relaxation, especially if you once used sugar as a sedative or food in general as a tranquilizer.

In our book *Worry-Free Living* (Minirth, Meier, Hawkins. Thomas Nelson, Nashville, TN: 1989) we discuss a number of techniques for dealing with tension and anxieties. Some of them are especially helpful for recovering overeaters.

1. *Progressive Relaxation*. Lie on your back in a comfortable place: bed, sofa, or floor. Close eyes. Inhale deeply. Release the air slowly. Repeat this cycle three more times. Now tense your leg muscles. Hold. Relax. Tense hip and abdomen muscles. Hold. Relax. Continue upward through every part of your body until you have worked upward to relax all the muscles of your face and scalp.

Now, counting backward from five, visualize yourself relaxing more and more thoroughly. Some of our patients think of themselves as floating upward on a soft cloud; others prefer to see themselves sinking downward into a deep, deep featherbed. Either way, tell yourself, *Five. I am relaxing more and more in every part of my body. Four. I am sinking deeper and deeper into total relaxation. It feels so-o-o good.* Continue on to, *One. I am totally relaxed.*

This would be an excellent time to play your positive self-talk tapes as your mind is very receptive in its relaxed state. Or you might want to let your subconscious mind surface if you've been looking for a creative solution to a problem at work. Or you might simply want to drift off to sleep. Even if you only have time for a brief nap, you will awaken refreshed because you relaxed so completely.

2. *Set Worry Limits*. If you are a "worrier," you may find yourself worrying throughout your day about maintaining your weight loss and staying on your recovery footpaths. If this happens, deal with it somewhat like you did negative thoughts in the positive self-

JUST FOR TODAY
(I Have a Choice)

1. JUST FOR TODAY I will try to live through this day only, not tackling my whole life problem at once. I can do something at this moment that would appall me if I felt that I had to keep it up for a lifetime.

2. JUST FOR TODAY I will try to be happy, realizing that my happiness does not depend on what others do or say, or what happens around me. Happiness is a result of being at peace with myself.

3. JUST FOR TODAY I will try to adjust myself to what is—and not force everything to adjust to my own desires. I will accept my family, my friends, my business, my circumstances as they come.

4. JUST FOR TODAY I will take care of my physical health; I will exercise my mind; I will read something spiritual.

5. JUST FOR TODAY I will do somebody a good turn and not get found out—if anyone knows of it, it will not count. I shall do at least one thing I don't want to do, and I will perform some small act of love for my neighbor.

6. JUST FOR TODAY I will try to go out of my way to be kind to someone I meet; I will be agreeable; I will look

as well as I can, dress becomingly, talk low, act courteously, criticize not one bit, not find fault with anything, and not try to improve or regulate anybody except myself.

7. JUST FOR TODAY I will have a program. I may not follow it exactly, but I will have it. I will save myself from two pests—hurry and indecision.

8. JUST FOR TODAY I will stop saying, "If I had time." I never will "find time" for anything. If I want time I must take it.

9. JUST FOR TODAY I will have a quiet time of meditation wherein I shall think of God, of myself, and of my neighbor. I shall relax and seek truth.

10. JUST FOR TODAY I shall be unafraid. Particularly, I shall be unafraid to be happy, to enjoy what is good, what is beautiful, and what is lovely in life.

11. JUST FOR TODAY I will accept myself and live to the best of my ability.

12. JUST FOR TODAY I choose to believe that I can live this one day.

THE CHOICE IS MINE!

talk process. Give yourself a ten-minute period once or twice a day when you can sit down and do a good job of worrying. When worries intrude during the day, jot them down and save them for your worry session, telling yourself, like Scarlett O'Hara, "I'll think about that tomorrow."

Businesses often develop a "worst case scenario" and a "best case scenario" when considering a new venture. Try imagining the worst that could happen, then the best that could happen. Reality will probably be somewhere in between. Then when it's time to worry, try to use the time creatively. Don't just go over and over the "what if . . ." worries, but take the offensive and try to think of ways to handle the situation if the worst does happen. Writing a Plan B in your journal will free your mind of that worry.

3. *Do Something Else.* Psychologists call this Competing Behavior, but it's really what our mothers did when they told us to "Go do something else." We sometimes instruct patients who are plagued with repeating worries to take their journals and write down what they are doing as the anxiety begins and describe all the symptoms of the anxiety attack. The journaling can contribute insight and also provides a competing behavior—the act of writing gives them something else to do. Going out for a walk or a session of aerobic exercises can do the same thing if one's schedule allows.

PRACTICING EMOTIONAL MAINTENANCE

Emotions Anonymous, one of the Twelve-Step, self-help support groups that we recommend to our patients, has a credo that emphasizes the importance of living one day at a time, choosing to be happy and stable for the day. With the permission of Emotions Anonymous International, we share these daily suggestions with you on page 188 and suggest that you read them every morning for two weeks, and then keep them handy to refer to whenever you need a refresher.

KEEPING IN TOUCH WITH GOD

In many self-help groups, people talk of a daily maintenance program. Many people take the step daily of admitting they are powerless over food and surrendering that problem to Christ on a daily basis. Some people on our recovery program may need to go back to footpath #1 every day and say, "I realize that I have a food addiction. I can't handle it in my own power. I surrender it to Christ."

Step Eleven of the Twelve Steps is particularly appropriate to the maintenance stage of your journey: "We have sought through prayer and Scripture meditation to improve our conscious contact with Christ, praying only for knowledge of His will for us and the power to carry that out." This was the case with Ralph.

Ralph has grown spiritually using his Twelve Step program. "Working the Twelve Steps was my first introduction to the concept of a spiritual life. Shortly after beginning recovery, I trusted Christ personally. Now I pray every morning. When I committed to recover from eating compulsivity, I started praying about my overeating. Then I learned to reach out—to take my spiritual life farther. I'm taking it to work now. I started praying about my honesty at work— about my feelings of being a fraud. Recently I've found I'm praying for others too—for people at work who need help. It's exciting to feel like you're growing."

When we tell some patients that they need a daily maintenance program, they say, "Wait a minute. If I'm having to do all this on a daily basis, that means I'm not healed. Christ hasn't spontaneously lifted this from me." One must realize that God heals in different ways. There are some rare cases of miraculous intervention when a person is touched by God and an addiction like food or drugs just seems to evaporate. Far more often, however, God heals by a slow educational process. He allows us to go through steps of healing.

When patients, like Ralph, yo-yo back and forth and get discouraged because they haven't had a spontaneous healing, we often tell them, "Well, maybe you've had the better healing. God has allowed you to work your way through the stages of healing. Now you understand your healing and yourself, and you can use these understandings to help others."

14

PATH TEN: DEALING WITH RELAPSE

THE THRILL Barbara felt when her scales dipped just below 135 pounds stayed with her for two days. She had expected it to last a lifetime. But that very night she and Tom had an argument—nothing too serious, but enough to take the shine off her feelings. The next day she didn't do as well on the final exam of her design class as she had expected to do. The third morning she woke up with a frightening desire to eat. Not just a desire to eat a healthy breakfast and get about her business, but a desire to eat and eat and eat until the pressures of her new life would be blotted out, at least temporarily.

In the same kind of blind panic with which a drowning swimmer would reach for a lifeline, Barbara called Dr. Hemfelt. "I want to eat. Really *eat*. I'm scared. I don't know what to do."

Just the sound of Dr. Hemfelt's gentle drawl was reassuring. "Now, Barbara, I want you to sit down right where you are and breathe deeply. Do you have a chair by the phone?"

Barbara sat. "Yeah. Okay."

Barbara did as she was directed. After a few deep breaths Barbara was feeling a little light-headed, but somewhat calmer. "Have you had breakfast yet, Barbara?"

She said she hadn't. She'd been planning to have oatmeal and an orange and coffee before she went out to see about applying for a job.

"That's fine. Eat just exactly what you've planned; then come see me. I've had a cancellation, so I can see you at ten o'clock this morning."

Two hours later Barbara sat in Dr. Hemfelt's green chair. "Dealing with relapse is part of your recovery program, Barbara. It's really dealing with fear. Everyone has to do that at some level all the time: Fear of big things like death and disease; fear of little things like burning the roast or meeting new people; fear for yourself; fear for others. The first step in pushing down the panic is to know that it's normal. Just knowing that relapse is likely to happen is your first line of defense against it.

"In working through your footpaths to recovery we've diffused most of the landmines that would have sent you into a major binge in the old days, but fear is a normal human emotion. We don't want to eliminate it, just teach you how to deal with it. In order to deal with relapse you need to know what can cause a relapse, know the warning signals, know the ten remedial steps."

KNOW WHAT CAN CAUSE RELAPSE

MESSAGES OF SHAME FROM OTHERS

Sometimes patients have people around them in their support system who aren't as supportive or as healthy as they should be. Although Tom had begun seeing a therapist, he was far from recovered from his compulsive workaholism and therefore projected many of his problems onto Barbara before she was strong enough to handle them.

Jared was another example of this. One night at his support group meeting he shared some problems he was having forgiving his parents and older brother for humiliating him as a child. Jared had passed the anger stage in his grief process and had moved on to sadness. He told his group he was not yet able to make the decision to accept what had happened in his past and forgive those responsible, but he knew that was next, and he looked forward to being able to achieve it. He asked for the prayers and support of his group as he worked through this.

After the meeting two young men who were new to the group met him in the hall. "We heard you. I mean really *heard* you. We've been talking about it, and we both had the same sort of stinking childhood. My dad rode me constantly. I never felt good about anything. Nothing was ever good enough."

The other one took over. "That's right. Only with me it was my sister and mother. And you know what? We don't think you *should* forgive those people. They treated you like dirt and messed up your life. What's to forgive?"

Fortunately, Jared was strong enough to disregard this negative message after talking it out with us, but it could have caused a serious setback.

Every diet, every recovery program, like everything else in life, has its plateaus and valleys. Sometimes a person is really struggling with a diet or hurting over old or recent pains or going through one of those grief periods when they miss food as a tranquilizer or a buffer. They're feeling, *I'm willing to do this, but it isn't much fun right now.* And just at that sensitive moment a spouse or close friend can step in and say, "Give yourself a weekend off. You deserve it. You've lost a lot of weight. Live a little."

The Johnsons came to us for evaluation. Ed Johnson drank a lot, but they weren't sure he was really an alcoholic, and they weren't willing to commit to an Alcoholics Anonymous program unless they were sure it was necessary. We directed that as part of the evaluation Ed should try to go for two weeks without taking a drink. Then he should come back and report to us.

At the end of the two weeks a crestfallen couple sat in front of us. "Well, how did it go?" we asked.

Alice answered. "Well, Doctor, Ed went for ten days without taking a drink, just like you said. Not a drop. But I couldn't stand to see him suffer. It was just too much for him, so I bought him a bottle."

SELF-IMPOSED GUILT CAN CAUSE RELAPSE

Often the messages are less overt than those Jared and Ed Johnson received. Often they are even imagined by an overweight patient. Remember when Ginger refused to see her friend from New Zealand because she had overeaten and imagined he would think she looked fat? "I was so grouchy with him on the phone," she recalled. "And all he said in that wonderfully proper accent of his was, 'Well, be nice to the dog.' Of course, it turned out that he never thought about my weight at all and would certainly never have noticed the extra pieces of chicken I ate. But I was so ashamed of losing control that I felt like a blimp."

And the messages don't even have to relate to food. Barbara imagined people would laugh behind her back because she didn't get an A+ on her exam. In her mind the old negative messages she had received as a child flooded back: "Barbara's drawings look like a kindergartener's." "She'll never be an artist." "Barbara can't make it—why does she even try?" The fact that in the heat of studying for her finals she hadn't taken time to play her positive self-talk tape for two weeks had helped pave the way for this flood of negative messages.

PERFECTIONISTIC THINKING CAN CAUSE RELAPSE

The greatest danger at this stage is not the actual harm done to your diet from two or three pieces of chicken, or even of chocolate pie. The real danger is of throwing the baby out with the bath water. This is a special danger for perfectionists or for black-and-white thinkers who will tell themselves, *Well, I've done it now. If I can't do it right, I might as well quit trying—go ahead and eat the whole gallon of ice cream. I knew I could never be thin.*

When such shame and guilt come back into play, one is back into the addiction cycle. Instead of shame helping one get back on the program, it drives self-esteem down and brings back the love hunger, propelling the person downward toward a new binge.

We challenge all our patients to be committed to their diets and to make a lifetime commitment to weight maintenance. But we also warn them not to be overly perfectionistic. This is really learning to walk a balanced rope. On the one side, you need to stay on your maintenance program forever. On the other side, you need to understand that it's not unusual and it's not terrible to slip the boundaries occasionally. Learn to balance between the dangers of relapse and the dangers of perfectionism.

KNOW THE WARNING SIGNALS OF A RELAPSE

Before Barbara left Dr. Hemfelt's office, he had also suggested that she might find it helpful to call Ralph, whom she had come to know well in the clinic therapy group. "Ralph is a 'pro' at relapse," the doctor said. "He's experienced it many, many times, and now he's doing a great job of preventing it. He can give you some first-hand tips if you need them."

For several days her visit to the doctor had carried her through, but on the following Tuesday Barbara woke up worrying about not having heard from her job application yet, and she felt a compelling desire to smother her worry with pancakes. She called Ralph.

Ralph laughed when he heard what the doctor had said about him. "Called me a 'pro' at relapse, huh? That's about the size of it. But one thing that's helped me stay on top of it this time is learning how to recognize the warning signals."

"Like craving pancakes, you mean?"

Ralph laughed again. "Well, that certainly is one, but the best thing is to head off the relapse before you get to a food craving. That's the last-ditch stand, and it's much harder to win the battle at that point. A big cause of relapse is going back into denial. If I wake up some morning hearing myself say, 'I wasn't really all that heavy,' I know I have to go back and face the truth and get out of denial, or I'll wind up being 'all that heavy' again. Listen carefully to the messages you're giving yourself. If you're hearing, 'I'm not really compulsive' or 'My relationships weren't in that much trouble,' you're on the brink of going back into denial, and that can trigger a major relapse."

"Oh!" Barbara's voice reflected the light that had come on in her mind. "I see. I'd been focusing so hard on this job thing that I was telling myself, 'If I just get the job, everything will be okay.' When really, the job would be great, but it doesn't really have anything to do with my compulsive behavior. Thank you, Ralph."

"Glad to help. Call anytime. And good luck with the job."

Now Barbara was perfectly satisfied eating a bowl of Fiber One with a fresh peach before she called the personnel manager about her application. Later she reviewed the other warning signals her doctor had told her to watch out for.

1. Are you aware of building anger and simmering resentment? If you suddenly realize that you feel picked on or if you are walking around feeling angry day after day and don't even know what or whom you are angry at, be warned. There is something down there in the emotional core that you haven't tapped or inventoried, or there is a new grief in your life you haven't dealt with.

2. Do you find yourself trying to rationalize your way out of your diet? If you are telling yourself: I don't have a food problem. I wasn't *that* heavy. I can do this on my own. This diet makes my legs ache. Dieting saps my energy. Be warned. This can be a new form of denial, and you'll have to go all the way back to footpath #1 and break through it.

3. Are you isolating, pulling back from your support network? Perhaps early in your recovery program you were seeing a therapist weekly, going to OA daily and to a Bible study twice a week. Now you look back over the past two weeks and realize you have found excuses to cancel your therapy, haven't been to an OA meeting in ten days, and only went once to Bible study, but didn't have your lesson done. Be warned. Disconnecting from your support groups is a major danger signal.

4. Do you find yourself being excessively preoccupied with food? If you discover yourself obsessing about what you're eating and what you're not eating, if you spend a lot of time thinking about old favorite restaurants, or if you start reading cookbooks like novels, be warned. You are moving to the edge of a relapse.

5. Are you gaining weight? Everyone's weight fluctuates normally within as much as a ten-pound range. Women are particularly aware of this near the onset of the menstrual cycle. But if your weight has gone up more than ten pounds and stayed there, be warned. You are eating too much, eating the wrong things, or not

exercising enough. An adjustment needs to be made in your program.

KNOW THE REMEDIAL STEPS

In another phone call Ralph told Barbara something she liked so much that she asked him to repeat it, so she could write it down: "Relapse does not mean the end of the whole program. Remember, the key is balance: do not give yourself permission to relapse; do not condemn yourself if it occurs."

If you lose your way in the woods, the most harmful thing you can do is to panic. If you suddenly discover you've lost your way on your recovery program, do not panic; calmly follow our ten remedial steps back to the security of your well-marked footpath.

1. Immediately acknowledge your relapse to yourself, to another person, and to God. You made a great victory in your initial breaking through denial. Don't go back into negation by denying your problem now. Ginger says, "Once I got out of denial, I didn't want to deny anything. Honesty is a wonderful, releasing thing. Denial is bondage: it's like being in prison, and I don't want any more of it."

If you were recovering from major surgery and suddenly began bleeding, you would not reach for the first aid kit; you would reach for the telephone. Do the same now. Call your sponsor or your therapist or your pastor. Get help. And reach out to God in prayer. Many patients quit praying at this time without even realizing it. This is the time when your prayer support needs to be strongest.

2. Now share your problem with your support group. The typical response is to stay home from meetings if things aren't going well. This is exactly the wrong thing to do. When you are feeling weakest is the time you most need the strength of your group. Some patients, however, will keep going to their group, but will not share. This is its own form of isolation. Secrecy leads to shame, and shame, as we saw in Chapter 4, is the feeling that keeps the entire addiction cycle going.

3. Forgive yourself. Be compassionate; be a friend to yourself. A friend does not persecute, punish, condemn, or shame. A friend forgives, accepts, encourages, and helps. Tell yourself: *This is normal. This is human. I accept it. I will deal with it.*

4. Endorse yourself. This is going a step beyond forgiveness by affirming the progress you've made. Walk back over your journey, the number of pounds lost, the support meetings attended, the foot-

paths successfully walked. Give yourself some new affirmations in your self-talk: I affirm my body. I enjoy taking care of my body. I affirm my right to heal.

One loses perspective when lost in the woods. Relapse is a case of not being able to see the forest for the trees. Don't focus on the one giant pine in front of you as if you had to climb it. Look behind you at all the woods, meadows, and deserts you've passed in recovery. Look ahead of you at the beautiful countryside you'll be walking through as recovery continues.

5. Put down a milestone. One of the most frustrating directions a footpath walker can encounter is "Turn left at the Martins' barn." Which barn is the Martins'? But one of the greatest securities is finding a milestone—a large, granite boulder with the directions literally carved in stone. Put down your own milestone by making a detailed inventory in your journal of the progress you've made. Write down in detail the recoveries you've made in every area of your life: emotional, intellectual, physical, relational, spiritual.

In the Old Testament, Samuel set up a stone to mark the defeat of the Philistines. He called it the Ebenezer, "Stone of Help," and it served as a reminder to the Children of Israel that "Hitherto has the Lord led us." Look back over your Ebenezers and say, "Hitherto has the Lord led me." Then look toward the future and say, "And He will lead me again."

6. Now you need to inventory the emotional and relationship issues that led up to your relapse. Although the symptom of a relapse is a desire to binge, the relapse itself usually has very little to do with food. Survey your emotional and relational life for the past two weeks. Patients have reported this as an eye-opening experience. Relapses look as if they come out of the blue with a sudden, inexplicable, overwhelming desire to EAT. But in reality, there will have been a long onset of gradually building tensions and disappointments. Ralph once told us after he relapsed, "I was angry for three weeks. Angry at my girlfriend, angry at my boss, angry at myself. All the time that rage was building inside me, and I didn't realize it at all. No wonder I finally went out and ordered three Big Macs. I had to go all the way back and work through the grief process over losing that big computer account before I could get on top of my eating issues again."

Once you've written your retrospective down, you need to share it. Call your closest support person and read it to him or her. Hearing your own words aloud will give you perspective, and your support person's insights will broaden the view.

7. Make new decisions about changes in your relationships and your food program. The typical response to a relapse is for pa-

tients to become more rigid in their diet and lifestyle. Rather than inflict punishment on yourself by drastically reducing your caloric intake, do your best to maintain a healthy, restricted calorie diet.

Constructively use your desire to relapse by redefining and re-establishing new boundaries. We talked in the last chapter about keeping in touch with your body. Your desire to relapse may be telling you that you've not been listening closely enough to your body. You may be losing weight too fast or too slowly. Your body might be missing a nutrient that's in short supply in your diet.

Often the message of experience is not nutritional, but emotional. Your feelings may be rebelling. Maybe you've jogged part of your footpaths rather than walking them. Now you need to go back at a more leisurely stroll and take care of any unfinished business.

Ralph said this was a major reason for his repeated relapses. "Path #2, the eating for success—I didn't jog that; I sprinted. When I would decide to lose weight, I'd just quit eating and double my exercise program. That's guaranteed to get the weight off *fast*, but it's no way to learn sensible eating. Until I took that class from Dr. Sneed, I didn't know anything about fats or carbohydrates. I could tell chocolate cake from an apple—that was about it. I've had to walk the eating right footpath very slowly and learn that material from the ground up. Now I love it, though. I'm even becoming a pretty good cook."

Or maybe you are rebelling against your diet. We've talked before about the emotional aspect of food. Maybe some part of your diet isn't meeting an emotional need. We had one patient who got depressed if her diet didn't contain enough fat. Since a healthy diet may be between 20 and 30 percent fat, this left room for her to make adjustments in her diet to suit her needs. Talk this over with your doctor, dietitian, or food sponsor.

8. Recommit to a revitalized recovery plan. Your relapse may be simply a reaction against boredom. Even for patients on a program as highly restricted as a liquid diet, boredom can be dealt with. At the clinic we have a recipe book which we don't give our liquid-dieting patients initially. But when they've been on the program a few weeks and boredom threatens, we show them how to add variety to their liquid diet with such items as low-calorie JELL-O or diet soda.

After six months of successful maintenance, Ralph came to us with a long face. "I don't know, Doc. I'm supposed to be your 'pro,' but I'm afraid the urge to relapse is bigger than I am this time."

"What have you done lately to beat boredom?" we asked him.

"Well, I've cooked all of Dr. Sneed's recipes several times, so I bought a new low-fat cookbook, and that helped for a while. Then I started experimenting on my own—I checked out the herb and spice shelves at the grocery store—and the gourmet section. Pickled onions are really something, and tarragon Dijon mustard can do incredible things to a turkey sandwich. But," he paused and shrugged, "I'm still bored."

We commended Ralph's culinary efforts but told him we suspected the problem was elsewhere this time. So, we gave him a growth survey to take home and work through. We suggest you do the same if you are feeling bored in any area of your life.

What am I doing to grow physically? Do I have a good exercise program? Do I need a new hairstyle or skin care program?

What am I doing to grow intellectually? Have I read a good book lately? Have I had a stimulating discussion with friends recently on important topics? Do I need to take a class on a subject I want to know more about?

What am I doing to grow in my career? Are there advancements I should consider applying for? Are there seminars I should be taking? What professional literature should I be reading?

What am I doing to grow spiritually? Am I having a daily devotional time? Do I need some new devotional literature? Have I found a church that helps me grow spiritually? Is my small group meeting my needs, or do I need to look further?

The impulse to chuck the whole thing, which often accompanies relapse, is actually a signal to do the exact opposite—make it more exciting, give yourself new challenges.

9. Find special ways to be nice to yourself. This is not rewarding relapse, but giving yourself the special nurturance you need right now. One patient of ours treats herself to a professional massage when she finds herself struggling with relapse. Another patient, who is self-employed, gives herself permission to sleep until ten o'clock and enjoy a cup of tea in bed. These are excellent examples because tension and fatigue can be major factors in triggering a relapse.

An important part of recovery is learning to be your own best friend. This is the time to show yourself what a good friend you can be by being extra nice to yourself. The message of relapse is, "Something is missing." It's your job to make it up to yourself.

10. Pursue a closer relationship with God. With any addiction, the most insidious liability of relapse is a tendency to pull away from God because the old feelings of shame and guilt come into play. This tendency is as old as the Garden of Eden where Adam and Eve hid themselves from God after they had sinned.

When Ralph returned with his growth survey completed, he reluctantly pinpointed this as a problem area in his life. "I had been doing great and was really growing spiritually, but I realize now I've been drawing away from God lately."

We told him that bitterness, or prolonged anger, is often at the root of a desire to withdraw from God. "Sometimes patients feel like, 'I turned this over to God, and He dropped the ball.'"

"That's right. That is how I felt. But I didn't realize it. I think I got mad at God when I felt a desire to relapse."

"That's exactly right," we said. "Such feelings are subconscious, but conscious, mechanical steps are needed to return to a close fellowship. First, remind yourself of all the Bible stories you ever heard of people who went to Jesus. Call your pastor or Sunday school teacher, and make a list. Notice how the vast majority of these people were sick, hurting, or distressed. Now put yourself in that group. Tell yourself, *God wants me to be close to Him. I can go to Him just like all those people in the Bible.* Then go to Him in prayer and tell Him."

Perhaps you, like Ralph, need to tap back into the spiritual strength on which your entire recovery is based. This is the one source that never fails, the one place you will never be condemned or misunderstood. Christ, who was tempted in all ways like us, knows our weakness. He knows, not just from an omniscient consciousness of the universe, but from the personal experience of being human, living on this earth, and experiencing all our weaknesses for thirty-three years. He has promised to be our ever-present help in time of trouble. But we must call on Him. He will never intrude where He's not invited. So reach out in prayer, meditation, and Bible reading to the ultimate source of strength in the universe that is also your closest, most intimate source of strength.

Barbara had recognized the reasons for her relapse as Dr. Hemfelt explained the situation to her. Back home in her room, she thought over them again. Disappointment over her exam was only a small part, the tip of the iceberg. Under that was the fear of now seriously entering the job market— and not just for any old job, but for the job she'd dreamed of all her life. Now her dreams were on the line. She needed to tell herself that she was well qualified for this opening at a local furniture store. It was work she could do well and would enjoy doing. She would do well on the interview. But it was not the only job in the world. If this one didn't work out, there would be others. She was still a worthwhile, lovable person. Just as her self-worth didn't rest in her reading on the scales that morning, neither did it rest on this job or any other she might apply for.

Look at all she'd achieved: Every day she and Tom were moving closer to the emotional intimacy in their marriage that Dr. Hemfelt talked about. She had finished her classwork and was ready to put her artistic ability to use. She had reached her ideal weight and was thoroughly enjoying her new attractiveness and new, energetic lifestyle. Barbara vowed to work as hard on the steps to prevent a relapse as she had on the pathways to recovery.

We hope you will too. As you have walked these footpaths with Ralph and Barbara and their friends, you have moved into your own recovery. We say to you, as we would to any patient who is leaving our care, congratulations! Congratulations on having been able to recognize your problem, congratulations on breaking out of denial and reading this book, and congratulations on walking our footpaths to recovery all the way to journey's end.

And yet, this isn't the end at all. In reality it's just the beginning. We know it sounds strange to a patient who has spent weeks, months, or even years in recovery to be told it's just the beginning, but it's exciting to realize that you now have years of emotional, spiritual, and relationship growth ahead of you. This growth will continue for the rest of your life as you continue to use our footpaths for personal development.

Remember what Ralph told his therapy group in Chapter 1: "Getting your life together, reaching recovery—it's tough, but it's worth it. If you really believe you deserve to be healthy and happy, then with personal effort, God's power, and the encouragement of others, you'll make it—one day at a time."

PART THREE

LOVE
HUNGER
COOKBOOK

COOKING TIPS AND MEAL PLANS

COOKING TIPS

BEFORE YOU use the recipes in this section of the book, we want to give you a list of things to help enhance the flavor and reduce the calories of your food. You don't have to sacrifice taste just because you're trying to lose weight. You'll want to follow these cooking tips forever, not just during weight loss.

1. *Learn to cook well.* Many people come into my office who don't eat certain healthy foods—specifically fish and vegetables—because they did not grow up with them. Because their mothers did not fix them, they never learned to cook these foods properly. If you have never learned to cook well, enroll in a community class or some type of cooking class. Investigate cookbooks, and after you've tried all 140 recipes in this book and have determined which ones meet your needs, then you might invest in some other low-calorie and/or low-fat cookbooks.

2. *Develop your own recipe file.* Certainly not all of the recipes in this book will be suitable for you or your family, but a good many of them will be. Take the ones you liked best, write them down on cards, and then you can easily select a dessert, for instance, that appealed to you—right from your own recipe file.

3. *Use the right equipment.* Nonstick cookware means that you don't have to cook with fat. In the past, fat in a cast-iron skillet reduced scrubbing. Today, a very important part of low-fat cooking is good nonstick cookware and nonstick cooking sprays, which come in regular flavor or butter flavor. We make heavy use of these in our recipes. Mazola Nonstick, PAM, and Marigold are good brands.

4. *Use butter substitutes*. These are primarily spray-dried butter products, which have been defatted. They have the essence of the butter flavor without all of the fat.

5. *Make use of the microwave*. Microwaves are excellent for cooking vegetables. To microwave a vegetable, put it in a small bowl, add 2 tablespoons of water, cover it with plastic wrap, and zap it for about 10 minutes, depending on the type of vegetable. This is also the easiest way to make nonfat popcorn. Take plain microwaved popcorn, spray it with the butter-flavored nonstick spray, and sprinkle one of the butter substitutes on it.

6. *Use a separating cup*. Separating cups may be obtained at culinary shops. Take the stock from any roast or baked chicken dish, pour it into the separating cup, and the fat will float to the top. Pour the fat-free bouillon off, and throw the fat away to make all types of fat-free gravy. For example, if you have a pot roast—a very lean pot roast, like the eye of the round roast—go ahead and Dutch oven cook it, pour the stock into the separating cup, pour the bouillon back into the pan, thicken it with cornstarch and water, and you have a very nice fat-free brown gravy. The same thing can be done with the stock from your Thanksgiving turkey.

7. *Dilute recipes*. Extend the volume of your recipes with high-fiber, low-calorie foods. For example, if you're going to make a tuna salad, you can double the volume size and dilute the calories by adding things like chopped celery, chopped dill pickles, and chopped apples—turning a lovely recipe into one that is also very low calorie.

8. *Limit oils*. When sautéing, use only a very small amount of oil or combination of a very small amount of oil and perhaps bouillon or water. Fat-absorbing vegetables such as potatoes should be cooked with as little oil as possible. For example, you would not want to put potatoes around a pot roast, because they will simply absorb all of the fat that's in the meat.

9. *Avoid regular salad dressings*. Never even consider a regular salad dressing. If you put one scoop of regular salad dressing on top of a salad, just imagine that, in terms of calories, you've put a cheeseburger on top of your salad. Regular salad dressings are about 80 to 90 calories per tablespoon, and we recommend 25 calories or fewer per tablespoon. We have some recipes in the book, or you can buy prebottled dressings. Read the label and make sure that the calorie content, which is going to be reflected by the fat content, is 25 calories per tablespoon or fewer.

10. *Substitute egg whites for whole eggs*. To decrease cholesterol, substitute 2 egg whites for each whole egg in most recipes.

For example, our muffin recipes call for 2 egg whites. Discard the egg yolks.

11. *Use skimmed evaporated milk.* Skimmed evaporated milk, which comes in little cans, is a very versatile product. It can be used in pies at holiday times; it can be whipped and used in place of whipping cream; it can be substituted for cream or half-and-half; and it goes very well in quiche.

12. *Avoid high-fat crackers.* When making a cracker selection, don't be fooled by high-fat crackers. Many of the variety crackers, even some whole wheat, are extremely high in fat. Take a facial tissue and place the cracker on it. A high-fat cracker will leave a little grease mark on the tissue. Also, you can just check the food label. Unfortunately, many labels list only the ingredients, not the calorie and fat contents specifically. You want to be on the lookout for hydrogenated fats as this usually indicates a high-fat cracker. Some that we can recommend include Cracklesnax, Cracklebred, Ry Krisp, Melba toast, Wasa, Norwegian Crisp Bread, and rice cakes.

13. *Don't fry corn tortillas.* When using corn tortillas, resist the urge to fry them before using them in an onchilada-type recipe. They just need to be steamed to soften them enough to roll.

14. *Use skimmed milk or ½ percent milk.* Don't even consider using whole milk or 2 percent milk. Whole milk is half fat. When using cheese, you should try to use a part-skim milk cheese or a reduced-calorie cheese or better yet, probably no cheese. The whole milk cheeses are out of the question. Get a grater that grates cheeses in very fine, long strands. Using cheese uncooked will make it fluffy and look like a greater amount.

15. *Low-caloric ice milk can be okay as a frozen dessert.* Whether it is okay depends on the fat content. You need to use your percent fat formula and determine that it is 25 percent fat or less.

16. *Fish is the best meat choice.* If you've never learned to like fish, make the effort. It's worth it, because fish is decidedly different from chicken or other types of poultry. Fish will help you to decrease your serum level of triglycerides and cholesterol, and it is lower in fat and lower in calories than either chicken or beef. Organ meats should absolutely be avoided. Liver once a week was good nutrition many years ago when vitamin and mineral supplements were not readily available. Many people, especially women, were suffering from anemia and needed to eat liver once a week for the iron content. Instead take a good vitamin/mineral supplement with the appropriate amount of iron and don't eat liver. Liver is one of the highest-fat, highest-cholesterol things you can put into your mouth.

17. *Choose vegetable oils.* When choosing an oil, always pick a

vegetable oil over anything like lard, bacon, fat, or cream. Canola oil is the most highly polyunsaturated and is available in most supermarkets. Olive oil is in the news now, because it helps you reduce the LDL cholesterol ratio and total cholesterol.

18. *Avoid high-fat breads.* When considering breads, steer away from high-fat breads such as biscuits, donuts, croissants, and any other type of pastries. Choose lower-fat breads including English muffins, bagels, French bread, regular bread, muffins, and pita bread. For chips and dips use the baked chips or the lighter chips, and homemade dips made out of low-fat cottage cheese instead of sour cream.

19. *Substitute yogurt for sour cream and cream cheese.* Instead of sour cream, use nonfat or low-fat yogurt, and instead of cream cheese, use the yogurt cheese described in the recipe section.

20. *Read labels and recipes carefully.* Learn which ingredients are good for you and which are not. Learn how to determine fat percentage from the label. Remember that many of your old recipes call for too much fat and too much sweetener. You might be able to take, for example, your all-time favorite oatmeal cookie recipe, reduce the fat content by 1/3, reduce the sugar content by 1/2, and have a relatively good food choice.

21. *Use lean sandwich meats.* Sandwiches can be an excellent food choice. Just make sure that you're not choosing one of the fatty processed meats such as bologna, salami, canned meats, sausages, or any other type of pressed meats. The only meats for your sandwiches are the very lean deli cuts such as turkey breast, lean ham, or chicken breast. Always buy water-packed tuna.

22. *Remove visible meat fat and skin.* Always cut away visible fat from all meat. Remove poultry skin prior to cooking, or cook it with the skin on to preserve moisture, then remove the skin and heat the meat for 10 minutes more.

23. *Use angel food cake.* Angel food cake, which is made from egg whites, contains no fat at all.

24. *Be an organized cook.* Make a grocery list, and plan out what you're going to have. This takes less time than having to make do with other ingredients or running to the store at the last minute.

25. *Cook on the weekends whenever possible, if you have a busy weekday schedule.* You can prepare up to a week's worth of food, put it into the proper storage container, and then reheat as you need it. If you find you are not eating raw vegetables, it's probably because you don't want to come home after a hard day's work and chop them up. One way to solve this problem is to cut vegetables on the weekend and put them into a tightly sealed container until needed.

26. *Avoid soggy packed lunches.* If you're packing sandwiches, take your vegetables in a separate plastic wrap, so that your sandwiches won't become soggy. This is especially important if you pack your lunch the night before.

27. *Substitute herbs and spices for fat and salt.* Use herbs and spices in everything to reduce the need for fat and salt. If you are using fresh herbs such as fresh chopped parsley, use about two to four times more fresh than dried.

NINE-DAY MEAL PLAN

1,000-CALORIE MENUS

―――――――――――― **Day 1** ――――――――――――

	Food Items	Exchanges
BREAKFAST	½ English muffin	1 bread
	8 oz. skim milk	1 milk
	1 tsp. diet margarine	½ fat
	Hot tea	
LUNCH	2 slices lite bread (40 calories/ slice)	1 bread
	1 oz. shredded turkey breast	1 meat
	Mustard, lettuce, tomato, sprouts	vegetables
	1 medium apple	2 fruit
SNACK	1 cup raw vegetables (carrots, celery, etc.)	vegetables
	2 tbsp. low-fat Italian dressing	
DINNER	1 barbecued chicken breast, no skin (sauce recipe p. 240)	3 meat
	1 small baked potato	1 bread
	1 tsp. diet margarine	½ fat
	Butter substitute sprinkles	
	1½ cup fresh spinach and oil-free Italian dressing	vegetables
SNACK	3 2½-inch graham cracker squares	1 bread
	8 oz. skim milk	1 milk

At the end of the day, you have had 4 bread exchanges, 4 meat exchanges, 2 milk exchanges, 2 fruit exchanges, plenty of vegetables, 1 fat exchange. This is just what has been recommended on pages 320–325, the Food Exchange Lists. Also, note that the calories and food exchanges have been spread out over the entire day.

――――――――――――――― **Day 2** ―――――――――――――――

	Food Items	Exchanges
BREAKFAST	8 oz. plain nonfat yogurt	1 milk
	½ cup fresh blueberries	1 fruit
	1 packet NutraSweet	
	1 small Unbelievable Oat-Bran Muffin (p. 246)	1 bread
LUNCH	Grilled cheese sandwich	
	1 slice lite bread	1 bread
	1 oz. low-fat cheese	1 meat
	1 tsp. diet margarine	½ fat
	V-8 juice	vegetables
	Tossed salad, lite dressing	vegetables
SNACK	½ cup grapes	1 fruit
DINNER	3 oz. Blackened Orange Roughy (p. 262)	3 meat, ½ fat
	1 cup Brown Rice Pilaf (p. 256)	2 bread
	¾ cup Spicy Green Beans (p. 248)	vegetables
SNACK	8 oz. skim milk	1 milk

――――――――――――――― **Day 3** ―――――――――――――――

	Food Items	Exchanges
BREAKFAST	2 slices lite toast	1 bread
	1 tsp. diet margarine	½ fat
	8 oz. skim milk	1 milk
	½ grapefruit	1 fruit
	1 tsp. sugar	
	Hot tea	
LUNCH	Chef salad	
	½ cup cottage cheese	1 milk
	2 oz. turkey and cheese	2 meat
	Vegetables, low-cal dressing	vegetables
	5 saltines	1 bread
DINNER	Vegetable/beef ka-bobs	
	2 oz. meat, tomatoes, onion, peppers	2 meat, vegetables
	½ cup wild rice/brown rice pilaf	1 bread, ½ fat

½ cup steamed broccoli	vegetables
Dessert	
1 1-inch slice angel food cake	1 bread
¾ cup sliced strawberries	1 fruit

Day 4

	Food Items	Exchanges
BREAKFAST	1 Breakfast Taco (p. 236)	1½ bread, 1 meat
	½ cup orange juice	1 fruit
LUNCH	Warm Tuna-Veggie Salad (p. 228)	2 meat, 1 fat, 1 vegetables
	on a bed of lettuce	vegetables
DINNER	Hungarian Beefsteak (p. 269)	2 meat, 1 fat
	1 cup cooked noodles	2 bread
	¼ canteloupe	1 fruit
SNACK	½ cup low-fat cottage cheese sprinkled with Mrs. Dash	1 milk

---

Day 5

	Food Items	Exchanges
BREAKFAST	½ whole wheat bagel, toasted	1 bread
	1 tsp. diet margarine	½ fat
	1 oz. low-fat cream cheese	1 meat
	1 cup fresh berries (strawberries, raspberries, blackberries)	1 fruit
LUNCH	2 slices lite bread	1 bread
	1 slice lite ham (approximately ¾ oz.), and 1 slice Borden Lite-line cheese	1 meat
	2 tsp. Dijon mustard	
	Lettuce, tomato	vegetables
	5 vanilla wafers	1 bread
SNACK	Vegetable sticks	vegetables
DINNER	Leek and Potato Soup (p. 230)	1 bread, 1½ milk, ½ fat

| | Tossed salad with 2½ oz. smoked turkey | 2½ meat, vegetables |
| SNACK | 8 oz. skim milk | 1 milk |

Day 6 (For a Day on the Go)

	Food Items	*Exchanges*
BREAKFAST	Granola bar (approximately 100 calories)	1 bread
	8 oz. skim milk	1 milk
LUNCH	Salad bar	
	2 cups raw vegetables	vegetables
	¼ cup cottage cheese	½ meat
	2 tbsp. meat or cheese bits	1 meat
	¼ cup low-cal dressing	1 fat
	4 saltine crackers	1 bread
SNACK	1 small banana	2 fruit
DINNER	Jack-in-the-Box*	
	Grilled chicken sandwich (order without any sauce and add your own mustard—sandwich contains 1 slice of cheese)	2 bread, 3 meat, vegetables, 1 milk

Day 7

	Food Items	*Exchanges*
BREAKFAST	½ cup Fiber One cereal (or other very high-fiber cereal equivalent), and ¼ cup raisin bran	1½ bread
	8 oz. skim milk	1 milk
	½ small banana	1 fruit
LUNCH	1 cup tomato soup	½ bread, ½ milk
	2 slices lite bread	1 bread

*Though we are not necessarily recommending fast-food as a staple in your nutritionally balanced weight-loss program, there may be some days in which this is a necessity to accommodate your lifestyle. Don't get off your diet just because you're in a rush. Choose one of the better fast-food meals such as the one above.

	½ cup Zesty Tuna Salad (p. 229)	½ fruit, 1½ meat, ½ fat
	Lettuce, tomato	vegetables
SNACK	1 peach	1 fruit
DINNER	½ cup spaghetti noodles	1 bread
	¾ cup tomato and ground beef sauce	2 meat, vegetables
	Tossed salad, all vegetables, low- cal dressing	vegetables
	1 tbsp. parmesan cheese	½ milk

Day 8

	Food Items	Exchanges
BREAKFAST	1 Unbelievable Oat-Bran Muffin (p. 246)	1 bread, ½ fruit
	8 oz. skim milk	1 milk
	Hot tea	
LUNCH	⅓ cup Curried Chicken Salad (p. 227)	1 meat, ½ fruit, 1 fat
	1 pita pocket bread	2 bread
	Lettuce, tomato, sprouts	vegetables
SNACK	Carrot sticks	vegetables
DINNER	4 oz. grilled or baked fish	3 meat
	½ cup rice, cooked in bouillon	1 bread
	Sliced tomatoes	vegetables
	Lettuce wedge	vegetables
SNACK	½ cup low-fat cottage cheese	1 milk
	½ cup fresh fruit	1 fruit

Day 9 (Party Day)

(Note that breakfast and lunch are smaller,
but not skipped, in preparation for an
at-home party in the evening.)

	Food Items	Exchanges
BREAKFAST	¾ cup cereal	1 bread
	8 oz. skim milk	1 milk

LUNCH	2 slices lite bread	1 bread
	1 oz. chicken breast	1 meat
	Mustard, lettuce, tomato	vegetables
DINNER	¼ cup Ricotta Vegetable Dip (p. 217)	½ milk, ½ fat
	Vegetable dippers	vegetables
	Chicken Parmesan (p. 267)	4 meat, 1 fat, vegetables
	Large tossed salad	vegetables
	Steamed vegetables (from free foods list)	vegetables
	Party Parfait (p. 275)	1 bread, ½ milk, ½ fruit, 1 fat

CHAPTER

16

Appetizers and Snacks

Fruit Smoothies

Nutritional Information
1-cup serving:
Calories 45
Fat 0
Protein 0
Carbohydrates 11.5g
% fat 0
Cholesterol 0

Exchanges
1 Fruit

1 cup fresh strawberries
1 small banana
1 teaspoon sugar
1–2 cups crushed ice and water
4 large, fresh strawberries

Combine all ingredients in a blender and mix until smooth. Pour equally into 4 glasses. Cut a strawberry partially in half (leaving the top intact) and wedge onto the side of the glass. Serve immediately. Serves 4.

Other fruits may be used instead of the strawberries. However, they are particularly low in calories.

Low-Fat Fruity Milkshakes (Honest!)

Nutritional Information
12-ounce serving:
Calories 195
Fat 1g
Protein 20g
Carbohydrates 26g
% fat 5
Cholesterol 0

Exchanges
½ Bread
1 Milk
1 Fruit

½ cup ice milk or low-fat ice cream, vanilla or other flavor
½ cup skim milk
½ cup fruit (such as banana or strawberries)

Place all ingredients in a blender and puree. This recipe works best with a vanilla ice cream base, but other flavors may be used as long as the nutritional value is the same. Serves 1.

Note: There should be no more than 3 percent fat

or 1 gram of fat per 100-calorie serving (usually ½ cup per serving).

Coke Float

Nutritional Information
18-ounce serving:
Calories 150
Fat 1.5g
Protein 5g
Carbohydrates 28g
% fat 9
Cholesterol 15mg

Exchanges
1 Bread
½ Milk
½ Fat

¾ cup vanilla ice milk or low-fat ice cream
12 ounces Diet Coke or equivalent

Combine these ingredients in a tall prechilled glass and prepare yourself for lots of bubbles and good taste. This snack is so low in fat that you can have one every day if you like. Serves 1.

Note: Should be no more than 1 gram of fat per 100-calorie serving.

Basic Yogurt Cheese

Nutritional Information
2-tablespoon serving:
Calories 24
Fat 0
Protein 2.3g
Carbohydrates 3.5g
% fat 0
Cholesterol 0

Exchanges
¼ Milk

16 ounces nonfat plain yogurt
Yogurt funnel or 15"x15" piece of cheesecloth

When using either a yogurt funnel or cheesecloth, simply place the yogurt into the meshed area and drain over a dish for approximately 24 hours. The watery whey will drain out of the yogurt, leaving a cheeselike substance similar in consistency to cream cheese. The longer the yogurt drains, the firmer it will become as more whey drains out. You can buy a yogurt funnel at many culinary cookshops. Serves 10.

Yogurt cheese is a wonderful low-fat alternative to any of the following:

Ricotta cheese (part-skim)	22 calories/tablespoon
Sour cream	30 calories/tablespoon
Cream cheese	52 calories/tablespoon
Mayonnaise	100 calories/tablespoon

By contrast yogurt cheese is 12 calories per tablespoon and has *no fat*. Yogurt cheese may be used as a substitute in cheese balls, spreads, dips, cheesecakes, etc.

Zesty Yogurt Cheese Mold

Nutritional Information
1/4-cup serving:
Calories 52
Fat 0
Protein 6.1g
Carbohydrates 7g
% fat 0
Cholesterol 0

Exchanges
3/4 Milk

8 cups nonfat plain yogurt
1/2 cup water
1 envelope unflavored gelatin
1 teaspoon Worcestershire sauce
1/2 teaspoon salt
1 teaspoon celery salt
1 teaspoon dry mustard
1/4 cup fresh parsley, minced
2 tablespoons chives, chopped
1/8 teaspoon cayenne or white ground pepper
Nonstick vegetable oil spray

Make 4 to 5 cups of Basic Yogurt Cheese (page 216). Stir the gelatin into the hot water in a saucepan over low heat until completely dissolved. Then combine gelatin, yogurt cheese, all remaining spices, and beat with a mixer. Spray the inside of a shallow gelatin mold with a nonstick vegetable oil spray, and pour in cheese yogurt mixture. Cover with plastic and chill until firm, at least 4 hours. When unmolding, loosen the edges with a sharp-tipped knife. Serves 20.

Serving Suggestion: Serve with low-fat crackers, pita bread, or vegetable slices.

Ricotta Vegetable Dip

Nutritional Information
1/4-cup-of-dip serving:
Calories 67
Fat 2.5g
Protein 6.5g
Carbohydrates 4.8g
% fat 33
Cholesterol 7mg

Exchanges
1/2 Milk
1/2 Fat

8 ounces part-skim milk ricotta
8 ounces Basic Yogurt Cheese (p. 216)
2 tablespoons green olives, minced
1/4 cup carrots, minced
1/4 cup celery, minced
2 tablespoons pecans, minced
Carrots, celery, cucumbers, and yellow squash

Combine ricotta, yogurt cheese, olives, minced carrots, minced celery, and pecans. Mix well. Make dipping sticks out of the carrots and celery, and slice the cucumbers and squash. Arrange the dip and vegetables on a party tray. Serves 10.

Dip (for Chips)

Nutritional Information
Heaping-¼-cup serving:
Calories 41
Fat 1.2g
Protein 14g
Carbohydrates 3.1g
% fat 26
Cholesterol 5mg

Exchanges
½ Meat

16 ounces 1 percent low-fat cottage cheese
2 tablespoons lemon juice
½–1 package Hidden Valley Ranch party dip mix

Empty the entire carton of cottage cheese into a food processor (a blender will not work in this recipe). Add the lemon juice and process until the cottage cheese resembles sour cream. Then add the Ranch party dip mix. (Note: Any other flavor packet or combination of herbs and spices may be used as a substitute for the Ranch mix.) Serve with a low-fat chip or cracker, such as Skinny Munchies, a baked chip, or Cracklesnax crackers. Also, this is great as a vegetable dip. Serves 8.

Green Tomatilla and Avocado Dip

Nutritional Information
⅓-cup serving:
Calories 48
Fat 3.3g
Protein 1g
Carbohydrates 3.8g
% fat 63
Cholesterol 0

Exchanges
½ Vegetable
1 Fat

6 medium tomatillos
1 medium avocado
1 serrano pepper
Juice of 2 fresh limes
2 tablespoons fresh cilantro, chopped
Salt, pepper, onion powder, garlic powder to taste

Boil whole tomatillos until soft. Cool, remove the outer green skin, pour off excess water, and mash the tomatillos until they form a green paste. Place the peeled and sectioned avocado in a food processor with all remaining ingredients (except tomatillo paste). Blend until smooth. Combine tomatillo mixture with avocado mixture, adjust spices, and serve. Serves 8.

Tomatillos are small vegetables that look similar to green tomatoes in a paperlike shell. *Do not* use green tomatoes as a substitute in this recipe, however. This recipe appears to be high in fat; all of the ingredients are very low in calories except for the avocado.

Buttery Popcorn

Nutritional Information
3-cup serving:
Calories 108
Fat 1.5g
Protein 3.6g
Carbohydrates 21g
% fat 12
Cholesterol 0

Exchanges
1 Bread
½ Fat

¹/₂ cup uncooked popcorn
Butter-flavored cooking spray
Molly McButter
Mrs. Dash, no pepper

Pop the popcorn in a microwave using a special plastic bowl designed for that purpose. Follow the directions that accompany the bowl. No oil should be necessary. When finished, spray with the cooking spray and sprinkle with Molly McButter and Mrs. Dash. Serves 3.

Party Cheese Ball

Nutritional Information
¹/₁₀ of the recipe serving:
Calories 94
Fat 7.7g
Protein 4.4g
Carbohydrates 2g
% fat 73
Cholesterol 26mg

Exchanges
1 Meat
½ Fat

8 ounces Philadelphia light cream cheese
4 ounces mozzarella cheese, finely grated
2 teaspoons Worcestershire sauce
1 tablespoon sesame seeds
1 dash Tabasco sauce
3 tablespoons dried parsley flakes

Soften the cream cheese. Mix the first 5 ingredients. This can easily be accomplished in a food processor. After it has been mixed, roll into a ball shape. Spread parsley flakes on a plate, and then roll the cheese ball in the flakes to coat completely. Serves 10.

Serving Suggestions: This is a wonderful hors d'oeuvre for Christmas parties. Top the green ball with slices of red pimento or red bell pepper in the shape of a poinsettia.

Any cheese ball is extremely high in fat. If you must have one, you can be moderate by eating only a small portion and by using these lower-fat cheeses.

Shell-Stuffed Scallop Ceviche[a]

Nutritional Information
1-shell serving:
Calories 44
Fat 0.5g
Protein 3.4g
Carbohydrates 6.3g
% fat 10
Cholesterol 5mg

Exchanges
¼ Bread
¼ Meat
1 Fruit

1 pound bay scallops
½ cup lime juice
⅔ cup red bell pepper, diced
⅔ cup fresh parsley, chopped
½ cup green onions, thinly sliced
2 tablespoons fresh cilantro, minced
2 teaspoons olive oil
¼ teaspoon salt
¼ teaspoon pepper
4–6 drops hot sauce
32 jumbo macaroni shells, cooked (prepared without salt or fat)

Cook scallops in a small amount of boiling water 1 minute; drain. Combine scallops and lime juice in a small bowl; toss well. Cover and marinate in refrigerator 1 hour, stirring occasionally. Add bell pepper and next 7 ingredients; stir well. Cover and chill 30 minutes. Drain. Stuff each shell with 1 tablespoon scallop mixture; arrange on serving platter. Serves 32.

Cheesy Spinach Dip

Nutritional Information
¼-cup serving:
Calories 36
Fat 1.4g
Protein 3.7g
Carbohydrates 2.1g
% fat 35
Cholesterol 5mg

Exchanges
½ Meat
½ Vegetable

8 ounces part-skim milk ricotta
8 ounces low-cal cottage cheese
2 tablespoons lemon juice
2 tablespoons purple onion, minced
1 10-ounce package fresh frozen spinach, chopped and drained
¼ teaspoon paprika
¼ teaspoon garlic powder

Combine the first 3 ingredients in a food processor, and blend until smooth. Fold the cheese mixture into a mixing bowl. Add the paprika, garlic powder, and minced onion. Unthaw and drain the frozen package of chopped spinach, and add to the cheese mixture. Fold together and serve with vegetable "dippers." Serves 16.

---

[a]All recipes noted [a] are contributed by Georgia Butler, Austin, TX.

Swedish Meatballs

Nutritional Information
¹/₈ recipe or about 6–8-
meatball serving:
Calories 215
Fat 8.1g
Protein 26g
Carbohydrates 9g
% fat 41.8
Cholesterol 72mg

Exchanges
3 Meat

1¹/₂ pounds very lean ground beef
2 egg whites
1 tablespoon dry minced onion
1 tablespoon parsley, chopped or dry
1¹/₂ teaspoons salt
1 teaspoon nutmeg
¹/₄ teaspoon pepper
¹/₄ cup skim milk
2 cups skim milk
4 stalks celery, diced
2 beef bouillon cubes
¹/₄ teaspoon pepper
1¹/₂ tablespoon flour

Combine the beef, egg, onion, parsley, 1¹/₂ teaspoons salt, nutmeg, ¹/₄ teaspoon pepper, and ¹/₄ cup milk. Shape into small balls. Broil. In a large saucepan, combine the 2 cups milk, celery, salt, pepper, and flour. Stir until the flour is dissolved. Heat until the sauce thickens, stirring constantly. Add the meatballs. Simmer 15 minutes. Add water if necessary. Serves 8.

This recipe makes a wonderful party meatball that is lower in calories and fat than many others.

Stuffed Mushrooms

Nutritional Information
3-mushroom serving:
Calories 76
Fat 1.7g
Protein 2g
Carbohydrates 13.3g
% fat 20
Cholesterol 0

Exchanges
¹/₂ Bread
1 Vegetable
¹/₂ Fat

12 large fresh mushrooms
2 teaspoons cooking oil
1 medium onion, minced
1 clove garlic, minced
¹/₂ cup coarse bread crumbs
¹/₈ teaspoon salt
¹/₄ teaspoon poultry seasoning
Dash of pepper
2 teaspoons fresh parsley, chopped
1 egg white

Carefully separate the stems from the mushroom caps. Finely chop the stems. In a Teflon skillet, sauté the onions and garlic in 1 teaspoon of the cooking oil. Add the chopped mushrooms and sauté until browned. Pour into a small bowl. Add bread crumbs, salt, poultry seasoning, pepper, parsley, and egg white. Mix well. In the same skillet, heat 1 teaspoon oil. Sauté mushroom caps with the stuffing. Bake in a preheated 400° oven for 10 minutes or until lightly browned. Serves 4.

───Crab and Cheese Ball[b]───

Nutritional Information
1-tablespoon serving:
Calories 14
Fat 0.1g
Protein 1.7g
Carbohydrates 1.4g
% fat 7

Exchanges
1/10 Meat
1/10 Milk

1 cup Basic Yogurt Cheese, made from nonfat yogurt (p. 216)
4 ounces crabmeat
1 tablespoon lemon juice
1 teaspoon prepared horseradish
1 teaspoon onion, minced
1 teaspoon fresh chives, finely chopped
1/4 teaspoon Worcestershire sauce

For this recipe you must leave the plain nonfat yogurt in the yogurt sieve for at least 48 hours so that your yogurt cheese will be as firm as cream cheese.

Squeeze excess water from crab. Chop crabmeat coarsely and blot well with paper towel. Combine all ingredients in a bowl. Blend well with a fork. Spoon mixture into serving dish. Refrigerate an hour.

To serve, spread on toast, crackers or serve with vegetables. If yogurt thins, serve as a dip with crackers or pita bread triangles. Serves 24.

───Party Chicken Balls───

Nutritional Information
3-ball serving:
Calories 40
Fat 0.5g
Protein 4.5g
Carbohydrates 4.2g
% fat 11
Cholesterol 10mg

Exchanges
1/4 Bread
1/4 Meat

2 whole chicken breasts, cooked, minced
1 small onion, minced
1 stalk celery, minced
1 small carrot, minced
1 teaspoon poultry seasoning
1 teaspoon salt
1/8 teaspoon pepper
4 tablespoons bread crumbs
2 egg whites
Nonstick spray

Combine all ingredients in a mixing bowl. Mix until chicken flakes apart. Roll about 1 tablespoon of

---

[b]All recipes throughout the section that are marked [b] have been taken from *Spa Specialties,* Debra Hart (Austin, TX: Hart Graphics, 1989).

the mixture into a ball (should make about 45 to 50 balls). Place balls on a cookie sheet, and bake at 400° for about 10 minutes, until golden brown. Serves 15.

These are truly wonderful. Try them at your next party.

Salads

Hearty Vegetable Salad

Nutritional Information
²/₃-cup serving:
Calories 72
Fat 2.2g
Protein 2g
Carbohydrates 11g
% fat 27.5
Cholesterol 0

Exchanges
¹/₂ Bread
1 Vegetable
¹/₂ Fat

1 red onion, sliced
1 stalk celery, sliced
1 carrot, thinly sliced
2 cucumbers, sliced
8 new potatoes, boiled, quartered or 1 large potato, diced
8 cherry tomatoes, halved
4 hard-boiled egg whites, sliced
¹/₂ teaspoon garlic salt
¹/₄ teaspoon pepper
¹/₄ teaspoon paprika
¹/₂ teaspoon salt
4 tablespoons lite mayonnaise
3 tablespoons plain low-fat yogurt
4 tablespoons fresh parsley, chopped

Combine all ingredients and toss gently so the shapes of the vegetables and egg whites will remain intact. Serves 10.

Centerpiece Coleslaw

Nutritional Information
¹/₂-cup serving:
Calories 25
Fat 0
Protein 1.5g
Carbohydrates 3.5g
% fat 0
Cholesterol 0

Exchanges
1 Vegetable

4 outside leaves from the cabbage
¹/₂ head cabbage, shredded
1 small can pimientos, chopped
¹/₃ bell pepper, chopped
¹/₂ teaspoon salt
¹/₄ teaspoon pepper
2 tablespoons wine vinegar
1 tablespoon sugar

Place the shredded cabbage in a large mixing bowl. Pour the juice from the pimientos over the cabbage.

Chop the pimientos. Add the remaining ingredients and toss. Arrange the cabbage leaves in a large serving bowl. Pour the coleslaw in the center of the leaves. The salad should have the appearance of a freshly picked head of cabbage with coleslaw in the center instead of the head. This is a very attractive salad, and it needs no garnish. Serves 8.

—————Fruit Salad with Fruity Dressing—————

Nutritional Information
¾-cup serving:
Calories 98
Fat 0
Protein 5.2g
Carbohydrates 19.3g
% fat 0
Cholesterol 0

Exchanges
¼ Meat
1½ Fruit

1 cup green seedless grapes
1 fresh peach, cut in chunks
1 large can pineapple chunks, no sugar added, drained, save juice
1 orange, cut in chunks
1 banana, sliced
½ cantaloupe, cubed
2 tablespoons fresh lemon juice
½ banana
½ cup low-fat cottage cheese
½ teaspoon poppy seed
2 teaspoons sugar (or 1 package Equal)

In a mixing bowl, combine the grapes, peach, pineapple, orange, banana, cantaloupe, and lemon juice. Toss lightly. Combine the ½ banana, ½ cup remaining pineapple juice, cottage cheese, poppy seed, and sugar in a blender and puree. Put fruit into 8 individual serving dishes. Top with ⅛ of the fruity dressing. Serves 8.

—————Polynesian Citrus Mold—————

Nutritional Information
½-cup serving:
Calories 48
Fat 1.1g
Protein 2g
Carbohydrates 7.5g
% fat 21
Cholesterol 0

Exchanges
1 Fruit

1 8-ounce can crushed pineapple
1 6½-ounce can mandarin orange slices
2 envelopes unflavored gelatin
2 packets NutraSweet (or 4 teaspoons sugar)
2 tablespoons walnuts, chopped
1 12-ounce can diet ginger ale, chilled

Drain fruit. Save juice. Put juice and gelatin in a small saucepan, heat and stir until gelatin is dissolved. Remove from heat. Stir in NutraSweet. Transfer to a medium-sized bowl and refrigerate about 45 minutes until chilled but not set. Stir in fruit, walnuts, and ginger ale. Stir gently until blended. Chill about 45 minutes until partially set. Spoon into desired molds. Chill until firm, about 1 hour. Unmold and serve. Serves 8.

Fresh Spinach, Artichoke, and Mandarin Orange Salad

Nutritional Information
About a 2-cup serving:
Calories 68
Fat 3.8g
Protein 2.1g
Carbohydrates 7g
% fat 51
Cholesterol 10mg

Exchanges
2 Vegetable
1 Fat

1-pound package fresh spinach
1 4-ounce jar marinated artichoke hearts
1 small can mandarin orange sections
2 tablespoons almond slivers
2 tablespoons balsamic vinegar

Wash, de-stem, and break the fresh spinach into bite-sized pieces. Empty the contents of the artichoke jar into the salad (except for 2 tablespoons of the marinade oil, which is to be discarded). Add the mandarin orange slices, vinegar, and almonds. Toss lightly and serve. Serves 8.

Remember that spinach contains very large amounts of vitamins and minerals, especially in comparison to lettuce.

Pasta Salad Alfredo

Nutritional Information
1/8-of-the-recipe serving:
Calories 281
Fat 5.7g
Protein 10.5g
Carbohydrates 47g
% fat 18
Cholesterol 8mg

Exchanges
2 Bread
1/4 Milk
1 Vegetable
1 Fat

2 medium yellow squash, sliced
2 medium zucchini, sliced
1 cup fresh mushrooms, sliced
1 medium onion, chopped
1 small bell pepper, chopped
2 large carrots, peeled and cut into julienne strips
2 tablespoons olive oil
1 8-ounce can evaporated skim milk
1 can chicken broth
1 cup Parmesan cheese
1 tablespoon cornstarch
1/2 teaspoon garlic powder
Salt and pepper to taste
10 ounces (dry weight) rotini noodles, cooked

In large nonstick skillet, heat olive oil. Sauté vegetables 7 to 8 minutes, do not overcook. Set aside. For sauce, combine milk, chicken broth, Parmesan cheese, cornstarch, garlic powder, salt, and pepper in large saucepan. Be sure cornstarch is fully dissolved. Simmer uncovered 15 minutes over low heat or until thickened, stirring frequently. Add vegetables to the sauce and simmer another 10 minutes. Add the cooked noodles and serve warm. Sprinkle with chopped fresh parsley for garnish. Serves 8.

Makes a great main dish when diced cooked chicken is added. See the Chicken Parmesan (p. 267), which is excellent chopped and tossed into the salad.

——————New Potato Confetti Salad——————

Nutritional Information
²/₃-cup serving:
Calories 81
Fat 2.1g
Protein 2g
Carbohydrates 13.7g
% fat 23
Cholesterol 0

Exchanges
³/₄ Bread
¹/₂ Vegetable
¹/₂ Fat

2 pounds new potatoes
¹/₄ cup Kraft Zesty Italian reduced-calorie salad dressing
¹/₄ cup Hellmann's cholesterol-free, reduced calorie
mayonnaise
¹/₂ red or green bell pepper, chopped
¹/₄ cup purple onion, chopped
2 tablespoons pimentos, diced
4 stalks celery, diced
Sprinkle to taste: Mrs. Dash, celery salt, pepper, garlic
powder, fresh parsley

Wash new potatoes and cut into ¹/₂-inch chunks (*do not peel*). Place potatoes in a microwavable mixing bowl with ¹/₄ cup water, cover with plastic, and microwave on high for 10 minutes. Stir at least once while cooking. Do not let potatoes become too soft. Drain water and add remaining ingredients. Serves 12.

——————Main Course Pasta Salad——————

Nutritional Information
1¹/₄-cup serving:
Calories 185
Fat 6.6g
Protein 12.1g
Carbohydrates 19.1g
% fat 32
Cholesterol 12mg

Exchanges
1 Bread
1 Meat
1 Fat

1 12-ounce package of vegetable-flavored, spiraled pasta
2 tablespoons olive oil
1 10-ounce package of frozen mixed vegetables, thawed
¹/₄ cup Parmesan cheese
3 ounces mozzarella cheese, cubed
1 cup celery, chopped
¹/₂ cup black olives, sliced
¹/₃ cup Kraft Zesty Italian reduced-calorie salad dressing
To taste: salt, pepper, garlic powder, Italian spice mix

Cook the noodles until just tender (noodles should still be firm). Add the olive oil and thawed mixed vegetables to the hot noodles and toss. When the mixture has cooled to a warm temperature, add all remaining ingredients, and fold together gently. This recipe is best when served warm or at room temperature. Serves 8.

Curried Chicken Salad

Nutritional Information
3/4-cup serving:
Calories 215
Fat 8.5g
Protein 27g
Carbohydrates 8.5g
% fat 35
Cholesterol 60mg

Exchanges
2 Meat
1 Fruit
1/2 Vegetable
2 Fat

4 chicken breasts, skinless, boneless
1 cup green seedless grapes, halved
1/4 cup walnuts, chopped
3 stalks celery, chopped
1/3 cup lite, no-cholesterol mayonnaise
1/4 cup raisins (golden seedless preferred)
1 green onion, chopped (optional)
1 tablespoon lemon juice
1 teaspoon curry powder
1 teaspoon celery salt
1/8 teaspoon black pepper

Boil the chicken until tender. Dice the chicken into 1/2 inch cubes. Combine the rest of the ingredients and mix. This delightful recipe may be used as a cool main dish on a bed of lettuce or as wonderful sandwich stuffer. Serves 6.

Most chicken salads are about 60 percent fat, because of the large amounts of mayonnaise that are traditionally used. Curried Chicken Salad comes in at a respectable 35 percent.

Taco Salad

Nutritional Information
Entire-recipe serving:
Calories 300
Fat 7g
Protein 21g
Carbohydrates 38g
% fat 21
Cholesterol 48mg

Exchanges
1 Bread
2 Meat
3 Vegetable

2 ounces ground taco meat, cooked
1–2 cups lettuce, chopped
1/2 medium tomato, chopped
1/4 cup kidney beans
1 6-inch corn tortilla, cut into julienne strips
1 tablespoon Kraft Catalina reduced-calorie dressing

Precook ground taco meat using lean ground round (or ground turkey) and a commercial seasoning packet for taco meat. Prepare the remaining ingredients as either a layered or tossed salad. Add the hot taco meat mixture to the top of the salad. Serve immediately. Serves 1.

The taco meat is usually prepared with 16 ounces ground beef and 1 seasoning packet. Use 2 ounces (cooked weight) of the mixture in this recipe. Ground turkey or extra-lean ground round may be used.

Grilled Chicken Salad with Julienne Tortilla Strips

Nutritional Information
1/2-of-recipe serving:
Calories 300
Fat 10g
Protein 27.2g
Carbohydrates 25.2g
% fat 30
Cholesterol 75mg

Exchanges
1 Bread
3 1/2 Meat
1 Fat

3 corn tortillas, cut in small julienne strips
1 tablespoon cooking oil
2 chicken breasts, cut into 1/2-inch julienne strips
2 tablespoons soy sauce
4 cups lettuce, cut into 1/2-inch slices
1 carrot, cut into small julienne strips
Butter-flavored cooking spray

Place the tortilla strips on a cookie sheet. Spray with butter-flavored nonstick cooking spray. Bake at 350° about 8 minutes or until crisp. In a Teflon skillet, brown the chicken, stirring frequently. Pour in the soy sauce, cooking and stirring 2 or 3 more minutes. Remove from the skillet, set aside. To serve, toss all ingredients with one of your favorite dressings. Serve immediately so the tortilla strips will stay crisp. Serves 2.

Nutritional values do not include a dressing.

Warm Tuna-Veggie Salad

Nutritional Information
1-cup serving:
Calories 103
Fat 3g
Protein 16.1g
Carbohydrates 3g
% fat 26
Cholesterol 33mg

Exchanges
2 Meat
1 Vegetable
1 Fat

2 6 1/2-ounce cans solid white albacore tuna, packed in water
1 tablespoon olive oil
1 medium bell pepper, cut into strips
1 green onion, diced
20 cherry tomatoes, halved
1/4 cup Spanish stuffed green olives, sliced
Lettuce leaves

Place olive oil in a large sauté pan. Sauté vegetables in the pan for 2 minutes, tossing frequently. After draining the tuna, add it to the vegetables and separate into large chunks. Serve immediately on a bed of lettuce leaves. Serves 6.

——Zesty Tuna Salad——

Nutritional Information
¹/₃-of-recipe serving:
Calories 130
Fat 3.8g
Protein 17g
Carbohydrates 8g
% fat 26
Cholesterol 21mg

Exchanges
¹/₂ Meat
¹/₂ Fruit
¹/₂ Fat

1 6¹/₂-ounce can white albacore tuna, packed in water
1 medium apple
2 stalks celery, minced
2 tablespoons lite mayonnaise
1 tablespoon lemon juice
2 tablespoons fresh parsley, minced
1 tablespoon sweet pickle relish
¹/₄ teaspoon dry mustard
¹/₄ teaspoon dill weed
Salt and pepper to taste
Lettuce, shredded (optional)

Combine all ingredients. This recipe is particularly nice when served on a bed of lettuce or spinach. Serves 3.

Notice that the calories are spread out by using low-calorie fruits and vegetables to give the entire recipe more volume.

Soups

——Vegetarian Vegetable Soup——

Nutritional Information
2-cup serving:
Calories 50
Fat 0.5g
Protein 2g
Carbohydrates 9.2g
% fat 10
Cholesterol 0

Exchanges
¹/₂ Bread
1 Vegetable

1 teaspoon olive oil
1 medium onion, chopped
3 stalks celery, cut lengthwise
1 medium bell pepper, chopped
4 cups water
4 bouillon cubes
2 16-ounce cans diced tomatoes
3 medium potatoes, cut into large chunks
Spices to taste: salt, pepper, basil, thyme, bay leaf, coriander, oregano, and garlic powder

Sauté the onion, celery, and bell pepper in the olive oil in a large Dutch oven. Add the other ingredients and simmer until softened. Serves 6.

———————Leek and Potato Soup———————

Nutritional Information
1-cup serving:
Calories 137
Fat 1.8g
Protein 7.5g
Carbohydrates 16.2g
% fat 12
Cholesterol 6mg

Exchanges
1 Bread
1/2 Milk
1/2 Fat

1 tablespoon butter
4 medium leeks, diced
4 cups water
1 1/2 teaspoons salt
3 medium potatoes, diced
2 cups skim milk
2 tablespoons flour
Fresh chives, chopped (optional)

Melt butter in a large saucepan. Sauté leeks until they have softened completely. Add water, salt, and potatoes. Boil covered, until potatoes are falling apart. Mix the milk and flour until completely dissolved. Stir milk mixture into the potato mixture, stirring constantly. Simmer for about 5 minutes, stirring frequently. Serve immediately. Top with chopped fresh chives if desired. Serves 6.

———————French Onion Soup———————

Nutritional Information
1 1/4-cup serving:
Calories 148
Fat 4.3g
Protein 7g
Carbohydrates 20g
% fat 26
Cholesterol 15mg

Exchanges
1 Bread
1/2 Meat
1/2 Fat

1 tablespoon butter
4 medium onions, thinly sliced
2 tablespoons flour
6 cups water
6 beef bouillon cubes
6 slices French bread, 3/4-inch thick
3 ounces Swiss cheese, grated
6 tablespoons bread crumbs

Melt butter in a large saucepan. Sauté the onion. Stir in the flour. When the flour begins to brown, add the water, stirring constantly. Add bouillon cubes. Cook over moderate heat, covered, about 15 minutes. Toast the bread, dry, under the broiler. Preheat oven to 400°. Fill individual ovenproof containers with soup. Lay 1 piece of the toasted French bread on top of each serving, top with 1/2 ounce cheese, sprinkle with 1 tablespoon bread crumbs. Place in oven for 20 minutes or until the cheese and bread crumbs have browned. Serve immediately. Serves 8.

Chicken and Vegetable Soup

Nutritional Information
About 2-cup serving:
Calories 160
Fat 1.8g
Protein 18.2g
Carbohydrates 17.8g
% fat 10
Cholesterol 35mg

Exchanges
1 Bread
1½ Meat
1 Vegetable

2 large potatoes, diced
3 carrots, scraped and sliced
½ bell pepper, diced
1 medium onion, diced
1 cup frozen peas
3 chicken breasts, boned, cooked, and diced
1½ quarts water
4 chicken bouillon cubes
Spices to taste: ground black pepper, thyme, parsley flakes

Combine all ingredients in a large stewpan, except the frozen peas. Cover and simmer 30 minutes or until potatoes begin to disintegrate. Add frozen peas (English peas may be substituted if preferred) and cook 5 more minutes. Serve immediately. Serves 6.

Remember that a hot liquid satisfies hunger pangs to a greater extent than a cold liquid. Include soups frequently.

Fresh Cream of Tomato Soup

Nutritional Information
1-cup serving:
Calories 60
Fat 1.2g
Protein 4.3g
Carbohydrates 7.5g
% fat 18
Cholesterol 0

Exchanges
¼ Bread
½ Milk
½ Vegetable

1 tablespoon low-cal margarine
1 clove garlic, minced
1 medium onion, minced
6 medium tomatoes, diced (do not lose juice)
1 cup water
8 ounces evaporated skim milk
1 teaspoon fresh parsley
1 tablespoon flour
1 teaspoon salt
⅛ teaspoon pepper

Sauté the garlic and onion in a large skillet until softened. Add the tomatoes and water. Simmer 5 minutes. In a blender or food processor, combine the remaining ingredients and puree. Pour the mixture back into the skillet, and bring almost to the boiling point. Garnish with minced fresh parsley. Serves 4.

Cream of Broccoli Soup

Nutritional Information
1½-cup serving:
Calories 240
Fat 7.1g
Protein 16.2g
Carbohydrates 28g
% fat 27
Cholesterol 22mg

Exchanges
1 Bread
1 Meat
½ Milk
1 Vegetable

2 cups Old-Fashioned Mashed Potatoes (p. 252)
1 10-ounce package frozen broccoli
¼ cup onion, chopped
2 cups skim milk
¼ cup cornstarch
4 ounces processed cheese
½ teaspoon salt
½ teaspoon garlic powder
¼ teaspoon pepper

Prepare Old-Fashioned Mashed Potatoes or use left-over mashed potatoes that have been either refrigerated or frozen. Thaw and cook the broccoli. Combine broccoli and all remaining ingredients (except mashed potatoes) in a blender and puree. Combine the broccoli/cheese mixture with the mashed potatoes in a Dutch oven. Cook over low heat to thicken, but *do not boil*. Thin with more milk, if necessary. Garnish with fresh parsley and serve as the main dish. Serves 4.

Mock creamed soups can be made from a potato-based stock for a tasty low-fat alternative.

Cauliflower Cheese Soup

Nutritional Information
2-cup serving:
Calories 263
Fat 16.5g
Protein 17.2g
Carbohydrates 12.1g
% fat 57
Cholesterol 45mg

Exchanges
½ Bread
1½ Meat
½ Milk
1 Vegetable

1 tablespoon low-cal margarine
1 medium onion, diced
2 cups cauliflower, chopped
1½ cups water
4 chicken bouillon cubes
⅛ teaspoon nutmeg
1 cup skim milk
1 tablespoon cornstarch
3 ounces sharp cheddar cheese, grated

In a large saucepan, heat the margarine. Sauté onion until golden brown. Add cauliflower, water, bouillon cubes, and nutmeg. Cover and simmer until cauliflower is tender, usually about 15 minutes. Combine milk and cornstarch and mix while cold. Add to the cauliflower mixture, and heat until thickened and slightly boiling. Reduce heat. Add grated cheese to soup and stir until thoroughly

·melted. Serve immediately. Fresh parsley may be used on top of individual servings for garnish. Serves 2.

——————————Savory Lentil Soup——————————

Nutritional Information
1³/₄-cup serving:
Calories 220
Fat 3g
Protein 17.2g
Carbohydrates 31g
% fat 12
Cholesterol 20mg

Exchanges
2 Bread
1 Meat

2 medium onions, sliced
2 medium carrots, sliced
1 cup celery, sliced
4 ounces lean ham, diced
1 16-ounce package of dry lentils
¹/₂ teaspoon salt
¹/₂ teaspoon thyme leaves
3 bay leaves
¹/₂ teaspoon pepper
¹/₄ teaspoon paprika
1 tablespoon lemon juice

Combine all ingredients in a large Dutch oven, and simmer for about 70 minutes. Discard the bay leaves. Adjust spices if necessary. Serve as a main course with salad and bread. Serves 6.

——————Clam Chowder-Manhattan Style——————

Nutritional Information
1²/₃-cup serving:
Calories 110
Fat 1g
Protein 10.2g
Carbohydrates 14.9g
% fat 8
Cholesterol 17mg

Exchanges
2 Meat
1 Vegetable

1 slice bacon
2 cups onion, diced
5 cups water
1¹/₂ cups carrots, sliced
1 cup celery, sliced
2 cups potatoes, cubed
3 tablespoons parsley
3 dozen clams, shucked, with liquid
1 28-ounce can tomatoes
2 bay leaves
1¹/₂ teaspoon salt
1 teaspoon thyme
¹/₄ teaspoon pepper

In a Dutch oven over medium heat, fry bacon until crisp. Set aside bacon and add onions. Cook until tender. Add 5 cups of water, clam liquid, and all remaining ingredients except clams. Simmer for 20 minutes. Chop the clams, add to mixture, and simmer 5 more minutes. Serves 8.

Cheddar Chowder

Nutritional Information
1 1/2-cup serving:
Calories 245
Fat 9.5g
Protein 10g
Carbohydrates 30g
% fat 35
Cholesterol 25mg

Exchanges
1 Bread
1 Meat
2 Fat

3 cups water
5 chicken bouillon cubes
4 medium potatoes, diced
1 medium onion, sliced
1 cup carrots, thinly sliced
1/2 cup green bell pepper, diced
1/4 cup diet margarine
1/3 cup all-purpose flour
3 1/2 cups skim milk
2 ounces pimiento, diced
2 stalks celery, sliced
6 ounces sharp cheddar cheese, grated
Spices to taste: Mrs. Dash (no pepper), garlic powder, thyme

Combine water and bouillon cubes in a heavy Dutch oven. Bring to a boil. Add vegetables, cover, and simmer 12 minutes or until vegetables are tender. Melt margarine in a heavy saucepan, blend in flour, and cook 1 minute. Gradually add milk and mix with a whisk. Cook over medium heat until thickened, stirring constantly. Add cheese, stirring over low heat until melted. Add all ingredients to the Dutch oven, stirring over a low heat. *Do not boil.* Cool for 5 minutes and serve. Serves 8.

Terrific Turkey Soup

Nutritional Information
1 1/2-to-2-cup serving:
Calories 168
Fat 1.5g
Protein 12g
Carbohydrates 26.6g
% fat 8
Cholesterol 24mg

Exchanges
1 Bread
1 Milk
1 Vegetable

1 pound turkey breast
Poultry seasoning
Sage
3 cups water
1 large onion
1/4 cup Scotch barley
2 large yellow potatoes, chopped into small pieces
1 cup fresh carrots, sliced
1 16-ounce can stewed tomatoes
1 16-ounce can kidney beans, drained
1 10-ounce can corn, drained
1 16-ounce can mixed vegetables
1 16-ounce can garbanzo beans, drained
1 16-ounce can green beans, drained
Salt and pepper to taste
1 teaspoon marjoram
1 teaspoon garlic powder

Boil turkey breast in Dutch oven until tender, putting poultry seasoning and sage into water. Remove turkey and set aside to cool, then chop into small pieces. Into reserved broth remaining in Dutch oven, add chopped turkey, onion, barley, potatoes, and carrots. Simmer for 30 minutes, until tender. Add remaining vegetables and spices, and simmer an additional 20 minutes. Serves 12.

You can substitute chicken for turkey, but turkey tastes much better. When reheating for successive meals, a can of chicken broth is good to have on hand to add for thinning. This recipe tastes great with corn bread.

Irish Stew

Nutritional Information
1-to-1½-cup serving:
Calories 251
Fat 5.4g
Protein 27.1g
Carbohydrates 23g
% fat 19
Cholesterol 71mg

Exchanges
1 Bread
2 Meat
1 Vegetable
½ Fat

1½ pounds lean beef, cut into 1½-inch cubes
½ cup flour
1 tablespoon cooking oil
2 large onions, cut into eighths
2 cloves garlic, chopped
1 16-ounce can tomatoes
2 carrots, sliced
2 stalks celery, sliced
2 large potatoes, cubed
1 medium turnip, diced
4 cups water
3 beef bouillon cubes
¼ cup red cooking wine
2 tablespoons parsley, chopped
2 teaspoons salt
¼ teaspoon pepper

Dredge the beef in flour. Use only enough flour to coat the beef. Heat the oil in a large stewpot. Brown the beef. Add onions and garlic. Brown, stirring constantly. Add the remaining ingredients (do not omit the turnip as it adds flavor). Stir well. Cover and simmer about an hour. Add water if necessary. Serves 8.

———————Easy Texas Chili and Pintos————————

Nutritional Information
1-to-1¹/₂-cup serving:
Calories 198
Fat 3g
Protein 25.5g
Carbohydrates 17.2g
% fat 14
Cholesterol 25mg

Exchanges
1 Bread
1¹/₂ Meat
¹/₂ Vegetable

¹/₂ pound dry pinto beans
¹/₂ pound dry kidney beans
8 cups water
¹/₂ teaspoon salt
1 pound ground round
2 packages commercial chili seasoning mix
1 16-ounce can tomatoes, diced
1 large onion, diced
2 cloves garlic, diced
1 4-ounce can green chilis (optional)
1 bell pepper, diced
4 tablespoons Masa Harina (masa flour)
4 tablespoons water

Rinse the beans and soak in tap water for 2 to 3 hours until the beans plump. Boil the beans, water, and salt until they are soft. Brown the ground round. Add all remaining ingredients (except Masa Harina) and simmer 10 minutes. Combine the meat mixture with the beans. In a mixing bowl, combine the Masa Harina with 4 tablespoons of water to form a thick paste. Add to the chili and heat while stirring for 2 to 3 minutes. Serves 10.

Sandwiches

———————Breakfast Sandwich———————

Nutritional Information
1-sandwich serving:
Calories 222
Fat 7.5g
Protein 17.1g
Carbohydrates 25g
% fat 30
Cholesterol 0

Exchanges
2 Bread
1 Meat
¹/₂ Fat

1 English muffin
¹/₄ cup Egg Beaters
1 thin slice Canadian bacon
1 slice reduced-calorie processed cheese
1 teaspoon diet margarine

Spread margarine over muffins and toast in the broiler. Cook the egg in a nonstick skillet as a very thin omelet until firm. Remove egg from skillet, fold, and place on bottom half of muffin. Lightly brown Canadian bacon in the same skillet, and place on top of egg. Place cheese on top of bacon, and top with the other half of the English muffin. Serve immediately. Serves 1.

Grilled Reuben Sandwich

Nutritional Information
1-sandwich serving:
Calories 350
Fat 13.6g
Protein 8g
Carbohydrates 48g
% fat 35
Cholesterol 10mg

Exchanges
2 Bread
1½ Meat
2 Fat

2 slices dark rye bread
1 tablespoon diet margarine
2 teaspoons reduced-calorie Thousand Island dressing
1 slice low-fat ham
1 thin slice Swiss cheese
1 heaping tablespoon sauerkraut
Nonstick cooking spray

Spread margarine over one side of bread slices. Place in a nonstick skillet sprayed lightly with nonstick spray. Spread dressing over bread and top with ham, cheese, and sauerkraut. Place top slice of bread (with dressing on one side and margarine on the other side) on top. Grill on both sides of the sandwich and serve hot. Serves 1.

Contrast this low-fat version with the 600-calorie, over-50-percent fat content of a traditional Reuben.

Club Sandwich

Nutritional Information
1-sandwich serving:
Calories 290
Fat 25.2g
Protein 25.5g
Carbohydrates 34.2g
% fat 18
Cholesterol 58mg

Exchanges
1½ Bread
3 Meat
¼ Milk
1 Fat

3 slices lite bread (40 calories/slice)
1 slice lite ham
1 slice turkey breast
1 slice Canadian bacon
1 slice lite processed cheese
2 thin slices tomato
Shredded lettuce and purple onion to taste
2 teaspoons lite mayonnaise

Toast the bread. Spread the mayonnaise on one side of the toast. Add in consecutive order: turkey breast, Canadian bacon, tomato, toast, ham, cheese, onion and lettuce, and the final piece of toast. Serves 1.

This makes a special sandwich to serve guests. Stay on your diet even when there are special occasions.

Fajita Pitas

Nutritional Information
¹/₄-of-recipe serving:
Calories 329
Fat 4g
Protein 33g
Carbohydrates 39g
% fat 12
Cholesterol 85mg

Exchanges
2 Bread
3 Meat
1 Vegetable
1 Fat

1 pound chicken breast fillets
Salt and pepper to taste
Fajita seasoning mix
1 clove garlic
1 tablespoon corn oil
1 medium onion, thinly sliced
1 bell pepper, sliced
4 pita breads, heated
1 medium tomato, diced
Picante sauce (commercial)

Cut the chicken into strips. Sprinkle with salt, pepper, and fajita seasoning mix. In a skillet, brown the chicken in the oil. Add garlic, onion, and bell pepper, stirring and browning until onion is soft. Slice pita breads in half, and open each to make a pocket. Fill each half with ¹/₈ of the chicken mixture and ¹/₈ of the diced tomatoes. Arrange on a platter. Serve hot with a side dish of picante sauce. Serves 4.

Note: This is a wonderful "made-at-home" southwestern fast-food that you will love. Lean beef may be substituted for the chicken.

The Italian Super Sub[c]

Nutritional Information
¹/₄-of-sandwich serving:
Calories 340 (depending
on bread density)
Fat 7g
Protein 30.1
Carbohydrates 40.2g
% fat 18
Cholesterol 75mg

Exchanges
3 Bread
2 Meat
1 Vegetable

1 loaf French bread (Choose one that is rather flat and about
   16″ long.)
4 ounces turkey breast, thinly sliced
2 ounces mozzarella cheese, thinly sliced
4 thin slices sharp cheddar cheese
¹/₄ cup Kraft Zesty Italian salad dressing
1 cup lettuce, finely shredded
2 (medium) tomatoes, thinly sliced
2 thin slices red onion, separated into rings (optional)
Pepper to taste

Slice the bread in half, lengthwise, and place both halves on a cookie sheet. Spread the Italian dressing evenly over both halves. Layer meat and then cheeses on both halves (cheese should be on top).

[c]All recipes marked [c] throughout this section are taken from *Prime Time: A Complete Health Guide for Women 35 to 65*, Sneed and Sneed (Irving, TX: Word, 1989), and are reprinted with permission.

Broil until bubbly. Add vegetables to bottom half. Then place top half of the loaf containing meat and melted cheese on the other half to form a giant submarine sandwich. Place 4 decorative toothpicks in the loaf and cut into 4 evenly sized pieces. This is a real hit at any party. Use a larger loaf (or more loaves) for larger crowds. Serves 4.

Note: This recipe is a real crowd pleaser as well as a party food that can keep you on a good eating program.

Low-Cal Grilled Cheese

Nutritional Information
1-sandwich serving:
Calories 150
Fat 4.7g
Protein 8g
Carbohydrates 18.9g
% fat 28
Cholesterol 5mg

Exchanges
1 Bread
½ Meat
1 Fat

2 slices lite bread (40 calories/slice)
1 slice lite processed cheese
2 teaspoons diet margarine

Spread margarine evenly over one side of each slice of bread. Place cheese in the middle. Heat on a grill, griddle, or skillet until browned on each side. Cheese in the center should be completely melted. Serves 1.

Regular, high-fat grilled cheese sandwiches are about 400–500 calories per sandwich.

Spicy Sloppy Joes

Nutritional Information
1-sandwich serving:
Calories 235
Fat 9.4g
Protein 19g
Carbohydrates 19.6g
% fat 36
Cholesterol 21mg

Exchanges
2 Bread
1½ Meat
1 Vegetable
1 Fat

Nonstick cooking spray
1 medium onion, diced
1 medium bell pepper, diced
½ pound lean ground beef
3 tablespoons taco seasoning mix
4 small hamburger buns, split and toasted
1 cup lettuce, shredded
1 tomato, diced
4 black olives, sliced

Sauté the onions, peppers, and ground beef in the cooking spray until browned. Blot excess fat with paper towels. Add tomato sauce and taco seasoning mix. Simmer 5 minutes, stirring frequently. To assemble, place bottoms of the buns on individual plates. Top each with ¼ of the meat mixture, ¼ cup lettuce, ¼ sliced tomato, and 1 slice black olive. Serve hot and enjoy. Serves 4.

Sauces and Dressings

——Sour Cream and Cucumber Topping——

Nutritional Information
2-tablespoon serving:
Calories 22
Fat 1.2g
Protein 0.8g
Carbohydrates 2g
% fat 48
Cholesterol 3mg

Exchanges
1 Fat

4 ounces lite sour cream
4 ounces plain nonfat yogurt
1 cucumber, minced
1/2 teaspoon curry (optional)

Combine the ingredients and mix until smooth. This is an excellent topping for oven-fried fish or salmon cakes. Serves 12.

————World-Class Barbeque Sauce————

Nutritional Information
2-tablespoon serving:
Calories 24
Fat 0.6g
Protein 0.6g
Carbohydrates 4g
% fat 20
Cholesterol 0

Exchanges
1/4 Bread

2 14-ounce bottles catsup
1 12-ounce bottle chili sauce
1/3 cup mustard
1 tablespoon dry mustard
2 teaspoons black pepper
1 1/2 cups wine vinegar
1/2 cup fresh lemon juice
4 ounces thick steak sauce
2 dashes Tabasco sauce
1/4 cup Worcestershire sauce
2 tablespoons soy sauce
2 tablespoons olive oil
2 cloves garlic, minced
2 cups brown sugar, firmly packed
1/2 cup honey

Combine all ingredients in a large cooking pot and stir well. Simmer over low heat uncovered for 1 to 2 hours or until thickened. This sauce may be stored in the refrigerator for several weeks or stored in the freezer for longer periods. It makes 6 pints. Serves 96.

Use this sauce over chicken, beef, or fish. It makes anything taste great.

Pico de Gallo Sauce

Nutritional Information
1/4–1/3-cup serving:
Calories 12
Fat 0
Protein 0.5g
Carbohydrates 3g
% fat 0
Cholesterol 0

Exchanges
1/2 Vegetable

3 large ripe tomatoes, chopped
1/3 cup red onion, chopped
1/4 bell pepper, chopped
1/3 cup fresh cilantro, chopped
1 large clove garlic, chopped
Juice of 2 fresh limes
Salt and pepper to taste

Combine all the ingredients. This can be used as a dip or over fresh-grilled meat, especially fish and chicken. Serves 8.

This can really be considered a free food. Additionally, it is loaded with Vitamin C.

Honey French Dressing

Nutritional Information
1-tablespoon serving:
Calories 28
Fat 0
Protein 0
Carbohydrates 7.0g
% fat 0
Cholesterol 0

Exchanges
1/2 Fruit

1/2 cup honey
1/4 cup water
1/4 cup cider vinegar
1/4 cup lite mayonnaise
1 teaspoon 72 percent less-sodium Worcestershire sauce

Combine all ingredients in a jar. Cover tightly and shake vigorously. Chill. Serves 24.

Faux Sour Cream and Chive Sauce

Nutritional Information
2-tablespoon serving:
Calories 22
Fat 0.4g
Protein 2.2g
Carbohydrates 3g
% fat 15
Cholesterol 5mg

Exchanges
1/4 Meat

2 cups low-cal cottage cheese
1/4 cup buttermilk
3 tablespoons fresh or frozen chives
1/2 teaspoon salt
1/4 teaspoon garlic juice

Liquefy all ingredients in a blender or beat with a mixer until smooth. Serves 18.

Blue Cheese Dressing

Nutritional Information
1-tablespoon serving:
Calories 27
Fat 2g
Protein 1g
Carbohydrates 1.2g
% fat 67
Cholesterol 24mg

Exchanges
$1/2$ Fat

1 cup low-cal cottage cheese
$1/2$ cup lite mayonnaise
$1/2$ teaspoon salt
$1/3$ cup blue cheese, crumbled

Place the cottage cheese, mayonnaise, and salt in a blender. Liquefy. Stir in the blue cheese. Refrigerate several hours before using. Serves 32.

Thousand Island Dressing

Nutritional Information
2-tablespoon serving:
Calories 34
Fat 1.2g
Protein 3g
Carbohydrates 3g
% fat 31
Cholesterol 14mg

Exchanges
$1/2$ Meat
$1/2$ Fat

$1^1/2$ cups low-cal cottage cheese
$1/2$ teaspoon dry mustard
2 tablespoons barbeque sauce
2 tablespoons lite mayonnaise
1 tablespoon sugar
2 tablespoons sweet pickle relish
2 hard-boiled eggs, chopped

Combine the cottage cheese, mustard, barbecue sauce, mayonnaise, and sugar in a blender. Liquefy. Stir in the pickle relish and eggs. Serves 20.

Brown Gravy

Nutritional Information
$1/4$-cup serving:
Calories 26
Fat 0.5g
Protein 1g
Carbohydrates 4.1g
% fat 2
Cholesterol 0

Exchanges
$1/4$ Bread

1 $10^1/2$ ounce can clear onion soup, condensed
5 ounces water
3 tablespoons flour or cornstarch

Mix all ingredients together with a wire whisk in a cold saucepan. Mix until most lumps have disappeared. Cook over medium heat, stirring frequently. Boil 10 seconds, cool, and serve. Serves 8.

Remember that there are two ways to mix a thickener (i.e., flour, cornstarch). You can mix them in the traditional way with melted fat to make a roux, or you can add the thickener to a cold liquid (i.e., water, milk, or bouillon). Gravies and sauces made in the second way are virtually fat-free and can be eaten daily. The gravies made with the roux (mixture of flour and fat) are very high in calories and fat and should not usually be eaten.

White Cream Gravy

Nutritional Information
1/4-cup serving:
Calories 38
Fat 0
Protein 3.5g
Carbohydrates 6g
% fat 0
Cholesterol 0

Exchanges
1/4 Bread
1/4 Meat

2 cups skim milk
4 tablespoons all-purpose flour
1/2 package Butter Buds
Salt and pepper to taste

Mix all ingredients together in a cold saucepan with a wire whisk. Heat over medium heat until slightly bubbling. Serves 8.

Who says you can't have gravy! Try this one with oven-fried chicken, mashed potatoes, and in other recipes requiring a sauce.

Herbed Butter Spread

Nutritional Information
1-teaspoon serving:
Calories 14
Fat 1.2g
Protein 0.5g
Carbohydrates 0
% fat 85
Cholesterol 8mg

Exchanges
1/2 Fat

1/2 cup diet margarine
2 tablespoons butter (optional)
3 tablespoons fresh parsley, minced
1 teaspoon garlic powder
1 teaspoon Italian seasoning
1/4 cup Parmesan cheese, grated

Melt the margarine and butter in a saucepan or microwave. Add spices. Cool to room temperature and add the Parmesan cheese. Mix and pour into a small soufflé dish, chill, and serve with warm bread or rolls. Serves 48.

Try this spicy/buttery spread instead of regular margarine or butter.

Breads

Bran Muffins

Nutritional Information
1-muffin serving:
Calories 110
Fat 1.5g
Protein 6.3g
Carbohydrates 17.7g
% fat 12
Cholesterol 0

Exchanges
1 Bread
1 Fat

1 cup whole-wheat flour
1 cup bran flakes
1/4 cup Miller's Bran
2 tablespoons golden raisins
2 teaspoons baking powder
1 teaspoon baking soda
1 teaspoon cinnamon
Dash of nutmeg
3/4 cup evaporated skim milk

2 tablespoons corn oil
³/₄ cup frozen apple-juice concentrate
1 teaspoon pure vanilla extract

In a mixing bowl, combine all the dry ingredients. Then add the liquids, mixing thoroughly. Fill muffin tins ²/₃ full and bake for 20 minutes at 375 °F. Serves 16.

Each muffin contains approximately 2 grams of crude fiber.

Popovers

Nutritional Information
1-popover serving:
Calories 53
Fat 1g
Protein 3.3g
Carbohydrates 8.5g
% fat 13
Cholesterol 41mg

Exchanges
²/₃ Bread

1 cup flour
¹/₂ teaspoon salt
1 cup skim milk
2 eggs, beaten
Nonstick cooking spray

Beat all ingredients just until smooth. Spray a 12-count muffin tin with nonstick cooking spray. Pour mixture into muffin tin to one-half full. Bake at 425° for 35 to 45 minutes until deep golden brown. This is a wonderful accompaniment to a soup. Serves 12.

Ham, Bran, and Cheese Muffins

Nutritional Information
1-muffin serving:
Calories 114
Fat 4.2g
Protein 7.9g
Carbohydrates 11g
% fat 33
Cholesterol 13mg

Exchanges
³/₄ Bread
1 Meat
1 Fruit
1 Fat

¹/₄ cup 100 percent bran cereal, crushed (no sweetener added)
1 cup whole wheat flour
¹/₂ cup all-purpose flour
1 tablespoon baking powder
1 teaspoon salt
¹/₈ teaspoon pepper
¹/₂ teaspoon dry mustard
4 ounces smoked ham, cooked, finely diced (no fat)
2 ounces sharp cheddar cheese, grated
¹/₄ cup cornmeal
1¹/₃ cup buttermilk
3 egg whites
1 tablespoon vegetable oil
Nonstick cooking spray

Preheat oven to 400°. Combine all ingredients in a large mixing bowl. Mix well. Spray a 12-count muffin tin with nonstick cooking spray, and spoon in the ham mixture. Bake 20 to 25 minutes until a toothpick inserted in the center comes out clean. Serve warm with a large salad for a complete dinner, or serve in the morning for a quick breakfast. Serves 12.

──────Oatmeal-Pumpkin Bread ──────

Nutritional Information
1/2-inch slice serving:
Calories 157
Fat 7g
Protein 3g
Carbohydrates 21.8g
% fat 40
Cholesterol 0

Exchanges
1 Bread

3 cups all-purpose flour, sifted
1 cup regular oats, uncooked
1 tablespoon plus 1 teaspoon baking powder
2 teaspoons ground cinnamon
1 teaspoon baking soda
1 teaspoon salt
1 teaspoon ground ginger
1 teaspoon ground mace
1/4 teaspoon ground cloves
1 cup honey
1/2 cup vegetable oil
8 egg whites (or 4 eggs or 1 cup Egg Beaters)
2/3 cup unsweetened orange juice
1 16-ounce can pumpkin
1 cup walnuts, chopped
Vegetable cooking spray
1 egg white, lightly beaten
1/4 cup regular oats, uncooked

Combine first 9 ingredients in a large bowl. Combine honey, oil, and eggs; add to flour mixture, stirring just until blended. Stir in orange juice, pumpkin, and walnuts. Spoon batter into 2 (8 1/2"x4 1/2"x3") loaf pans coated with cooking spray. Brush tops with egg white; sprinkle each with 2 tablespoons oats. Bake at 350° for 1 hour or until a wooden pick inserted in center comes out clean. Cool in pans 10 minutes. Remove from pans, and let cool completely on wire racks. Yield: 2 loaves. Serves 36.

This is a higher-fat/higher-calorie bread than most of the others in this book, and should be reserved for special events. However, you can eliminate the walnuts and decrease the fat and calorie content substantially.

Unbelievable Oat-Bran Muffins[c]

Nutritional Information
1-muffin serving:
Calories 110
Fat 3g
Protein 7.8g
Carbohydrates 13g
% fat 36
Cholesterol 0

Exchanges
1 Bread
1 Fat

1½ cups oat-bran flour (This is oat bran milled very finely; oat bran may be used.)
1½ cups Quick Oats
1 cup all-purpose flour
¼ cup sugar
⅓ cup wheat bran
2 teaspoons baking soda
1 teaspoon salt
2 teaspoons cinnamon
4 egg whites, raw
16-ounce canned crushed pineapple in own juice (fruit and juice used)
2 cups bananas, mashed
½ cup vegetable oil
¼ cup honey
1 tablespoon vanilla extract

Mix the dry ingredients together. In a separate bowl, mix wet ingredients. Combine the wet and dry mixtures, and mix gently. Spray muffin pan with nonstick vegetable oil such as PAM and bake at 350° for 20 to 25 minutes. Serves 30.

Remember that oat-bran fiber can reduce your serum cholesterol levels when eaten routinely.

Savory Dinner Rolls

Nutritional Information
1-roll serving:
Calories 120
Fat 4g
Protein 2g
Carbohydrates 19g
% fat 30
Cholesterol 15mg

Exchanges
1 Bread
1 Fat

1 package frozen yeast rolls (Bridgeford or other brand name), 24 rolls per package
¼ cup diet margarine (50 calories/tablespoon)
2 tablespoons butter (or regular margarine)
1 teaspoon Italian seasoning mix
2 teaspoons parsley flakes
½ teaspoon garlic powder
2 tablespoons Parmesan cheese
Vegetable oil coating spray

Thaw the rolls until soft but still cold. Melt margarine and butter in a saucepan, and then add herbs and spices to the butter mixture. Do not add cheese until mixture is removed from heat and is warm instead of hot. At this time mix in Parmesan cheese (do not reheat). Dip the thawed rolls into the butter mixture and coat lightly on all sides. Spray 2 10-

inch pie plates or 1 larger pan with a vegetable oil coating spray, place rolls in pans 1 inch apart and let them rise for 2 hours. Bake as directed on package (usually 15 minutes at 350°). Serves 24.

It is unnecessary to serve additional butter or margarine with this bread recipe.

Vegetables and Side Dishes

Ratatouille

Nutritional Information
3/4–1-cup serving:
Calories 44
Fat 1g
Protein 1.5g
Carbohydrates 7.3g
% fat 19
Cholesterol 0

Exchanges
1 1/2 Vegetable

1 small eggplant, diced
1/2 pound zucchini, scraped and diced
1 red bell pepper, seeded and diced
1 green bell pepper, seeded and diced
2 teaspoons olive oil
1 medium onion, minced
2 cloves garlic, minced
1 large tomato, chunked
1/4 cup tomato juice
Fresh basil, chopped (to taste)
Ground pepper
Fresh parsley
1/4 teaspoon salt

Heat 1/2 teaspoon of the oil in a Teflon skillet. Sauté the onion and garlic until soft. Add the eggplant and sauté for 3 minutes. Transfer the eggplant, onion, and garlic to a bowl. In the same skillet, add 1/2 teaspoon oil and sauté the zucchini for 3 minutes. Add to the eggplant. Sauté the peppers until crisp-tender, about 2 minutes. Combine with the eggplant and zucchini. Pour the remaining oil into the pan. Add the tomato, cook and stir, adding the tomato juice to make a sauce. Gently add the sautéed vegetables to the tomato sauce. Season with basil, pepper, parsley, and salt. Serve warm or cold, garnished with fresh parsley. Serves 8.

This is a nice accompaniment to rice and grilled fish.

Spicy Green Beans

Nutritional Information
¹/₂-cup serving:
Calories 40
Fat 1.3g
Protein 1g
Carbohydrates 6g
% fat 29
Cholesterol 0

Exchanges
1 Vegetable

1 10-ounce package frozen French-style green beans
1 tablespoon diet margarine
1 tablespoon water
¹/₂ cup celery, finely chopped
¹/₄ cup onion, finely chopped
2 tablespoons pimientos, chopped
1 tablespoon vinegar
¹/₄ teaspoon dill seed
Salt and pepper to taste

Place water and margarine in a 1¹/₂-quart saucepan. Add frozen beans and heat slowly, using a fork to separate beans. Cover and cook until the beans are just tender, taking care not to overcook. Add the remaining ingredients, toss lightly, and heat briefly. Remove from heat and serve. The celery should remain crisp. Serves 4.

Carrots with Cardamom

Nutritional Information
³/₄-cup serving:
Calories 45
Fat 1g
Protein 1g
Carbohydrates 8g
% fat 20
Cholesterol 0

Exchanges
1 Vegetable

3 cups carrots, scraped and sliced into thin strips
¹/₂ cup water
2 teaspoons diet margarine
1 teaspoon brown sugar
¹/₂ teaspoon ground cardamom

In a medium saucepan, combine the carrots and water. Cover and simmer until the carrots are crisp-tender. Drain the carrots and set aside. Melt the margarine in a saucepan. Stir in the brown sugar and the cardamom. Cook over low heat until sugar is dissolved. Add carrots. Cook over low heat, stirring gently until carrots are coated and well-heated. Serves 4.

Carrots with Cilantro

Nutritional Information
1/2-cup serving:
Calories 58
Fat 1.8g
Protein 1.2g
Carbohydrates 9.2g
% fat 28
Cholesterol 0

Exchanges
1 Vegetable
1/2 Fat

1 pound carrots, peeled and cut into julienne strips
1 tablespoon olive oil
1/4 cup fresh cilantro leaves, chopped
Dash of salt and pepper

Lightly sauté carrot strips in olive oil. When the carrots are slightly tender, add spices. Sauté for 1 minute more and serve immediately. Serves 6.

Carrots are one of your best sources of the vitamin A precursor, carotene. Include them frequently. Olive oil helps lower your total serum cholesterol levels.

Buttery Stir-Fried Vegetables

Nutritional Information
3/4-cup serving:
Calories 47
Fat 1.5g
Protein 2g
Carbohydrates 6.4g
% fat 29
Cholesterol 5mg

Exchanges
1 Vegetable
1/2 Fat

1 tablespoon low-cal margarine
1 medium onion, sliced
1 clove garlic, minced
1 cup broccoli florets
1 yellow squash, sliced
1/2 cup fresh mushrooms, sliced
1 bell pepper, sliced
2 medium tomatoes, cut into wedges
2 teaspoons Molly McButter
2 teaspoons sesame seeds
1/2 teaspoon pepper

In a large Teflon skillet, heat the margarine. Add the onion and garlic and cook until lightly crisp. Add broccoli, squash, mushrooms, and bell pepper. Stir-fry until lightly crisp. Add tomatoes. Stir-fry 1 minute. Add remaining ingredients and stir-fry until well-blended. Serves 6.

Pennsylvania Dutch Cabbage

Nutritional Information
³/₄-cup serving:
Calories 35
Fat 0
Protein 2g
Carbohydrates 6.5g
% fat 0
Cholesterol 0

Exchanges
1½ Vegetable

4 cups red cabbage, thinly sliced
1 apple, diced
2 tablespoons lemon juice
1 chicken-flavored bouillon cube
⅛ teaspoon allspice
³/₄ cup water
Salt and pepper to taste
½ teaspoon caraway seeds
1 tablespoon sugar

Combine all ingredients in a large saucepan. Cover and simmer until cabbage is tender (about 20 to 30 minutes). Serves 6.

Broccoli and Cauliflower Parmesan[c]

Nutritional Information
¼-of-recipe serving:
Calories 120
Fat 4.5g
Protein 5.1g
Carbohydrates 14.6g
% fat 34
Cholesterol 25mg

Exchanges
½ Meat
2 Vegetables
1 Fat

1 10-ounce package frozen broccoli florets, thawed
1 10-ounce package frozen cauliflower florets, thawed
2 ounces sharp cheddar cheese
3 tablespoons Parmesan cheese, grated
2 tablespoons bread crumbs
1 tablespoon diet margarine
Garlic salt, pepper, parsley, dry Italian seasoning mix to taste
Nonstick cooking spray

Spray a 1- to 1½-quart casserole dish with a non-stick cooking spray. Arrange 1 layer of thawed broccoli and cauliflower in the bottom of the dish. Sprinkle with half of the remaining ingredients. Add another layer of vegetables, and top with the rest of the cheeses and spices. Cover and bake at 350° for 30 minutes or until the cheese bubbles. Serves 4.

Artichokes Parmesan

Nutritional Information
2/3-cup serving:
Calories 80
Fat 1.5g
Protein 2g
Carbohydrates 14.5g
% fat 17
Cholesterol 9mg

Exchanges
1/2 Meat
1 Vegetable
1/2 Fat

1/4 cup bread crumbs
2 tablespoons Parmesan cheese, grated
3 tablespoons Italian low-cal salad dressing (7 calories/
    tablespoon)
1 10-ounce package frozen artichoke hearts, thawed and
    drained
1 tablespoon Italian low-cal salad dressing
2 medium tomatoes, quartered

Combine bread crumbs, cheese, 3 tablespoons of dressing, and mix. Sprinkle 1 tablespoon of dressing over the artichoke hearts, and arrange the artichokes and tomatoes in a 1-quart baking casserole. Sprinkle the bread crumb mixture over the vegetables. Bake at 350° for 30 to 35 minutes or until topping is lightly browned. Serves 4.

Cheesy Spinach Casserole

Nutritional Information
1/2-cup serving:
Calories 125
Fat 2.7g
Protein 16.5g
Carbohydrates 8.5g
% fat 19
Cholesterol 7mg

Exchanges
1 Milk
1 Vegetable
1 Fat

2 10-ounce packages frozen spinach, chopped, cooked, and
    drained
1 cup low-fat cottage cheese
1/4 cup onions, chopped
1/4 cup flour
1/2 cup Egg Beaters
1/2 teaspoon salt
1/2 teaspoon Worcestershire sauce
1/4 teaspoon nutmeg
1/4 teaspoon pepper
1/4 teaspoon thyme
1/2 cup Parmesan cheese, grated
Nonstick vegetable spray

Preheat oven to 350°. Combine all ingredients except Parmesan cheese. Spray a 1 1/2-quart casserole with nonstick vegetable spray and pour in spinach mixture. Sprinkle Parmesan on top. Bake, uncovered, for 35 to 40 minutes or until heated and browned. Serves 6.

———Old-Fashioned Mashed Potatoes———

Nutritional Information
²/₃-cup serving:
Calories 94
Fat 1.4g
Protein 3.5g
Carbohydrates 17g
% fat 18
Cholesterol 0 (if margarine is used)

Exchanges
1¹/₂ Bread
¹/₂ Fat

4 large baking potatoes
¹/₂ cup skim milk
1 tablespoon margarine or butter
Salt and pepper to taste
Dry butter substitute (Butter Buds or Molly McButter)

Peel, cube, and boil potatoes until soft. Mash with a potato masher and add remaining ingredients. Continue mashing until smooth. Serves 8.

Note: Traditional recipes do not have to be taboo on a low-calorie program. You really can have crispy chicken (Spicy Oven-Fried Chicken, p. 265), White Cream Gravy (p. 243), and mashed potatoes and remain on your low-fat regimen.

———New Potatoes Parmesan———

Nutritional Information
¹/₂-cup serving:
Calories 112
Fat 2g
Protein 2g
Carbohydrates 21.5g
% fat 23
Cholesterol 0

Exchanges
1 Bread
1 Fat

10 medium new potatoes
2 tablespoons diet margarine
¹/₄ cup Parmesan cheese
Mrs. Dash (original flavor)
Garlic salt
Parsley flakes
1 tablespoon lemon juice
Nonstick vegetable spray

Wash, but do not peel, the new potatoes. Cut into ¹/₄-inch slices. Place in a microwavable casserole dish. Add ¹/₄ cup water, cover with plastic, and cook on high in the microwave for 14 minutes. The potatoes should be soft, but not mushy. After cooking, drain in a colander. Spray the casserole with nonstick vegetable spray, and layer ¹/₃ of potatoes in bottom. Sprinkle lightly with ¹/₃ of the suggested flavorings. Add two more layers of potatoes, followed by a light coating of flavorings on top of each. Bake at 350° for 15 minutes or until hot throughout. Serves 6.

Cheddar Potato Bake

Nutritional Information
1/2-cup serving:
Calories 115
Fat 3.2g
Protein 7.2g
Carbohydrates 14.4g
% fat 25
Cholesterol 12mg

Exchanges
1 Bread
1 Meat

1³/₄ cups water
1¹/₃ cups potato flakes
1 tablespoon low-cal margarine
1 small onion, chopped
1 clove garlic, minced
³/₄ cup part-skim milk ricotta cheese
2 egg whites
1 ounce Parmesan cheese, grated
2 teaspoons dried parsley flakes
¹/₂ teaspoon salt
¹/₈ teaspoon pepper
2 ounces sharp cheddar cheese, grated
Nonstick cooking spray
Paprika

In a medium size saucepan bring water to a boil. Remove from heat and add potato flakes. Stir until smooth. Preheat oven to 350°. Sauté the onions and garlic in the margarine until softened. In a mixing bowl combine the potatoes, sautéed onions, and the remaining ingredients except cheddar cheese and paprika. Spray a casserole dish with nonstick cooking spray. Put potato mixture into the casserole and sprinkle the cheddar on top. Bake until the top is lightly browned, 25 to 30 minutes. Sprinkle the top with paprika. Serves 8.

Potato Pancakes

Nutritional Information
1-pancake serving:
Calories 75
Fat 2.8g
Protein 4.2g
Carbohydrates 8.3g
% fat 32
Cholesterol 0

Exchanges
1 Bread
¹/₂ Fat

1 small onion, chopped
1 clove garlic, minced
2 egg whites
4 large potatoes, grated
1 teaspoon salt
¹/₄ teaspoon pepper
2 tablespoons diet margarine
Butter-flavored nonstick cooking spray

Combine all ingredients into a mixing bowl. Stir well. Spray a Teflon skillet with butter-flavored nonstick cooking spray and heat. Drop heaping tablespoons of the potato mixture into the skillet, and spread to form a pancake. Make 3 or 4 at a time.

Brown well on both sides. Spray the skillet each time a new batch is made. Should make a total of 8 potato pancakes. Serves 8.

Quick Potato Wedges

Nutritional Information
1/2-potato serving:
Calories 117
Fat 3.4g
Protein 6g
Carbohydrates 16g
% fat 26
Cholesterol 15mg

Exchanges
1 Bread
1/4 Meat
1 Fat

3 large baked potatoes, cut lengthwise in quarters
Salt, pepper, paprika, Italian seasoning
3 tablespoons Parmesan cheese
3 tablespoons diet margarine
Butter-flavored nonstick cooking spray

Spray a baking sheet with butter-flavored nonstick cooking spray. Arrange the precooked baked potato wedges on the cooking sheet, skin side down. Spray the potatoes with cooking spray, and dot with margarine, salt, pepper, and paprika. Evenly distribute the cheese over the potatoes. Broil until the cheese browns. Serve immediately. Serves 6.

Skinny French Fries[c]

Nutritional Information
1/2-potato serving:
Calories 120
Fat 2g
Protein 2g
Carbohydrates 23g
% fat 15
Cholesterol 0

Exchanges
1 1/2 Bread
1/2 Fat

2 large Idaho potatoes, unpeeled and cut in strips
PAM butter-flavored cooking spray
Seasoned salt, pepper, or Cajun seasoning mix

Wash and prepare the potatoes. Dry the surface of the potato strips by placing them on paper towels. Spray a nonstick cookie sheet with PAM. Spray the potatoes with PAM and then sprinkle with seasoning of choice (you might try shaking them in a clear plastic bag). Bake at 350° for 30 to 35 minutes until tender and golden brown. Turn occasionally with a spatula. Serves 4.

Corn Casserole

Nutritional Information
1/8 of casserole serving:
Calories 132
Fat 4.2g
Protein 8.6g
Carbohydrates 15g
% fat 28
Cholesterol 44mg

Exchanges
1/2 Bread
1/2 Milk
1/2 Vegetable
1 Fat

1 16-ounce can whole-kernel corn
1 small onion, chopped
1/2 red bell pepper, chopped
1/4 cup green chilies, chopped
   (optional)
1 tablespoon margarine
2 tablespoons flour
1 teaspoon salt
1/2 teaspoon paprika
1/4 teaspoon dry mustard
3/4 cup skim milk
1 egg, beaten
1/3 cup cracker crumbs
2 ounces sharp cheddar cheese, grated

Preheat oven to 350°. Sauté the onions and bell pepper in the margarine until tender. Remove from heat. Stir in the flour, salt, paprika, mustard, and green chilies. Cook over low heat, stirring until the mixture is bubbly. Gradually stir in the milk. Heat to boiling, stirring constantly, and boil 1 minute. Stir in corn and egg. Pour into an ungreased casserole dish. Combine cracker crumbs and cheese. Sprinkle over the casserole. Bake, uncovered, for 30 to 35 minutes or until lightly browned. Serves 8.

Spanish Rice

Nutritional Information
2/3-cup serving:
Calories 130
Fat 2g
Protein 4.7g
Carbohydrates 23.3g
% fat 14
Cholesterol 0

Exchanges
1 1/2 Bread
1/4 Vegetable
1 Fat

2 tablespoons diet margarine
1/2 cup onion, chopped
1/4 cup green pepper, chopped
1/4 teaspoon fresh garlic, crushed
1 cup uncooked long-grain rice
2 1/4 cups water
1/2 cup tomato sauce
1/4 teaspoon oregano leaves
1/8 teaspoon ground black pepper
Dash of Tabasco sauce

In large skillet, melt margarine over medium heat. Stir in onion, green pepper, and garlic; sauté until tender, stirring occasionally, 2 to 2 1/2 minutes. Stir in rice; cook and stir until golden, about 1 1/2 to 2 minutes. Add water, tomato sauce, oregano, pepper, and hot pepper sauce. Cook and stir until mixed. Reduce heat to low; cover and cook until rice is tender and liquid is absorbed, 20 to 25 minutes. Fluff rice with fork and serve hot. Serves 6.

Try this wonderful side dish with the Mexican Oven-Fried Chicken (p. 265).

Brown Rice Pilaf

Nutritional Information
1/2-cup serving:
Calories 104
Fat 0.7g
Protein 5g
Carbohydrates 18.7g
% fat 6
Cholesterol 0

Exchanges
1 Bread
1/4 Vegetable
1/4 Fat

2 cups brown rice
2 1/2 cups chicken stock, defatted
1 tablespoon diet margarine
1/4 teaspoon garlic powder
Dash of white pepper
Dash of black pepper
1/4 cup green pepper, chopped
1/4 cup onion, chopped
1/4 cup celery, chopped
2 tablespoons pimiento
Nonstick cooking spray

Spray baking dish with a nonstick cooking spray. Add rice to baking dish. Combine chicken stock, margarine, garlic powder, and peppers. Add to rice. Stir in green pepper, onion, celery, and pimiento. Cover with aluminum foil. Bake in 350° preheated oven for 50 minutes. Serves 8.

Hawaiian-Style Sweet Potatoes

Nutritional Information
1/2-cup serving:
Calories 120
Fat 2g
Protein 1.2g
Carbohydrates 24g
% fat 15
Cholesterol 10mg

Exchanges
1 Bread
1 Fat

4 large sweet potatoes
1/4 cup pineapple juice
1 tablespoon regular margarine (or 2 tablespoons diet margarine)
1/4 cup pineapple, chopped
1/4 teaspoon cinnamon
1/4 teaspoon nutmeg
1/4 teaspoon allspice
1 tablespoon molasses (or honey)
1 tablespoon diet margarine

Boil potatoes until tender, then cool and remove skins. Mash the peeled potatoes and fruit juice, spices, and 2 tablespoons of diet margarine. Whip until fluffy. Turn into a 1-quart baking dish. Spread molasses over the top, dot with margarine, and bake at 425° until lightly browned. Serves 8.

This is a wonderful substitute for the heavy, sugary sweet potato recipes which usually surface at Christmastime.

Main Dishes and Casseroles

Breakfast Tacos

Nutritional Information
1-taco serving:
Calories 180
Fat 2.4g
Protein 12.4g
Carbohydrates 27.1g
% fat 12
Cholesterol 0

Exchanges
2 Bread
1 Meat
1/2 Vegetable

1 8-inch flour tortilla
Nonstick cooking spray
1/4 cup potatoes, diced and parboiled
1/4 cup Egg Beaters℗
2 tablespoons picante sauce

In a skillet sprayed with a nonstick cooking spray, mix the Egg Beaters and potatoes (which have previously been boiled to a firm texture). Cook as you would a scrambled egg, scraping the bottom and sides with a spatula. Use salt and pepper if desired. Place the egg mixture in the middle of the tortilla and serve warm with picante sauce. Serves 1.

Low-Cholesterol Egg Casserole

Nutritional Information
1/10 of recipe serving.
Calories 275
Fat 8g
Protein 27g
Carbohydrates 24g
% fat 26
Cholesterol 52mg

Exchanges
1 Bread
2 Meat
1 Milk

1 pound turkey sausage
2 tablespoons onions, minced
2 tablespoons green bell pepper, minced
1 teaspoon dry mustard
12 slices white bread, no crust
2 tablespoons diet margarine
8 ounces reduced-fat, medium cheddar cheese, grated
2 cartons Egg Beaters, unthawed (equivalent to 8 eggs)
2 cups skim milk
1/2 teaspoon salt
1/8 teaspoon black pepper
2 teaspoons Worcestershire sauce
Nonstick cooking spray

Cook sausage in a nonstick skillet. Drain any excess grease. Mix in onion, bell pepper, and dry mustard, and continue to cook until vegetables are softened. Spread margarine lightly over bread (all crust trimmed off), and place in the bottom of an 8"x12" baking dish sprayed with nonstick cooking spray. Pour sausage mixture over bread and top with cheese. Place remaining 6 slices of bread on top of cheese to form the top layer. Beat the Egg Beaters, milk, and spices together in a separate mixing bowl. Pour over bread and refrigerate overnight. Bake for 75 minutes at 350°. Let this casserole stand for 15 minutes to set before serving. Serves 10.

Turkey sausage is simply ground turkey with sausage seasonings mixed throughout. You can make it yourself or it can be found at many butcher shops.

—Spinach Quiche—

Nutritional Information
1/6 of pie serving:
Calories 192.5
Fat 9.5g
Protein 10.8g
Carbohydrates 15.9g
% fat 44
Cholesterol 5mg

Exchanges
1 Bread
1 1/2 Meat
1 Vegetable
1 Fat

1 pre-prepared piecrust
1 10-ounce package frozen spinach
1 clove garlic, minced
1 cup Egg Beaters
1 cup reconstituted, evaporated skim milk
1/3 cup Parmesan cheese
2 tablespoons Romano cheese
1 teaspoon dried basil
1/2 teaspoon salt
1/8 teaspoon cayenne pepper

Bake the piecrust for 5 minutes. In a medium bowl, combine eggs, milk, cheeses, basil, salt, and pepper and mix thoroughly. Add the spinach and garlic. Pour spinach and egg mixture into the piecrust, and bake for 1 hour at 325°. Let the quiche cool and set for 10 minutes before serving. Serves 6.

Who says quiche must be made from whole eggs and cream? Try this delightful low-fat rendition of a traditional favorite.

Manicotti Casserole

Nutritional Information
2-shell serving:
Calories 340
Fat 17g
Protein 17g
Carbohydrates 37.1g
% fat 34
Cholesterol 20mg

Exchanges
2 Bread
2 Meat
1 Fat

12 manicotti shells
1 cup low-fat cottage cheese
⅔ cup part-skim milk ricotta
4 ounces mozzarella cheese, grated
4 egg whites
½ cup low-fat milk
¼ cup fresh parsley, chopped
½ teaspoon oregano
1 tablespoon vegetable oil
½ cup bell pepper, chopped
½ cup onion, chopped
1 16-ounce can spaghetti sauce

Preheat oven to 350°. Prepare manicotti shells according to the directions on package. Drain. Combine in a large bowl the cheeses, egg whites, and milk. Mix well. Add parsley and oregano. Stir well. Stuff the manicotti shells with the mixture. In a Teflon skillet, heat the oil. Sauté the onion and bell pepper. Add spaghetti sauce. Coat the bottom of a baking dish with the sauce mixture. Place the filled manicotti shells on top of the sauce. Cover the shells with the remaining sauce. Bake, covered, 40 to 45 minutes. Serves 6.

Easy Homemade Pizza

Nutritional Information
2-slice serving:
Calories 330
Fat 10.1g
Protein 20.5g
Carbohydrates 37g
% fat 28
Cholesterol 19mg

Exchanges
2 Bread
2 Meat
1 Vegetable

1 boxed pizza crust (dry)
1 cup thick spaghetti sauce
½ teaspoon Italian seasoning mix
¼ cup Parmesan cheese
3 ounces grated mozzarella cheese, made with part-skim milk
¼ cup green bell pepper, slivered
¼ cup purple onion, slivered
¼ cup fresh mushrooms, slivered
Nonstick cooking spray

Make the pizza crust as described by instructions on the box. Spread the crust out onto a 14-inch pizza pan. Top with the spaghetti sauce, Italian seasoning, and cheeses. In a skillet sprayed with the cooking spray, brown the vegetables until soft. Spread evenly over the top of the pizza, and bake at 375° 15 to 25 minutes until bubbly and browned. Cut into 8 slices. Serves 4.

—————Red Snapper Veracruzano[b] —————

Nutritional Information
5-ounce serving:
Calories 153
Fat 1.5g
Protein 29g
Carbohydrates 4.8g
% fat 9
Cholesterol 0

Exchanges
3 Meat
1/2 Vegetable

4 5-ounce snapper fillets
1 tablespoon lime juice
2 shallots, minced
1 garlic clove, minced
1/4 cup dry white cooking wine
4 canned tomatoes, drained and chopped
3 tablespoons fresh cilantro, chopped
1 tablespoon fresh oregano, chopped (or 1 1/2 teaspoons dried)
1 tablespoon fresh thyme, chopped (or 1 1/2 teaspoons dried)
1 teaspoon Tabasco sauce
Vegetable coating spray

Spray a baking dish with vegetable coating spray, and place fillets in dish. Sprinkle with lime juice. Sauté minced shallots and garlic in white cooking wine. Add tomatoes and Tabasco and cook 5 minutes. Add herbs. Pour tomato mixture over fish and cover. Place in a preheated 350° oven and bake 20 to 25 minutes. Use lime slices and fresh cilantro for garnish. Serves 4.

—————Cheesy Flounder Fillets[b] —————

Nutritional Information
5-ounce serving:
Calories 158
Fat 2.3g
Protein 27.2g
Carbohydrates 5.3g
% fat 14
Cholesterol 0

Exchanges
1/10 Bread
2 1/2 Meat
1/3 Milk
1/10 Vegetable

1 1/2 pounds flounder fillets
1/3 cup Basic Yogurt Cheese (p. 216)
2 teaspoons cornstarch
2 tablespoons Parmesan cheese, grated
2 tablespoons fresh parsley, chopped
1/4 cup onion, minced
1 tablespoon fresh lemon juice
1 tablespoon fresh dill (or 1 teaspoon dried—or use tarragon
    or marjoram)
Vegetable coating spray

Arrange fillets in a 13"x9" baking pan sprayed with vegetable coating spray. Combine remaining ingredients; spread mixture evenly over fillets. Bake at 350° for 15 minutes or until fish flakes easily. If desired, place under broiler for 1 to 2 minutes until cheese mixture begins to brown. Serves 4.

Savory Salmon Cakes

Nutritional Information
2-cake serving:
Calories 225
Fat 8g
Protein 22g
Carbohydrates 16g
% fat 32
Cholesterol 35mg

Exchanges
1/2 Bread
3 Meat
1 Fat

1 16-ounce can pink salmon, coarsely chopped
2 egg whites
1/4 cup low-cal sour cream
1 small onion, minced
1 tablespoon lemon juice
1/2 cup Progresso Italian bread crumbs
1/2 teaspoon dill weed

Preheat oven to 375°. Blend all ingredients except bread crumbs and dill weed. Stir until well mixed and salmon flakes. Form 8 cakes. Combine the bread crumbs and the dill weed in a bowl. Roll the cakes in the mixture. Place cakes on a nonstick baking sheet, and bake 10 to 15 minutes or until golden brown. Serve with the Sour Cream and Cucumber Topping on page 240. Serves 4.

Pink salmon contains much less fat than Chinook and Atlantic salmon. Even though salmon is a fatty fish, the fish oil tends to bring down serum triglyceride and cholesterol levels.

Oven-Fried Fish[b]

Nutritional Information
4-ounce serving:
Calories 149
Fat 1.9g
Protein 22.3g
Carbohydrates 8.8g
% fat 12
Cholesterol 0

Exchanges
1/2 Bread
2 Meat
1/10 Milk
1/10 Fat

20 ounces white fish fillets (4 5-ounce pieces)
1/2 cup low-fat buttermilk
1/2 cup Melba toast crumbs
2 tablespoons fresh parsley, minced
1 teaspoon paprika
Vegetable coating spray

Put buttermilk in a shallow bowl. Mix crumbs, parsley, and paprika and put in a shallow bowl. Dip fish fillets in buttermilk, then in crumb mixture. Place on a baking sheet that has been sprayed with vegetable coating spray. Bake at 450° for 12 minutes or until fish flakes easily. Serves 4.

Blackened Orange Roughy[c]

Nutritional Information
4-ounce serving:
Calories 190
Fat 3.7g
Protein 32g
Carbohydrates 7.8g
% fat 16
Cholesterol 75mg

Exchanges
4 Meat
1 Fat

20-ounces orange roughy fillets, raw
Nonstick butter-flavored cooking spray
1½ tablespoons butter (or oil)
McCormick's blackened redfish mix (or something similar in
    another brand)
2 fresh lemons

Sprinkle fillets with seasoning mix. Spray a heavy skillet (such as copper lined with stainless steel) with butter-flavored nonstick cooking spray, and place on rangetop over medium heat. Melt butter in pan. Place fillets in hot skillet and cook 3 to 5 minutes on each side until fish is flaky. Turn off pan, sprinkle with fresh lemon juice. Serve immediately with more lemon juice, brown rice pilaf, and a vegetable. Serves 4.

Cornish Game Hens à l'Orange

Nutritional Information
½-hen serving:
Calories 210
Fat 6g
Protein 23g
Carbohydrates 16g
% fat 26
Cholesterol 41mg

Exchanges
3 Meat
1 Fat

2 Cornish game hens (about 1½ pounds each)
¼ cup frozen orange juice concentrate
1 cup chicken stock
2 teaspoons cornstarch dissolved in 1 tablespoon water
2 tablespoons Molly McButter or other noncaloric butter flavor
    substitute
2 tablespoons brown sugar
¼ teaspoon ground cloves
Dash of salt, pepper, garlic powder, and onion powder

Bake hens on a roasting rack for 50 minutes at 350° or until almost done. Meanwhile, combine remaining ingredients in a saucepan, cook over medium heat until thickened. Split hens in half. Remove excess skin and fat and place breast side up. Spoon sauce over chicken and bake 20 minutes, basting occasionally. Avoid eating most of the skin. Serves 4.

This is a lovely cook-ahead meal for entertaining. Note that using a butter substitute for basting saves many of the wrong type of calories.

Italian Chicken and Squash

Nutritional Information
1/4 of-recipe serving:
Calories 429
Fat 9.5g
Protein 30g
Carbohydrates 56g
% fat 20
Cholesterol 72mg

Exchanges
2 Bread
4 Meat
2 Vegetable
1 Fat

4 chicken breasts, boiled and diced into bite-sized pieces (no skin)

2 medium zucchini, sliced

2 medium yellow squash, sliced

1 medium onion, chopped

1/2 cup fresh mushrooms, sliced

1 small bell pepper, thinly sliced

2 1-pound cans Italian-flavored stewed tomatoes

1 can chicken broth

2 tablespoons olive oil

1/2 teaspoon marjoram

1/2 teaspoon basil

1/2 teaspoon powdered garlic

1 tablespoon cornstarch

1 dash Worcestershire sauce

Ground pepper to taste

4 cups cooked rice

Boil chicken breasts until tender. Drain and set aside to cool. Prepare rice. Substitute 1/2 can chicken broth for same amount of water. In large nonstick skillet, heat olive oil. Sauté all the vegetables until onions become tender (about 5 minutes). Add remaining 1/2 can of chicken broth and simmer 5 minutes. While simmering, empty tomatoes into bowl and add marjoram, basil, garlic, cornstarch, Worcestershire sauce, sugar, and ground pepper. Stir until cornstarch is mixed. Crush all the tomatoes. Cut chicken into small bite-sized pieces. Add tomato mixture and chicken to vegetables. Cover skillet and simmer 5 minutes. Serve over rice. Serves 4.

Chicken can be deleted and recipe used as a vegetable side dish. As is, it makes a wonderful one-dish meal.

30-Minute Chicken Stroganoff

Nutritional Information
About 1-cup serving:
Calories 255
Fat 10.5g
Protein 29.1g
Carbohydrates 11.1g
% fat 37
Cholesterol 47mg

Exchanges
3½ Meat
½ Vegetable
2 Fat

6 chicken breasts, boneless, skinless
1 tablespoon vegetable oil
½ teaspoon salt
½ teaspoon sage
2 cups fresh mushrooms, sliced
2 tablespoons onion, chopped
½ cup liquid Butter Buds
1 teaspoon thyme
¼ teaspoon paprika
2 teaspoons cornstarch
4 tablespoons water
½ cup white cooking wine
1 cup lite sour cream

Slice chicken breasts into strips ½ inch wide, and sprinkle with salt and sage. Sauté the chicken until brown in vegetable oil. Add mushrooms, onion, Butter Buds, thyme, and paprika. Sauté until browned. Combine cornstarch and water. Stir into the chicken. Simmer, stirring, until sauce thickens. Stir in cooking wine. Simmer, covered, 3 or 4 more minutes. Stir in sour cream. *Do not boil.* Serve plain or over noodles. Serves 6.

Nutritional calculations do not include rice or noodles.

Grilled Chicken Breasts with Raspberry Sauce

Nutritional Information
1-piece serving:
Calories 217
Fat 6.5g
Protein 28g
Carbohydrates 11.7g
% fat 27
Cholesterol 72mg

Exchanges
3½ Meat
1 Fruit

2 tablespoons Worcestershire sauce
¼ cup soy sauce
1 tablespoon brown sugar
2 tablespoons wine vinegar
1 teaspoon garlic salt
4 chicken breasts, boned, skinned
2 cups raspberries
4 tablespoons soy sauce
2 tablespoons brown sugar
1 tablespoon cooking oil

In a deep mixing bowl, combine the Worcestershire sauce, ¼ cup soy sauce, 1 tablespoon brown sugar, vinegar, and salt. Add chicken breasts. Marinate at least 30 minutes. Combine raspberries, 4 tablespoons soy sauce, and 2 tablespoons brown sugar. Puree. Pour the raspberry mixture into a small saucepan over low heat. Put cooking oil into a Teflon skillet. Place over medium heat. Remove chicken from marinade and grill until browned. Place chicken on individual serving plates or a platter. Pour raspberry sauce over the chicken and serve immediately. Serves 4.

Spicy Oven-Fried Chicken

Nutritional Information
1-piece serving:
Calories 185
Fat 5g
Protein 28.2g
Carbohydrates 6.8g
% fat 24
Cholesterol 72mg

Exchanges
1/4 Bread
3 1/2 Meat

4 chicken breasts, boneless, skinned
1/2 cup skim milk
Salt, pepper, paprika
1 cup bread crumbs
Butter-flavored nonstick cooking spray

Preheat oven to 350°. Put milk in a small mixing bowl. Put bread crumbs in another. Dip the chicken in milk. Without blotting chicken, sprinkle with spices and roll in the bread crumbs. Place chicken on a baking dish that has been sprayed with butter-flavored nonstick cooking spray. Now spray the chicken. Bake until chicken is golden brown, about 35 minutes at 350°. Spray once during cooking time. Serves 4.

Mexican Oven-Fried Chicken[b]

Nutritional Information
1-piece serving:
Calories 206
Fat 5.5g
Protein 28.1g
Carbohydrates 13.4g
% fat 23
Cholesterol 0

Exchanges
1/2 Bread
2 Meat
1 1/2 Vegetable
2 Fat

4 chicken breast halves, skinned
1 cup Snap-E-Tom (or spiced tomato juice)
1/2 cup crushed corn flakes cereal (or wheat flakes)
1/4 cup wheat bran
1/2 teaspoon dried oregano
1/2 teaspoon ground cumin
1/2 teaspoon chili powder
1/2 teaspoon paprika
1/4 teaspoon dried minced onion
1/4 teaspoon garlic powder
Vegetable coating spray

Combine chicken and Snap-E-Tom mix in a large bowl; cover chicken and refrigerate 6 hours or overnight.

Combine next 8 ingredients. Drain chicken, and dredge in cereal mixture. Place chicken breasts in a baking pan covered with vegetable coating spray. Bake at 350° for 50 to 60 minutes or until done. Serves 4.

——————Chicken Enchiladas Verdes[b] ————

Nutritional Information
2-enchilada serving:
Calories 250
Fat 4.4g
Protein 16.6g
Carbohydrates 37.2g
% fat 16
Cholesterol 0

Exchanges
1¾ Bread
1 Meat
¹/₁₀ Milk
¹/₁₀ Vegetable
1¹/₃ Fat

2 cups cooked chicken, chopped (remove all skin and visible fat)
2 green onions, chopped
¹/₈ teaspoon garlic powder
10 corn tortillas
1 cup chicken broth, defatted
¹/₂ cup nonfat yogurt
2 teaspoons skim milk
Thinly sliced onion
Salsa verde (below)

Make salsa verde. Combine chicken, green onions, garlic powder, and 3 tablespoons salsa verde. Mix well. Heat ¹/₄ cup chicken broth in small skillet, until hot. Slip 1 tortilla into skillet, cook until softened (or soften tortillas in microwave). Drain on paper towel. Repeat with remaining tortillas, adding additional chicken broth every 3 to 4 tortillas or as needed. Fill each tortilla with 3 tablespoons of chicken mixture; roll up. Fill all tortillas and arrange seam-side down, in a single layer in shallow baking dish. Pour salsa verde over tortillas. Bake until sauce is bubbly, about 20 minutes in 350° oven. Mix yogurt and skim milk and spoon over enchiladas. Top with onion slices. Serves 5.

——————Salsa Verde (Green Sauce) ————

Nutritional Information
1-tablespoon serving:
Calories 6
Fat 0g
Protein 0.1g
Carbohydrates 1.4g
% fat 2
Cholesterol 0

Exchanges
¹/₈ Vegetable

1 small onion
1 medium jalapeno, stemmed and chopped
1 tablespoon cilantro, chopped
1 small garlic clove, chopped
1 pound fresh tomatillos

Combine onion, jalapeno, cilantro, and garlic in blender.

Blanch fresh tomatillos in boiling water to soften slightly, 2 minutes; drain. Add to blender container. Process all ingredients until smooth. Serves 32.

Chicken Jambalaya[b]

Nutritional Information
¼-recipe serving:
Calories 229
Fat 5.9g
Protein 28.4g
Carbohydrates 16.6g
% fat 23
Cholesterol 0

Exchanges
½ Bread
2 Meat
1 Vegetable
2⅓ Fat

4 chicken breast halves, skinned
1 cup chicken broth, defatted
½ cup dry white cooking wine
1 16-ounce can tomatoes, chopped
½ cup onion, chopped
¼ cup green pepper, chopped
2 tablespoons fresh parsley, chopped
½ teaspoon dried basil
¼ teaspoon thyme
1 bay leaf
½ teaspoon black pepper
¾ cup raw long-grain brown rice
Vegetable coating spray

Combine broth, cooking wine, tomatoes, onion, green pepper, parsley, basil, thyme, bay leaf, and pepper in a large saucepan. Bring to a boil. Reduce heat and cover; simmer for 5 minutes. Remove from heat. Remove bay leaves and add rice. Spray a 13″x9″ baking dish with vegetable coating spray. Pour rice mixture into dish. Place chicken on top of mixture. Cover and bake 55 to 65 minutes at 350° or until done. Add water if rice is dry. Serves 4.

Chicken Parmesan

Nutritional Information
1-breast-with-sauce serving:
Calories 349
Fat 7g
Protein 31g
Carbohydrates 38g
% fat 18
Cholesterol 80mg

Exchanges
4 Meat
2 Vegetable
1 Fat

4 chicken breasts, skinless, boneless
1 cup commercially prepared bread crumbs
⅛ cup Parmesan cheese
4 egg whites
1 tablespoon basil
Vegetable coating spray
2 cans Italian-flavored crushed tomatoes
1 tablespoon cornstarch
½ teaspoon garlic powder
½ teaspoon marjoram
½ teaspoon basil
1 dash Worcestershire sauce
1 teaspoon sugar
Ground pepper to taste

Preheat oven to 350°. Combine bread crumbs, Parmesan cheese, and basil in a small mixing bowl. Dip chicken in egg and dredge in bread crumb mixture. Lay in baking dish sprayed with vegetable coating spray. Bake 50 to 60 minutes or until done.

Sauce: Combine tomatoes, cornstarch, garlic, marjoram, basil, Worcestershire sauce, sugar, and ground pepper. Simmer 15 minutes.

To Serve: Place 1/3 cup sauce on the plate. Place chicken fillet on top of sauce, a dot of sauce on top, and garnish with chopped fresh basil or parsley. Serves 4.

The basic chicken recipe is great when sliced and placed on top of chef salad or used in sandwiches. This recipe goes well with linguini or spaghetti noddles.

Chicken Cordon Bleu

Nutritional Information
1-chicken breast serving:
Calories 275
Fat 10.1g
Protein 32.8g
Carbohydrates 13.2g
% fat 33
Cholesterol 126mg

Exchanges
1/4 Bread
5 Meat

4 thin slices lean cooked ham
4 thin slices Swiss cheese
4 chicken breasts, boneless, skinned, split, and pounded thin
    (3 to 4 ounces each)
1/3 cup seasoned bread crumbs
1/4 teaspoon salt
1/8 teaspoon pepper
1/8 teaspoon tarragon
1/8 teaspoon garlic powder
1 package Butter Buds made into liquid
Nonstick cooking spray

Preheat oven to 350°. For each serving, place 1 slice ham and 1 slice cheese on each chicken breast. Roll up and secure with toothpick. Combine bread crumbs and seasonings. Dip each chicken roll in Butter Buds, then roll in bread crumbs. Arrange in baking dish sprayed with nonstick cooking spray. Drizzle with remaining Butter Buds. Bake approximately 40 minutes or until chicken is tender and golden brown. Serves 4.

Stuffed Bell Peppers

Nutritional Information
1-stuffed pepper serving:
Calories 350
Fat 10g
Protein 35g
Carbohydrates 30g
% fat 26
Cholesterol 95mg

Exchanges
1 Bread
3 Meat
2 Vegetable

4 large bell peppers
1 pound ground turkey (may use extra-lean ground beef)
1 cup tomatoes, chopped
2 teaspoons allspice
1/2 cup instant rice, uncooked
1/2 cup whole-kernel corn
2 tablespoons Parmesan cheese
2 tablespoons onion, minced
1 clove garlic, minced
1 tablespoon fresh basil, chopped
1 tablespoon fresh parsley, chopped
1/8 teaspoon pepper
1/4 teaspoon salt
1 small can tomato sauce
Nonstick cooking spray

Cut off the tops of the peppers, core, and remove seeds. In a mixing bowl combine the remaining ingredients except the tomato sauce. Stuff the peppers. Place the peppers in a baking dish that has been sprayed with nonstick cooking spray. Put tomato sauce on top of the peppers, and bake at 350° for 1 hour. Serves 4.

This is another one of those wonderful one-dish meals. It contains vegetable, starch, and meat. Serve with a salad to complete your nutritional requirements.

Hungarian Beefsteak

Nutritional Information
3/4-cup serving:
Calories 216
Fat 9.5g
Protein 22.2g
Carbohydrates 9.8g
% fat 39
Cholesterol 58mg

Exchanges
2 Meat
1 Fat

1 pound round steak, trimmed and thinly sliced
2 tablespoons olive oil
1/8 cup onion, chopped
1 clove garlic, minced
3/4 cup water
1/3 cup catsup
2 tablespoons brown sugar
2 tablespoons Worcestershire sauce
1 1/2 teaspoons paprika
1 teaspoon salt
1 teaspoon dry mustard
1 tablespoon cornstarch

Add oil to a nonstick 10-inch skillet. Sauté steak strips until all are well browned. Add the onion and garlic and sauté 3 to 5 minutes. Stir in ½ cup of water and all other ingredients except cornstarch. Cover and simmer on low for 30 minutes. Combine cornstarch with remaining ¼ cup water and mix thoroughly. Add to the skillet and stir as the mixture thickens. Serve with noodles or rice. Serves 6.

Note: Noodles are not included in the nutritional calculations. If desired, simply add 1 bread exchange for each ½ cup of noodles.

— Beef Stroganoff —

Nutritional Information
About ¾-cup serving:
Calories 225
Fat 8.2g
Protein 31.3g
Carbohydrates 7.4g
% fat 33
Cholesterol 74mg

Exchanges
3 Meat

2 pounds round steak, about ½ to ¾ inch thick
1 tablespoon diet margarine
1 onion, chopped
1 can mushrooms, sliced
1 clove garlic, chopped
2 cups water
3 tablespoons flour
1 teaspoon salt
⅛ teaspoon pepper
2 beef bouillon cubes
1½ cups low-cal cottage cheese
½ cup skim milk
2 tablespoons vinegar

Trim all fat from the steak, cut into 1½-inch squares, and broil. In a large Teflon skillet, sauté the onion, mushrooms, and garlic in the margarine. Combine the water, flour, salt, and pepper. Mix until the flour is completely dissolved. Pour into the skillet with the onions. Simmer until thickened, stirring frequently. Add beef and bouillon cubes. Simmer 15 minutes. Liquefy the cottage cheese and skim milk in a blender (or beat until smooth with a mixer), and add to the beef mixture. Cook only until heated, add vinegar, and serve immediately. This dish is traditionally served over ½ cup of noodles. Serves 10.

Note: Noodles are included in the nutritional calculations. If desired, simply add 1 bread exchange for each ½ cup of noodles.

Great Meat Loaf

Nutritional Information
1/8-recipe (about 3 1/2
ounces) serving:
Calories 198
Fat 8g
Protein 25g
Carbohydrates 6.5g
% fat 36
Cholesterol 68mg

Exchanges
2 1/2 Meat

1 1/2 pounds extra-lean ground beef
1 cup Special K cereal
4 egg whites
1 onion
2 teaspoons salt
1/2 teaspoon pepper
1/4 teaspoon dry mustard
1/8 teaspoon sage
2 cups V-8 juice
1 tablespoon flour
1 can green beans, finely chopped
1 teaspoon salt
1/4 teaspoon pepper

Combine the ground beef, Special K, eggs, onion, salt, pepper, mustard, and sage. Mix well, preferably with hands. Shape into a rectangle about 1 1/2 inches thick. Place on a broiling pan, and bake at 350° for about 1 hour. Place the V-8 juice, flour, chopped green beans, salt, and pepper in a saucepan. Dissolve the flour before heating. Simmer over low heat until thickened. Pour the sauce over the meat loaf and serve. Serves 8.

Stovetop Apricot-Glazed Ham

Nutritional Information
3 1/2-ounce (cooked
weight) serving:
Calories 325
Fat 12g
Protein 25g
Carbohydrates 29g
% fat 33
Cholesterol 76mg

Exchanges
4 Meat
1 Fruit
1 Fat

1 pound ham steak, precooked, no fat
1/3 cup reduced-sugar apricot jam
1/3 cup orange juice
6 fresh apricots, thinly sliced
2 tablespoons white cooking wine
1/2 teaspoon mustard
2 tablespoons currants (or raisins)
1/4 teaspoon ground cloves

In a Teflon skillet, brown the ham on both sides. Remove the ham from the skillet. In the same skillet, combine the remaining ingredients. Simmer 4 or 5 minutes, turning the ham to coat both sides. Arrange the ham on a serving platter. Pour apricot sauce on top. Serves 4.

Ham-Stuffed Baked Potatoes

Nutritional Information
1-potato serving:
Calories 283
Fat 8.1g
Protein 17.4g
Carbohydrates 35.1g
% fat 26
Cholesterol 17mg

Exchanges
1½ Bread
2 Meat
1 Fat

4 large potatoes, baked
2 green onions, diced
½ teaspoon garlic salt
1 tablespoon fresh parsley, chopped
½ teaspoon pepper
1 cup ham, cooked, diced
2 teaspoons Molly McButter
4 teaspoons margarine
3 tablespoons sharp cheddar cheese, grated
Nonstick cooking spray

Cut off the top ⅓ of the prebaked potato. Scoop out the bottom half of the shell. In a mixing bowl, combine the potatoes, onion, garlic salt, parsley, ham, Molly McButter, margarine, and pepper. Mash and mix well. Stuff the potato shells with this mixture. Spray an appropriate baking dish with nonstick cooking spray. Place stuffed shells in the baking dish, and sprinkle with cheese. Bake in a preheated 400° oven for 10 to 12 minutes or until lightly browned. Serves 4.

Desserts and Baked Fruits

Classic Banana Split

Nutritional Information
Entire-recipe serving:
Calories 302
Fat 7g
Protein 7g
Carbohydrates 52g
% fat 21
Cholesterol 0

Exchanges
1 Bread
1 Milk
1 Fruit
1 Fat

⅓ cup chocolate ice milk
⅓ cup strawberry ice milk
½ small banana
1 tablespoon strawberry jam
1 tablespoon crushed pineapple
1 tablespoon walnuts, chopped

In a banana split dish, put ⅓-cup scoops of chocolate and strawberry ice milk. Slice the banana lengthwise, and place ½ on each side of the ice milk. Top the scoops of ice milk with the fruit toppers. Finish with the chopped nuts. Serves 1.

Sure it's a splurge—but only a 300-calorie splurge instead of 1,000 calories. Have this great dessert on some special occasion.

——Creamy Three-Fruit Sherbet[a] ——

Nutritional Information
1/2-cup serving:
Calories 107
Fat 0.6g
Protein 1.8g
Carbohydrates 25g
% fat 5
Cholesterol 1mg

Exchanges
1/2 Bread
1/4 Milk
1 Fruit

1 3/4 cups fresh strawberry halves
2 1/2 cups ripe bananas (3 medium), sliced
1/4 cup sugar
1 6-ounce can frozen orange juice
1/4 teaspoon almond extract
1/2 cup plain low-fat yogurt

Position knife blade in food processor bowl; add first 5 ingredients. Cover and process until smooth. Place mixture in a medium bowl; add yogurt, stirring well. Pour mixture into a freezer can of a 1-gallon ice cream freezer. Freeze mixture according to manufacturer's instructions. Serves 10.

——Baked Apples with Raspberry Sauce ——

Nutritional Information
1-apple serving:
Calories 140
Fat 1g
Protein 4.5g
Carbohydrates 28g
% fat 7
Cholesterol 0

Exchanges
3 Fruit

4 large apples
Nonstick cooking spray
2 teaspoons low-cal margarine
1/2 cup water
1/4 cup sugar
4 teaspoons raspberry jelly

Preheat oven to 400°. Wash apples, wipe dry, and core. Spray a baking dish with nonstick cooking spray. Arrange apples in the dish, put 1/2 teaspoon margarine on each apple, add water, and place in the oven. Bake for 15 minutes, sprinkle each apple with sugar, and return to the oven. Bake 30 minutes more or until tender. Remove the apples from the oven. Spoon 1 teaspoon jelly on each apple. Serve warm. Serves 4.

Banana Pudding Bake

Nutritional Information
⅛-recipe serving:
Calories 136
Fat 1g
Protein 6.2g
Carbohydrates 25.5g
% fat 6
Cholesterol 0

Exchanges
1 Bread
½ Meat
½ Fruit

1 package vanilla pudding mix
2 cups skim milk
3 bananas
2 tablespoons lemon juice
¼ cup cold water
4 egg whites
1 teaspoon cream of tartar
¼ cup sugar

Prepare the vanilla pudding mix as indicated on the package, using skim milk. Let cool. Slice the bananas, and soak for at least 10 minutes in a bowl with the lemon juice and water. Layer a casserole with the banana slices, and then spoon the pudding on top. In another bowl, beat the egg whites until stiff. Add the cream of tartar and sugar and mix thoroughly. Spread over the pudding, and bake for 5 to 10 minutes at 425° or until the meringue is set. Let cool to serve. Serves 8.

Baked Rice and Fruit Pudding

Nutritional Information
⅔-cup serving:
Calories 139
Fat 1g
Protein 4g
Carbohydrates 28.5g
% fat 6
Cholesterol 33g

Exchanges
¾ Bread
¼ Milk
1 Fruit

½ cup regular rice, uncooked
1 cup water
¾ cup sugar
1 tablespoon cornstarch
Dash of salt
2 eggs
2½ cups skim milk
1 tablespoon lemon juice
½ cup raisins
2 apples, finely diced

In a saucepan, combine the rice and water. Heat to boiling, stirring occasionally. Reduce heat, cover, and simmer 15 minutes. All water should be absorbed. Preheat oven to 350°. In a mixing bowl, combine the sugar, cornstarch, and salt. Beat the eggs and milk until smooth. Stir into the cornstarch mixture. Add the lemon juice, raisins, and apples, and mix well. Pour into a casserole dish. Place casserole in a pan of very hot water 1 inch deep. Bake about 1½ hours or until a knife comes out clean. Serves 12.

Party Parfait

Nutritional Information
1-parfait serving:
Calories 180
Fat 3g
Protein 6g
Carbohydrates 32g
% fat 15
Cholesterol 0

Exchanges
1 Bread
1/2 Milk
1/2 Fruit
1 Fat

1 package pistachio pudding mix
2 cups skim milk
4 fresh strawberries, sliced
1 large fresh banana, sliced
1 tablespoon lemon juice
4 tablespoons whipped cream (or whipped cream substitute)

Soak the banana slices in 1/4 cup cold water and 1 tablespoon of lemon juice. Prepare the pistachio pudding as indicated on the package. Place 2 table-spoons of pudding in the bottom of each of 4 parfait glasses. Top each with 1/4 of the drained banana slices. Apply 2 more tablespoons of pudding to each parfait (all of the pudding should now be in the parfait glasses). Apply 1/4 of the strawberry slices to each of the parfait glasses, saving 4 of the slices. Top each parfait with 1 tablespoon of whipped cream and the last slice of strawberry. Serves 4.

Sugar-free alternatives may be used in this recipe to make a delicious diabetic dessert and save about 60 calories per serving.

Chocolate Roll[a]

Nutritional Information
1-slice serving:
Calories 173
Fat 7.4g
Protein 3.8g
Carbohydrates 27.5g
% fat 38
Cholesterol 55mg

Exchanges
1 Bread
1/2 Fruit
2 Fat

2 cups frozen whipped topping, thawed
1 tablespoon instant coffee powder
Vegetable cooking spray
4 egg whites
1/3 cup sugar
2 eggs
1/2 cup sugar
2 1-ounce squares unsweetened chocolate, melted and cooled
1 teaspoon vanilla extract
1/4 cup plus 2 tablespoons all-purpose flour, sifted
1/4 teaspoon baking powder
1/4 cup cocoa powder
Chocolate leaves (optional)

Fold whipped topping and coffee powder together until well blended; cover and chill. Coat a 15"x10"x1" jelly roll pan with cooking spray. Line pan with waxed paper; coat paper with cooking spray, and set aside. Beat egg whites (at room temperature) until soft peaks form. Gradually add ⅓ cup sugar, 1 tablespoon at a time, beating until stiff peaks form; set aside. Beat eggs and ½ cup sugar in a medium mixing bowl until thick and lemon colored. Add chocolate and vanilla, beating well. Stir ¼ of egg whites into chocolate mixture; gently fold remaining egg whites into chocolate mixture. Sprinkle flour and baking powder over chocolate mixture; fold in gently. Spread batter evenly in prepared pan. Bake at 350° for 18 minutes. Cool in pan 5 minutes. Sift cocoa in a 15″x10″ rectangle on a towel. Loosen cake from sides of pan, and turn out onto cocoa. Peel off waxed paper. Cool 1 minute. Starting at narrow end, roll up cake and towel together, then cool cake for 1 hour on a wire rack, seam side down. Unroll cake and remove towel. Stir reserved whipped topping mixture, and spread evenly over cake; reroll. Place on serving plate, seam side down. Garnish with chocolate leaves, if desired. Chill 1 hour before serving. Serves 10.

Fruit Shortcake with Buttermilk-Chocolate Sauce[a]

Nutritional Information
1-shortcake (and 2 tablespoons of sauce) serving:
Calories 211
Fat 4.8g
Protein 4.7g
Carbohydrates 40.6g
% fat 20
Cholesterol 74mg

Exchanges
1 Bread
2 Fruit
1 Fat

6 ¾-ounce commercial shortcakes
1½ cups unpeeled nectarines or peaches (about 1 large), cubed
½ cup fresh raspberries (about ½ pint)
1 tablespoon lemon juice

Place shortcakes on individual serving plates. In a small bowl, combine the fruit. Spoon 1 tablespoon Buttermilk-Chocolate Sauce (see next page) over each shortcake. Top with ⅓ cup fruit; drizzle each shortcake with 1 additional tablespoon Buttermilk-Chocolate Sauce. Serves 6.

———Buttermilk-Chocolate Sauce[a]———

Nutritional Information
1-tablespoon serving:
Calories 32
Fat 0.7g
Protein 0.8g
Carbohydrates 6.2g
% fat 20
Cholesterol 0

Exchanges
¹/₄ Fruit
¹/₂ Fat

¹/₃ cup Dutch-process cocoa
¹/₄ cup brown sugar, firmly packed
¹/₂ cup nonfat buttermilk
1 teaspoon orange extract

Combine cocoa and sugar in a small saucepan. Gradually add buttermilk, stirring well. Place over medium heat, and cook until sugar dissolves. Stir in extract; remove from heat. Yield: ³/₄ cup. Serves 12.

———Oatmeal Brownies[a]———

Nutritional Information
2x2¹/₂-inch-square
serving:
Calories 126
Fat 4.1g
Protein 2.4g
Carbohydrates 20.1g
% fat 29
Cholesterol 0

Exchanges
1¹/₂ Bread
1 Fat

²/₃ cup sugar
¹/₂ cup water
3 tablespoons vegetable oil
¹/₂ teaspoon vanilla extract
2 egg whites, lightly beaten
¹/₂ cup all-purpose flour
¹/₃ cup quick-cooking oats, uncooked
¹/₄ cup unsweetened cocoa
³/₄ teaspoon baking powder
¹/₈ teaspoon salt
Vegetable cooking spray
1 teaspoon powdered sugar, sifted

Combine sugar, water, vegetable oil, and vanilla in a medium bowl; stir well. Add egg whites, and stir well. Combine flour and next 4 ingredients; add sugar mixture, stirring well. Pour batter into an 8-inch-square baking pan coated with vegetable cooking spray. Bake at 350° for 23 minutes, or until wooden pick inserted in center comes out clean. Cool; sprinkle with sugar. Serves 12.

——————No-Cholesterol Brownies ——————

Nutritional Information
1-square serving:
Calories 105
Fat 4g
Protein 7.1g
Carbohydrates 10.1g
% fat 34
Cholesterol 0

Exchanges
1 Bread
1 Fat

¼ cup **corn oil margarine**
½ cup **sugar**
½ cup **brown sugar, firmly packed**
½ cup **all-purpose flour**
2 tablespoons **unsweetened cocoa**
2 **egg whites**
1 teaspoon **vanilla extract**
¼ cup **walnuts, chopped**
Nonstick cooking spray

Melt the margarine in a large bowl. Add all other ingredients except walnuts. Mix well. Stir in walnuts. Spread out batter evenly in an 8″x8″x2″ metal pan sprayed with nonstick cooking spray. Bake at 350° for 30 minutes or until just done. The middle portion should still be soft. Cool before cutting into 2-inch squares. Serves 16.

Any cookie recipe may be modified in a similar way as has been done with this one to yield a lower-fat, lower-calorie, lower-cholesterol product.

——————No-Bake Fruity Pecan Bars ——————

Nutritional Information
1-cookie serving:
Calories 70
Fat 3g
Protein 4.2g
Carbohydrates 6.5g
% fat 39
Cholesterol 0

Exchanges
½ Bread
½ Fruit

⅓ cup **margarine**
½ cup **light brown sugar, firmly packed**
⅓ cup **honey**
⅓ cup **wheat germ**
¼ teaspoon **ground cinnamon**
1½ cups **old-fashioned oats, uncooked**
1 cup **dried apricots, chopped**
¼ cup **pecans, coarsely chopped**
¼ cup **golden raisins**

Combine margarine, brown sugar, and honey in a saucepan. Bring to a boil over medium-high heat, stirring constantly. Reduce heat and simmer for 4 minutes, stirring constantly. Remove from heat. Mix in wheat germ and cinnamon. Stir in oats, apricots, pecans, and raisins. Drop mixture by level tablespoonfuls onto waxed paper, shaping into a mound. Chill until firm. Store in refrigerator in a tightly covered container. Serves 36.

Key Lime Pie[b]

Nutritional Information
1/10-pie serving:
Calories 111
Fat .02g
Protein 7.8g
Carbohydrates 20.9g
% fat 0
Cholesterol 0

Exchanges
6/10 Bread
8/10 Milk
1/10 Fruit

2 envelopes unflavored gelatin
1 cup boiling water
1/2 cup sugar
2/3 cup fresh lime juice
2 tablespoons zest of lime, finely grated
3 cups Basic Yogurt Cheese (p. 216)

Mix sugar and gelatin in a large bowl. Pour in boiling water, stir 1 minute until gelatin is dissolved. Stir in lime juice and peel; mix well. Add yogurt cheese 1 cup at a time and mix until well-blended and smooth.

Pour into a 9-inch glass pie pan and chill until firm (2 to 3 hours). Garnish with fresh mint sprigs and lime slices if desired. Serves 10.

Fresh Peach Pie

Nutritional Information
1/8-of-pie serving:
Calories 115
Fat 4.5g
Protein 4.2g
Carbohydrates 14.4g
% fat 35
Cholesterol 12mg

Exchanges
1/2 Bread
1/2 Meat
1/2 Fruit
1 Fat

Nonstick cooking spray
4 canned biscuits
4 fresh peaches, sliced
1 egg white
1 cup part-skim milk ricotta
1/4 cup skim milk
2 tablespoons brown sugar
1 teaspoon vanilla
1 teaspoon allspice

Preheat oven to 375°. Roll out biscuits. Spray a 9-inch pie plate with nonstick cooking spray. Press biscuits over the bottom and sides to form a shell. Trim around edges and flute. Arrange peaches in the shell. Combine the remaining ingredients in the blender until smooth. Pour over the peaches. Bake approximately 45 minutes until a knife inserted comes out clean. Serves 8.

Quick Apple Pies

Nutritional Information
1-pie serving:
Calories 166
Fat 8.1g
Protein 7g
Carbohydrates 16.2g
% fat 44
Cholesterol 10mg

Exchanges
1 Bread
1 Fruit
1½ Fat

1 tablespoon low-cal margarine
2 large apples, diced
Apple pie spice
2 teaspoons brown sugar
4 canned biscuits, unbaked
Butter-flavored nonstick cooking spray

Preheat oven to 400°. Sauté the apples in the margarine until soft. Roll each biscuit out to about 5-inch circles. Spread ½ of each circle with ¼ of the apple mixture. Sprinkle with apple pie spice and ½ teaspoon brown sugar. Fold each circle in half, and press the edges to seal with a fork. Place the pies on a baking sheet that has been sprayed with butter-flavored nonstick cooking spray, and then spray the pies. Bake until golden brown, about 10 to 12 minutes. Serve hot! Serves 4.

Classic Cheesecake

Nutritional Information
⅛-of-recipe serving:
Calories 103
Fat 1.8g
Protein 6g
Carbohydrates 23.7g
% fat 16
Cholesterol 0

Exchanges
½ Bread
1 Milk

32-ounce carton low-fat vanilla-flavored yogurt
4 tablespoons granulated sugar
1 tablespoon cornstarch
1 tablespoon lemon juice
1 teaspoon vanilla
½ cup Egg Beaters (or 2 whole eggs)
Nonstick cooking spray

Prepare Basic Yogurt Cheese (p. 216) substituting vanilla yogurt for plain. Use the entire carton of yogurt. Use nonstick cooking spray on an 8-inch pie pan or 7-inch springform pan. In a mixing bowl, combine the yogurt cheese with all remaining ingredients. Prepare Crumb Crust for Pies (p. 282), pour mixture into crust, and bake in a 325° preheated oven for 20 to 25 minutes in a pie pan or 40 to 45 minutes in a springform pan. Cool and refrigerate until serving. Add fresh strawberries to the top, if desired. Serves 8.

Nutritional calculations assume that this recipe was made with Egg Beaters and the Crumb Crust for Pies on page 282.

Pineapple Cheesecake

Nutritional Information
1/8-of-pie serving:
Calories 105
Fat 1g
Protein 10g
Carbohydrates 15g
% fat 8
Cholesterol 20mg

Exchanges
1/2 Bread
1/2 Milk
1/2 Fruit

2 envelopes unflavored gelatin
1/4 cup sugar
1/4 teaspoon salt
1/2 cup unsweetened pineapple juice
1 cup low-fat milk
3 egg whites
8 ounces low-fat cottage cheese
1/2 cup crushed pineapple, drained
1 tablespoon lemon peel, grated
1/2 cup graham cracker crumbs
1 teaspoon vanilla
1 tablespoon diet margarine
3 tablespoons pineapple juice
1 tablespoon lemon juice
2 tablespoons sugar
3 tablespoons crushed pineapple, drained

In a saucepan, mix gelatin, 1/4 cup sugar, salt, 1/2 cup pineapple juice, milk, and 1 egg white. Cook over low heat until mixture thickens. Cool slightly, pour into blender. Add cottage cheese. Liquefy. Stir in pineapple and lemon peel. In a small bowl, combine graham cracker crumbs, vanilla, 3 tablespoons pineapple juice, lemon juice, and 2 tablespoons sugar. Mix and pack into a 9-inch pie plate. Pour in cheese mixture. Chill until firm, and top with remaining 3 tablespoons of drained pineapple. Serves 8.

Strawberry-Glazed Cheesecake[a]

Nutritional Information
1/16-of-recipe serving:
Calories 210
Fat 14.9g
Protein 7.4g
Carbohydrates 13.9g
% fat 61
Cholesterol 113mg

Exchanges
1 Bread
1 Meat
3 Fat

Vegetable cooking spray
1 tablespoon graham cracker crumbs
4 8-ounce packages Philadelphia light cream cheese, softened
3/4 cup sugar
4 eggs
1/2 teaspoon vanilla extract
2 cups fresh strawberries, hulled
1 tablespoon water
1/2 teaspoon cornstarch
8 fresh strawberries, halved

Coat an 8-inch springform pan with vegetable cooking spray. Sprinkle bottom of pan with graham cracker crumbs; set aside. Combine cheese and sugar in a large mixing bowl; beat at high speed until fluffy. Add eggs, 1 at a time, beating well after each addition. Stir in vanilla; pour into prepared pan. Place springform pan in a 13"x9"x2" baking pan, filled halfway with water. Bake at 325° for 1 hour or until firm. Remove from oven, and refrigerate 8 hours. Place 2 cups strawberries in a blender or food processor, and process until smooth. Strain through a sieve to yield ½ cup puree. Combine puree, water, and cornstarch in a nonaluminum saucepan. Bring to a boil; cook 1 minute or until thickened. Chill. Remove sides of pan, place on a serving plate; spoon strawberry sauce over top. Arrange strawberry halves decoratively on top. Serves 16.

Crumb Crust for Pies

Nutritional Information
⅛-of-recipe serving:
Calories 48
Fat 1.4g
Protein 2.8g
Carbohydrates 6g
% fat 26
Cholesterol 0

Exchanges
½ Bread

¾ cup crumbs (use graham crackers—usually 4½ whole
   crackers—or 9 Zwieback slices)
2 tablespoons diet margarine
1½ tablespoons sugar
Nonstick cooking spray

Grind the crackers into crumbs in a food processor. Add granulated sugar in food processor to mix briefly. Pour crumb/sugar mixture into a bowl. Drizzle melted margarine over top, and mix with a fork. Pat crumb mixture into the bottom and sides of the desired pan, which has been sprayed with a nonstick cooking spray. Fill with pie filling and bake. If the pie is a no-bake dessert, then set the crust before filling by baking for 4 minutes at 375° Serves 8.

    Suitable for 8-inch pie pan or 7-inch springform pan.

Holiday Fare

Holiday Eggnog

Nutritional Information
$^1/_2$-cup serving:
Calories 55
Fat 1g
Protein 10.8g
Carbohydrates 11.3g
% fat 2
Cholesterol 0

Exchanges
$^1/_2$ Meat
$^1/_2$ Milk

3 cups $^1/_2$ percent low-fat milk, cold
1 cup evaporated skim milk, undiluted, cold
1 teaspoon rum flavoring
1 cup Egg Beaters
4 packets NutraSweet (or 2 tablespoons sugar)
1 teaspoon vanilla
Dash of nutmeg

Combine all ingredients except nutmeg in blender. Process on low speed about 30 seconds or until frothy. Pour mixture into a saucepan, and beat until steamy on a low heat. *Do not boil.* Chill and serve with a dash of nutmeg. Serves 8.

Cranberry Chutney

Nutritional Information
2 rounded-tablespoon serving:
Calories 60
Fat 0
Protein 1.2g
Carbohydrates 13.8g
% fat 0
Cholesterol 0

Exchanges
1$^1/_2$ Fruit

1 cup seedless golden raisins
4 ounces pitted dates, chopped
4 cups (1 pound) fresh cranberries
$^2/_3$ cup white granulated sugar
$^1/_8$ teaspoon salt
$^1/_4$ teaspoon ginger, cinnamon, and allspice
$^1/_8$ teaspoon ground cloves
$^3/_4$ cup cider vinegar

Combine all ingredients and cook, stirring occasionally for 30 minutes. Spoon into hot sterilized jars for keeping several months, or serve immediately. Serves 80.

This will be a nice accompaniment to your holiday turkey dinner.

——Fresh Cranberry and Orange Salad——

Nutritional Information
1/3-cup serving:
Calories 64
Fat 3g
Protein 2.2g
Carbohydrates 7g
% fat 42
Cholesterol 0

Exchanges
1 Fruit
1 Fat

1 package fresh cranberries, chopped
2 oranges, chopped
1 orange peel, chopped
1/2 cup walnuts, chopped
1/2 cup sugar

A food processor makes this recipe very quick and easy. Combine all ingredients in a mixing bowl. Chill. Toss and put into a serving dish. Serves 12.

Note: This makes a very nice relish/salad accompaniment at holiday dinners.

——Holiday Gelatin Salad——

Nutritional Information
1/8-of-recipe serving:
Calories 90
Fat 4.3g
Protein 3.8g
Carbohydrates 9g
% fat 43
Cholesterol 0

Exchanges
1 Meat
1/2 Fruit
1/2 Fat

1 package black cherry sugar-free gelatin
1 can sweet dark pitted cherries, drained
1/4 cup walnuts, chopped
4 ounces lite cream cheese

Prepare gelatin as directed on package. Add cherries after draining well. Add walnuts. Cut cream cheese into small cubes and add to mixture. Stir and place in a decorative mold or other dish. Refrigerate until gelatin is set. Serves 8.

——Holiday Bread Spread——

Nutritional Information
1/4-cup serving:
Calories 47
Fat 1.8g
Protein 4.1g
Carbohydrates 3.6g
% fat 34.4
Cholesterol 0

Exchanges
1/4 Milk
1/4 Fruit
1/2 Fat

3/4 cup low-cal cottage cheese
1/2 cup crushed pineapple, no sugar added
2 tablespoons walnuts, minced

Combine cottage cheese and pineapple in a food processor and puree. Add walnuts. Spread over holiday fruit breads such as the Oatmeal-Pumpkin Bread found on page 245. Serves 6.

Remember that walnuts are one of your best choices for nuts as they are high in polyunsaturated fatty acids.

Hot Curried Fruit

Nutritional Information
¹/₂-cup fruit and juice
serving:
Calories 128
Fat 3.7g
Protein 0.5g
Carbohydrates 23g
% fat 26
Cholesterol 11mg (if butter
is used)

Exchanges
¹/₂ Bread
1 Fruit
1 Fat

1 29-ounce can of peach halves, light syrup
1 15-ounce can of pineapple slices, no sugar added
1 29-ounce can of pear halves, light syrup
¹/₄ cup butter (or margarine)
¹/₂ cup brown sugar, firmly packed
4 teaspoons curry powder

Preheat oven to 350°. Drain fruit. Pat individual pieces of fruit with a paper towel until thoroughly dry. Arrange fruit in a baking dish. Melt butter. Add the brown sugar and curry. Spoon over the fruit and bake 30 minutes. Serve hot with holiday buffets. Serves 12.

Holiday Turkey Gravy

Nutritional Information
¹/₄-cup serving:
Calories 24
Fat 0.7g
Protein 3.2g
Carbohydrates 1g
% fat 26
Cholesterol 0

Exchanges
¹/₄ Meat

Turkey Stock from baked turkey, defatted
2 cups skim milk
4 tablespoons all-purpose flour
¹/₂ 10¹/₂-ounce can cream of chicken soup
Salt and pepper to taste

To defat turkey stock, place pan drippings in the freezer so that the fat layer can harden for easy removal. Or, a separating cup may be used if a quicker process is desired. Add the flour to the cold skim milk in a large saucepan. Mix in soup and defatted stock with a wire whisk. Heat the entire mixture until bubbly. Remove from heat. Season to taste and serve. Serves 16.

Thanksgiving Turkey Dressing (or Stuffing)

Nutritional Information
¹/₂-cup serving:
Calories 120
Fat 2g
Protein 3g
Carbohydrates 23g
% fat 15
Cholesterol 5mg

Exchanges
1 Bread
1 Fat

3 cups crumbled corn bread
1 cup bread cubes, white bread, no crust
2 cups fat-free turkey or chicken broth
3 stalks celery, finely chopped
1 large Jonathan apple, finely chopped
3 egg whites
Salt and pepper to taste
¹/₂–1 teaspoon poultry seasoning
Vegetable cooking spray

Combine all ingredients in a mixing bowl. Mix well, but gently. Turn the mixture gently into a baking dish that has been coated with a nonstick vegetable cooking spray. Bake at 350° for 45 minutes. This recipe is better when cooked in a baking dish; however, it may also be used as a turkey or chicken stuffing. Serves 10.

Use a corn bread recipe that produces a coarse product. Most corn bread recipes using buttermilk will be suitable.

Thanksgiving Pumpkin Pie

Nutritional Information
1/10-of-recipe serving:
Calories 175
Fat 4.7g
Protein 12g
Carbohydrates 21.2g
% fat 24
Cholesterol 0

Exchanges
1 Bread
1/2 Milk
1 Fruit

1/2 cup Egg Beaters
1 16-ounce can pumpkin, solid-pack
3/4 cup brown sugar, firmly packed
1/2 teaspoon salt
1 teaspoon ground cinnamon
1/2 teaspoon ground ginger
1/4 teaspoon ground cloves
1 12-ounce can evaporated skim milk
1 9-inch deep-dish pastry piecrust

Combine all the ingredients, except the piecrust, in the order given. Mix until smooth. Pour into the 9-inch piecrust, and bake 15 minutes at 425°. Reduce the temperature to 350°, and bake an additional 40 to 50 minutes or until a knife inserted in the center comes out clean. Serves 10.

Party Chex Mix

Nutritional Information
1/2-cup serving:
Calories 100
Fat 3.4g
Protein 4.9g
Carbohydrates 12.3g
% fat 31
Cholesterol 27mg

Exchanges
1/2 Bread
1 Fat

1/4 cup butter (or margarine)
1 tablespoon Worcestershire sauce
1/4 teaspoon celery salt
1/4 teaspoon seasoned salt
1/4 teaspoon garlic salt
2 cups Rice Chex cereal
2 cups Wheat Chex cereal
2 cups Corn Chex cereal
1 cup Cheerios, plain
1 cup pretzel sticks or oyster crackers
1/4 cup sunflower seeds, shelled
Butter-flavored nonstick cooking spray

Preheat oven to 325°. In a small saucepan, heat the butter and seasonings. In a very large bowl, toss the remaining ingredients with the butter mixture. Spray a large cookie sheet with 1-inch sides with the butter-flavored nonstick cooking spray. Spread the cereal mixture evenly over the cookie sheet. Bake 20 minutes, stirring occasionally. Serve immediately or store in an airtight container. This makes a nice gift or a chip alternative for brown-bag lunches. Makes 8 cups total. Serves 16.

APPENDICES

APPENDIX A

Guide to Nutrition and Calories

Chart 1
CALORIE COUNTER

Food Eaten	Amount	g Fat	g Fiber	Calories
TOTALS				

Chart 2

THE CALORIE GUIDE*

Almonds, roasted in oil, 1 oz.	178	soft drinks, 12 oz.	
Apple, 1 raw with skin,		cola	144
3″ diam.	96	cream soda	156
Apple butter, 1 tbsp.	33	fruit drinks	168
Apple juice, 1 cup	117	ginger ale	109
Apple sauce, unsweetened,		root beer	156
1 cup	100	tea, 1 cup	
Apricots, raw, 3 medium	55	no sugar	0
Artichoke, globe, cooked	53	with sugar	30
Artichoke hearts, 3 frozen	22	with sugar & milk	40
Asparagus, cooked 4 spears	12	Biscuits, 1 medium	130
Avocado, 1 medium	378	Blackberries, 1 cup	65
		Blueberries, 1 cup	85
Bacon		Bran, 1 cup, raw	120
cooked, 2 slices	86	Branflakes, 1 cup	106
Canadian, 1 slice cooked	58	Breads, 1 slice or piece	
Bagel, medium	170	banana	135
Banana, 1 medium	101	corn	95
Barbecue sauce, 2 tbsp.	28	French	44
Beans, cooked, 1 cup		pumpernickel	80
kidney, navy, northern	200	raisin	66
Bean sprouts, 1 cup raw	45	white or whole wheat	74
Beef, cooked, 4 oz.		Breadcrumbs, ¼ cup	98
chuck roast, lean	219	Broccoli, cooked, 1 stalk	47
flank steak, lean	222	Brussels sprouts, 1 cup	56
round steak, lean	214	Butter	
sirloin steak, lean	235	regular, 1 tbsp.	102
Beets, canned, 1 cup	63	whipped, 1 tbsp.	67
Beverages			
cider, 4 oz.	125	Cabbage, cooked, 1 cup	29
cocoa, with milk, 1 cup	175	Cakes, 1/12 of cake, no icing	
coffee, 1 cup		angel food	161
black	5	cupcake	172
with sugar	35	fruit cake	163
with sugar & cream	65	pound	142
lemonade, 8 oz.	105	Candy	
milk, 8 oz.		butterscotch, 1 piece	20
chocolate	205	candy corn, 10 pieces	51
skim	80	chocolate kisses, 1 oz.	150
whole	160	marshmallows, 1 regular	23
milk shake, 8 oz.	420	Cantaloupe, ½ melon	60

*Information for this table was taken from: (1) *Bowes and Church's Food Values of Portions Commonly Used*, 14th ed., J. Pennington and H. Church, J. B. Lippincott Company, Philadelphia, 1985; and (2) *The LEARN Program for Weight Control*, K. Brownell, University of Pennsylvania School of Medicine, Philadelphia, 1988. Also note that prepackaged foods have not been included on this list to any great extent. Your best resource for calorie and fat levels for prepackaged foods is on the food label.

Carrots		sugar	36
raw, 1	30	sugar wafers	46
cooked, 1 cup	48	vanilla wafer	19
Cashew nuts, 9 medium	80	Corn, cooked, 1 cup	137
Cauliflower, 1 cup	28	Cornstarch, 1 tbsp.	30
Celery, 1 stalk	7	Crab, canned, 4 oz.	116
Cereals, 1 cup		Crackers	
Alpha Bits	110	cheese	15
branflakes	106	matzo	80
Cap'n Crunch	151	Melba toast	15
Cheerios	89	oyster	3
corn flakes	95	Ritz	15
Cream of Wheat	130	Ry-Krisp	20
Grape Nuts, ¼ cup	110	saltine	15
Kix	100	Wheat Thins	10
oatmeal	150	Cranberries, raw, 1 cup	44
Product 19	110	Cranberry juice, 6 oz.	124
puffed rice	50		
Rice Krispies	105	Dates, pitted, 10	219
shredded wheat, 1 oz.	85	Donuts, raised, yeast, or cake	125
Sugar Smacks	110		
Trix	112	Eggs	
Wheat Chex, ½ cup	100	fresh, 1 large	82
Cheese, 1 oz.		fresh, whites, 1	17
American	105	fresh, yolks, 1	59
Cheddar	111	Eggplant, cooked, 1 cup	38
cottage, ½ cup	120		
Gorgonzola	112	Figs, 1 medium	40
Monterey	102	Fish, 4 oz., cooked, most types	200
mozzarella	79	Flour, 1 tbsp.	25
Parmesan	110	Fruit cocktail, water pack,	
Swiss	104	1 cup	91
Velveeta	90		
Chicken, broiled, 4 oz., no skin	154	Gelatin	
Chicken pot pie, small pie	545	plain, 1 tbsp.	35
Chow mein, chicken, 1 cup	255	fruit flavors, ½ cup	80
Clams		diet, ½ cup	8
cherrystone, 6 large	56	Grapefruit, ½ medium	40
steamers, 4 large or 9 small	80	Grapefruit juice, 1 cup	96
Coconut, shredded, 1 cup	345	Grapes, ½ cup	50
Collards, cooked, 1 cup	59	Grape Juice, 1 cup	167
Cookies, 1 piece			
Animal Crackers	10	Honey, 1 tbsp.	64
brownies, nuts, not iced	97		
chocolate chip	50	Ice cream, 1 cup	
chocolate fudge sandwich	100	chocolate	256
creme sandwich	46	French vanilla	323
fig bar	50	Ice milk, vanilla, 1 cup	200
gingersnaps	30		
graham cracker	30	Jams, 1 tbsp.	54
macaroon	90	Jellies, 1 tbsp.	55
oatmeal, with raisins	59		
Oreo	40	Kale, raw, 4 oz.	80

Ketchup, 1 tbsp.	20
Lamb, loin chops, lean, 4 oz.	213
Lard, 1 tbsp.	117
Leeks. raw, 1	17
Lemon, peeled	20
Lemon juice, 1 tbsp.	4
Lettuce, fresh, iceberg, 1 head	70
Lima beans, 1 cup	185
Liver, cooked, beef, 4 oz.	260
Lobster, cooked, 1 cup	138
Macadamia nuts, 6	106
Macaroni, cooked, 1 cup	155
Mangoes, 1 fruit	152
Margarine	
1 pat or 1 tsp.	36
1 tbsp.	102
Marshmallow, 1 reg.	23
Mayonnaise 1 tbsp.	100
light, 1 tbsp.	45
Melba toast, 1 slice	25
Milk, 1 cup	
whole, 3.5% fat	159
skim	88
low-fat, 2% fat	145
Molasses, 1 tbsp.	46
Mushrooms, sliced, 1 cup	20
Muskmelons	
cantaloupe, 1 cup	60
honeydew, 1 cup	65
Mussels, 4 oz.	108
Mustard, 1 tsp.	5
Nectarine, 1 average	88
Noodles	
egg, cooked, 1 cup	200
chow mein, canned, 1 cup	220
Nuts, mixed, 8–12	95
Oils, all vegetable, 1 tbsp.	120
Okra, sliced, 1 cup	36
Olives, 5 small	16
Onions, 1 medium	40
Oranges, large	71
Orange juice, 1 cup	120
Oysters, 13–19 medium	158
Pancakes, 1 large	164
Papaya, medium	119
Peaches, 1 medium	38
Peanuts, 10 nuts	105
Peanut butter, 1 tbsp.	94

Pears, 1 medium	100
Peas, ½ cup, canned	82
Pecans, 10 medium	96
Peppers, sweet, 1 cup	18
Pickles	
dill, 1 medium	7
sweet, Gerkins, 1	22
relish, sweet, 1 tbsp.	21
Piecrust, ⅛ crust	112
Pineapple	
fresh, diced, 1 cup	81
canned, water pack, 1 cup	96
Pineapple juice, 1 cup	138
Pizza, ⅛ of 14″ pie, cheese	153
Plums, prune type, 1	21
Popcorn	
popped, plain, 1 cup	23
popped in oil, 1 cup	41
Potatoes	
baked, 1 medium	145
French fried, 4 oz.	311
mashed, with milk, 1 cup	137
sweet potatoes, 4 oz.	125
Potato chips	
10 chips	114
1 oz.	161
Pretzels	
Dutch, 1 large	60
10 sticks or 1 three-ring	20
Prunes, dried, 1 cup	253
Puddings, ½ cup, made with	
skim milk	
banana	150
butterscotch	165
chocolate	165
rice	125
tapioca, vanilla	155
Pumpkin, canned, 1 cup	81
Radishes, 10 medium	8
Raisins, 1 tbsp.	26
Raspberries, 1 cup	70
Rice	
brown, cooked, 1 cup	232
white, cooked, 1 cup	223
Rice mixes (commercial)	
beef, 1 cup	320
chicken, 1 cup	314
wild, 1 cup	282
Rolls and buns	
brown & serve	84
Danish pastry, plain	317
hard roll, Kaiser	156

hot dog or hamburger bun, small	119	Spaghetti		
		dry, 4 oz.	419	
hamburger bun, large	210	cooked, tender, 1 cup	155	
		Spinach, 1 cup	14	
Salad dressings, 1 tbsp.		Squash		
blue cheese	86	acorn, 1 squash	190	
blue cheese, light	25	zucchini, sliced, 1 cup	22	
French	66	Strawberries, 1 cup	55	
French, light	15	Sugar		
Italian	83	brown, packed, 1 cup	821	
Italian, light	8	granulated, 1 cup	770	
mayonnaise	100	granulated, 1 tbsp.	46	
mayonnaise, light	40	granulated, 1 lump (2 cubes)	19	
Thousand Island	80	powdered, 1 cup	462	
Thousand Island, light	27	Sunflower seeds, hulled, 1 oz.	159	
Sardines, in oil, 4 oz.	352	Sweet potatoes, baked, 4 oz.	125	
Sauces, 1 tbsp.				
barbecue	17	Tangerines	39	
cheese, ¼ cup	130	Tomatoes		
chili	15	fresh, 1 medium	27	
chocolate	45	canned, 1 cup	51	
tartar	95	puree, canned, 1 cup	100	
tomato, canned, ¼ cup	30	Tomato juice, canned, 1 cup	46	
Worcestershire	10	Tomato juice, cocktail, 1 cup	51	
Sauerkraut, 1 cup	42	Tomato paste, canned, 4 oz.	93	
Scallops, 4 oz.	127	Tortilla		
Sesame seeds, 1 tbsp.	47	5″ corn	60	
Shortening, 1 tbsp.	100	6″ flour	100	
Shrimp, fresh, 4 oz.	103	Tuna, canned, in water, 4 oz.	144	
Soft drinks, 12 oz., regular	120	Turkey, roasted, 4 oz. no skin	216	
Soup, commercial, 1 cup		Turnips, 1 cup	39	
bean	200			
beef broth (bouillon)	31	Veal, cooked, 4 oz.	270	
celery, cream	86	Vegetables, mixed, 1 cup	116	
chicken, consomme	22	Venison, roasted	166	
chicken, cream	94			
chicken, noodle	62	Waffles, 7″ diam.	209	
chicken with rice	48	Walnuts, shelled, 1 oz.	178	
clam chowder, Manhattan	76	Water chestnuts, 4 oz.	69	
clam chowder, New England	175	Watermelon	42	
minestrone	105	Wheat germ, 1 tbsp	29	
mushroom, cream	134	Yeast, baker's, dry, 1 oz.	80	
tomato	88	Yogurt, 1 cup		
vegetable	65	plain, skimmed milk	123	
vegetable beef	70	plain, whole milk	153	
Soybeans, cooked, 1 cup	234	fruit-flavored, low-fat	250	
Soybean curd (tofu), 1 oz.	20	frozen, low-fat	250	

Chart 3

PERCENT FAT AND NUTRIENT CONTENT OF SELECTED FOODS*

This list is provided as a means to make nutritional comparisons between general types of foods. It is not an exhaustive list, but is included primarily so that you can make a comparison of fat content of different meats, dairy products, and other potentially high-fat foods. The % fat content is based on its portion of the total calorie value.

Food, Amount	Calories (kcal)	Fat (g)	Protein (g)	Carbo-hydrate (g)	Choles-terol (mg)	% Fat**
Meat, Fish, and Eggs						
Ground beef, X-lean, cooked, 3 oz.	185	10	23	0	72	49
Ground beef, regular, cooked, 3 oz.	235	17	20	0	75	65
Round roast or steak, lean, cooked, 3 oz.	165	7	25	0	68	38
Ribs or rib roast, cooked, 3 oz.	375	33	17	0	75	79
Liver, beef, cooked, 3 oz.	195	9	22	0	407	42
Liver, chicken, cooked, 3 oz.	185	9	21	0	633	44
Pork loin, roasted, lean, 3 oz.	225	12	25	0	76	48
Lean ham, cooked, 3 oz.	195	11	24	0	76	50
Chicken, light meat, cooked, no skin, 3 oz.	142	4	27	0	72	25
Chicken, dark meat, cooked, no skin, 3 oz.	151	6	24	0	78	36
Turkey, light meat, cooked, no skin, 3 oz.	151	3	28	0	58	18

*Portions of this table are from *Prime Time: A Complete Health Guide for Women Age 35 to 65*, Sneed and Sneed, Word Books, Waco, TX, 1989.
**% fat as a portion of the total calories.

Food, Amount	Calories (kcal)	Fat (g)	Protein (g)	Carbo-hydrate (g)	Choles-terol (mg)	% Fat**
Turkey, dark meat, cooked, no skin, 3 oz.	174	7	26	0	72	36
Halibut, cod, cooked, 3 oz.	120	1	24	0	52	8
Shrimp, steamed, shelled, 3 oz.	100	2	23	0	175	18
Crab, meat only, cooked, 3 oz.	90	2	22	0	86	20
Oysters, shucked, cooked, 3 oz.	120	2	23	0	54	15
Egg, whole, large	80	6	7	0	274	68
Egg, yolk	70	6	3	0	274	77
Egg, white	10	0	4	0	0	0
Milk, Yogurt, and Cheeses						
Milk, whole, 8 oz.	160	9	8	12	33	50
Milk, 2% low-fat, 8 oz.	120	5	8	12	18	37
Milk, 1% low-fat, 8 oz.	105	2	8	12	10	17
Milk, skim, 8 oz.	90	1	9	12	5	10
Yogurt, nonfat, plain, 8 oz.	90	1	9	12	5	10
Yogurt, fruit-flavored, 8 oz.	230	2	8	47	5	8
Cottage cheese, creamed, ½ cup	120	5	15	4	17	37.5
Cottage cheese, low-fat, ½ cup	90	2	15	4	5	20
Natural cheddar cheese, (Swiss, Jack, munster, etc.), 1 oz.	115	9	7	1	30	70
Mozzarella, part-skimmed milk, 1 oz.	90	6	5	1	17	60
Sour cream, 1 tbsp.	26	3	0	1	5	95

*Portions of this table are from *Prime Time: A Complete Health Guide for Women Age 35 to 65*, Sneed and Sneed, Word Books, Waco, TX, 1989.
**% fat as a portion of the total calories.

Food, Amount	Calories (kcal)	Fat (g)	Protein (g)	Carbo- hydrate (g)	Choles- terol (mg)	% Fat**
Borden Lite-line cheese slices, 1 slice	35	1	5	1	7	26
Fats and Oils						
Beef fat, 1 tbsp.	126	13	0	0	14	100
Chicken fat, 1 tbsp.	126	13	0	0	11	100
Butter, 1 tbsp.	107	11	0	0	31	100
Corn oil (or other vegetable oil), 1 tbsp.	126	14	0	0	0	100
Margarine, stick or tub, 1 tbsp.	108	11	0	0	0	100
Diet margarine, 1 tbsp.	50	6	0	0	0	100
Shortening, vegetable	124	13	0	0	0	100
Mayonnaise, 1 tbsp.	100	11	0	0	8	100
Mayonnaise-type salad dressing, 1 tbsp.	60	5	0	0	4	100
Thousand Island, regular, 1 tbsp.	70	6	0	0	4	100
Italian, regular, 1 tbsp.	77	7	0	0	0	100
Nuts						
Peanuts, dry roasted, salted, 2 tbsp.	170	14	9	5	0	75
Walnuts, chopped, 2 tbsp.	98	9	2	2	0	83
Pecans, 12 halves, 2 tbsp., chopped	104	9	2	2	0	78
Peanut butter, 2 tbsp.	175	14	8	6	0	72

*Portions of this table are from *Prime Time: A Complete Health Guide for Women Age 35 to 65*, Sneed and Sneed, Word Books, Waco, TX, 1989.
**% fat as a portion of the total calories.

Chart 4

NUTRITIONAL VALUE OF CEREALS
(values are for 1 ounce serving)

Cereal	Calories	Grams of Fiber	Grams of Sugar	Grams of Fat
Nabisco Shredded Wheat N' Bran	110	4	0	1
Nabisco Spoon Size Shredded Wheat	110	3	0	1
Nabisco Shredded Wheat	110	3	0	1
Fiber One	60	12	2	1
Frosted Mini-Wheats	110	3	6	0
All Bran	70	9	5	1
Nutri-Grain Wheat	110	2	2	0
Grape-Nuts	110	2	3	0
Post Natural Bran Flakes	90	5	5	0
Wheat Chex	100	2	2	0
Nutri-Grain Corn	110	2	2	1
Special K	110	0	3	0
Bran Chex	90	5	5	0
Cheerios	110	2	1	2
Nutri-Grain Wheat & Raisins	100	1	6	0
Sun Country Granola & Raisins	130	1	6	5
Grape-Nuts Flakes	100	2	5	1
Kellogg's Bran Flakes	90	4	5	0
Life	120	1	6	2
Sun Flakes Crispy Wheat & Rice	110	0	0	1
Total	130	2	3	1
100% Natural Cereal Raisin & Date	130	0	5	5
Wheaties	110	2	3	1
Crispix	110	0	3	0
Fruit & Fibre Harvest Medley	90	4	7	1
Fruit & Fibre Mountain Trail	90	4	7	1
Fruit & Fibre Tropical Fruit	90	4	6	1
Kellogg's Corn Flakes	110	0	2	0
100% Natural Cereal	140	0	6	6
Quaker Corn Bran	110	5	6	1
Fruitful Bran	90	4	8	0
Product 19	110	0	3	0

Cereal	Calories	Grams of Fiber	Grams of Sugar	Grams of Fat
Raisin Life	100	1	10	1
Rice Chex	110	0	2	0
Rice Krispies	110	0	3	0
Super Golden Crisp	110	0	14	0
Corn Chex	110	0	3	0
Honey Smacks	110	0	16	0
Post Natural Raisin Bran	90	4	9	0
Kellogg's Raisin Bran	80	4	9	1
Almond Delight	110	1	8	2
Corn Pops	110	0	12	0
Cracklin' Oat Bran	120	4	8	4
Apple Jacks	110	0	14	0
Froot Loops	110	0	13	1
Cocoa Krispies	110	0	10	0
Crispy Wheats & Raisins	110	0	10	1
Frosted Flakes	110	0	11	0
Honey-Comb	110	0	11	0
Lucky Charms	110	0	11	1
Cocoa Pebbles	110	0	13	1
Fruity Pebbles	110	0	12	1
Golden Grahams	110	0	9	1
Honey Nut Cheerios	110	0	10	1
Trix	110	0	12	1
Cocoa Puffs	110	0	11	1
Cap'n Crunch	120	0	12	2

Notes: Copyright 1986 by Consumers Union of United States, Inc., Mount Vernon, NY 10553. Excerpted by permission from *Consumer Reports*, October 1986. The article in *Consumer Reports* also contained figures for protein and sodium.

Fiber levels shown as "0" were listed as "trace" amounts in the original article from *Consumer Reports*. Therefore, levels shown as 0 refer to less than 1 gram.

Chart 5

FOODS AND FAT CONTENT

% Fat Compared with the Total Calories	Foods
100%	Meat fat, oils (all types), shortening, nonstick sprays, butter, margarine, oleo
90–95%	Most regular salad dressings (including Italian, French, Ranch, Thousand Island, Green Goddess, etc.), olives (all types), cream cheese, macadamia nuts, sour cream, cream
80–89%	Avocados, fresh coconut, sesame seeds, light cream cheese, most nuts (including walnuts, almonds, pecans, etc.)
70–79%	Most brick cheeses (including cheddar, brick, Swiss, etc.), peanuts, peanut butter, American cheese, ribs or rib roast, egg yolk
60–69%	Whole egg, ricotta whole-milk cheese, mozzarella whole-milk cheese, Romano cheese, cheese sauce, regular ground beef
50–59%	Mozzarella part-skim milk cheese, parmesan cheese, chocolate bars with nuts, lean ham, whole milk
40–49%	Ground round, beef liver, roasted and lean pork loin, sardines (no oil), cakes with frosting, biscuits, waffles, cream pies, pastries, ice cream
30–39%	Round steak (no fat); dark meat chicken (no skin); dark meat turkey (no skin); fatty fish (flounder, salmon, pompano); creamed cottage cheese; milk chocolate; most granolas, brownies, and many cookies; cheesecake; muffins; fruit pies
20–29%	Light meat chicken (no skin), 2% low-fat milk, low-fat cottage cheese, rice mixes
9–19%	Light meat turkey (no skin), shellfish (crab, oysters, lobster), flour tortillas, ice milk

% Fat Compared with the Total Calories	Foods
Less than 9%	Lean fish (cod, halibut, hake), skim milk, nonfat yogurt, most flakes or nugget breakfast cereals, most breads, corn tortillas, frozen yogurt
0%	Egg white, rice, most vegetables and fruits, sugar candy (jelly beans, hard candy)

Chart 6

FAST FOOD CHART

	Calories	Fat (g)	Cholesterol (mg)	% Fat
Arby's				
*Roast Beef, reg.	350	15	39	39
*Roast Beef, jr.	218	8	20	33
Roast Beef, super	501	22	40	40
Roast Beef, deluxe	486	23	59	43
Beef'n Cheddar	490	21	51	39
Chicken Breast Sandwich	592	27	57	41
Potato Cakes, 2	201	14	1	63
French Fries	211	8	6	34
Bac'n Cheddar Deluxe	561	34	78	55
*Hot Ham & Cheese	353	13	50	33
Turkey Deluxe	375	17	39	41
Baked Potato, plain	290	1	0	3
Superstuffed Potato, Deluxe	648	38	72	53
**Roasted Chicken Breast	254	7	200	25
Chicken Salad Sandwich	386	20	30	47
Tossed Salad, plain	44	0	0	0
Vanilla Shake	295	10	30	31
Chocolate Shake	384	11	32	26
Burger King				
Whopper	640	41	94	58
Whopper, with cheese	723	48	117	60
*Whopper Junior	370	17	41	41
Whopper Junior, cheese	420	20	52	43
*Hamburger	275	12	37	39
Cheeseburger	317	15	48	43
Bacon Double Cheeseburger	510	31	104	55
French Fries, reg.	227	13	14	52
Onion Rings, reg.	274	16	0	53
Apple Pie	305	12	4	35
Whaler Fish Sandwich	488	27	84	50
Whaler, with cheese	530	30	95	51
Chicken Sandwich	688	40	82	52
Chicken Tenders	204	10	47	44

*Reasonable Choices
**Best Choices

	Calories	Fat (g)	Cholesterol (mg)	% Fat
Breakfast Croissanwich				
Bacon, Egg, Cheese	355	24	249	62
Sausage, Egg, Cheese	538	41	293	69
Ham, Egg, Cheese	335	20	262	54
Scrambled Egg Platter	468	30	370	58
Scram. Egg Plat. & Sausage	702	52	420	67
French Toast Platter/Bacon	469	30	73	58
Salad, plain	28	0	0	0
Cherry Pie	357	13	6	33
Pecan Pie	459	20	4	39
Chocolate Shake, med.	320	12	N/A	34
Vanilla Shake, med.	321	10	N/A	28
Church's				
Fried Chicken				
Breast	278	17	N/A	55
Wing-Breast	303	20	N/A	59
Thigh	306	22	N/A	65
Leg	147	9	N/A	55
Crispy Nuggets	55	3	N/A	49
Hush Puppies	78	3	N/A	11
*Dinner Roll	83	2	N/A	22
French Fries	256	13	N/A	45
Cole Slaw	83	7	N/A	76
Pecan Pie	367	20	N/A	49
Dairy Queen				
Cone, small	140	4	10	26
Cone, large	340	10	25	26
Dipped Cone, small	190	9	10	43
Dipped Cone, large	510	24	30	42
Sundae, small	190	4	10	19
Sundae, large	440	10	30	20
Shake, small	490	13	35	24
Shake, large	990	26	70	24
Malt, small	520	13	35	23
Float	410	7	20	15
Banana Split	540	11	30	18
Parfait	430	8	30	17
Hot Fudge Brownie Delight	600	25	20	38
Mr. Misty, small	190	0	0	0
Buster Bar	460	29	10	57

	Calories	Fat (g)	Cholesterol (mg)	% Fat
Dilly Bar	210	13	10	56
DQ Sandwich	140	4	5	26
*Single Hamburger	360	16	45	40
Single Hamburger, cheese	410	20	50	44
Double Hamburger	530	28	85	48
Double Hamburger, cheese	650	37	95	51
Hot Dog	280	16	45	51
Hot Dog & Chili	320	20	55	56
Hot Dog & Cheese	330	21	55	57
*Fish Filet Sandwich	400	17	50	38
Chicken Sandwich	670	41	75	55
French Fries, small	200	10	10	45
Onion Rings	280	16	15	51
Hardee's				
*Hamburger	305	13	N/A	38
Cheeseburger	335	17	N/A	46
Big Deluxe	546	26	77	43
1/4 Pound Cheeseburger	506	26	61	46
Roast Beef Sandwich	377	17	57	41
Big Roast Beef	418	19	60	41
Hot Dog	346	22	42	57
*Hot Ham & Cheese	376	15	59	36
Fisherman's Fillet Sandwich	514	26	41	46
Chicken Fillet	510	26	57	46
Bacon Cheeseburger	686	42	295	55
Sausage Biscuit	413	26	29	57
Sausage & Egg Biscuit	521	35	293	60
Bacon & Egg Biscuit	405	26	305	58
French Fries, small	239	13	4	49
Apple Turnover	282	14	5	45
Milkshake	391	10	42	23
Jack In The Box				
*Hamburger	276	12	29	39
Cheeseburger	323	15	42	42
Jumbo Jack, with cheese	630	35	110	50
Bacon Cheeseburger Supreme	724	46	70	57
Mushroom Burger	477	27	87	51
Moby Jack	444	25	47	51
Taco, reg.	191	11	21	52
Super Taco	288	17	37	53

	Calories	Fat (g)	Cholesterol (mg)	% Fat
**Club Pita	284	8	43	25
Chicken Supreme	601	36	60	54
Sausage Crescent	584	43	187	66
*Pancakes Breakfast	626	27	85	39
Scrambled Eggs Breakfast	719	44	260	55
Bacon, 2 slices	70	6	10	77
*Chicken Strips Dinner	689	30	100	39
Shrimp Dinner	731	37	157	46
*Sirloin Steak Dinner	699	27	75	35
Cheese Nachos	571	35	37	55
Pasta Seafood Salad	394	22	48	50
Taco Salad	377	24	102	57
French Fries, reg.	221	12	8	49
Onion Rings	382	23	27	54
Apple Turnover	410	24	15	53
Vanilla Shake	320	6	25	17
Chocolate Shake	330	7	25	19
Kentucky Fried Chicken				
Wing, original recipe	181	12	67	60
Wing, extra crispy	218	16	63	66
Breast, original recipe	276	17	96	55
Breast, extra crispy	354	24	66	61
Drumstick, original recipe	147	9	81	55
Drumstick, extra crispy	173	11	65	57
Thigh, original recipe	278	19	122	61
Thigh, extra crispy	371	26	121	63
Kentucky Nuggets (one)	46	3	12	59
Kentucky Fries	268	13	2	44
**Mashed Potatoes & Gravy	62	1	1	15
Buttermilk Biscuit	269	14	1	47
Potato Salad	141	9	11	57
Baked Beans	105	1	1	9
Corn on the Cob	176	3	1	15
Cole Slaw	103	6	4	52
Long John Silver's				
3 Pc. Fish & Fryes	853	48	106	51
2 Pc. Fish & Fryes	651	36	75	50
3 Pc. Fish Dinner	1180	70	119	53
3 Pc. Chicken Planks Dinner	885	51	25	52
6 Pc. Chick. Nuggets Dinner	699	45	25	58

	Calories	Fat (g)	Cholesterol (mg)	% Fat
Seafood Platter	976	58	95	53
Clam Dinner	955	58	27	55
Fried Shrimp Dinner	711	45	127	57
Fish Sandwich Platter	835	42	75	45
Seafood Salad	426	30	113	63
Ocean Chef Salad	229	8	64	31
Fryes	247	12	13	44
Cole Slaw	182	15	12	74
Hush Puppies	145	7	1	43
McDonald's				
Chicken McNuggets	323	21	73	59
Hamburger	263	11	29	38
Cheeseburger	328	16	41	44
Quarter Pounder	427	24	81	51
Quarter Pounder, cheese	525	32	107	55
Big Mac	570	35	83	55
Filet-O-Fish	435	26	45	54
Mc D.L.T.	680	44	101	58
French Fries, reg.	220	12	9	49
Biscuit, Sausage, Egg	585	40	285	62
Biscuit, Bacon, Egg, Cheese	483	32	263	60
Sausage McMuffin	427	26	59	55
Sausage McMuffin, Egg	517	33	287	57
Egg McMuffin	340	16	259	42
Hot Cakes, butter, syrup	500	10	47	18
Scrambled Eggs	180	13	514	65
Sausage	210	19	39	81
English Muffin, butter	186	53	15	N/A
Hash Brown Potatoes	125	7	7	50
Strawberry Sundae	320	9	25	25
Hot Fudge Sundae	357	11	27	28
Caramel Sundae	361	10	31	25
Apple Pie	253	14	12	50
Cherry Pie	260	14	13	40
McDonaldland Cookies	308	11	10	32
Chocolate Chip Cookies	342	16	18	42
Chef's Salad	220	13	125	53
Shrimp Salad	99	3	187	27
Garden Salad	91	6	110	59
French Dressing, 1 packet	228	10	1	39
House Dressing, 1 packet	326	17	7	47

	Calories	Fat (g)	Cholesterol (mg)	% Fat
Blue Ch. Dress., 1 packet	342	17	16	45
Vanilla Shake	352	8	31	20
Chocolate Shake	383	9	30	21

Pizza Hut (serving size—2 slices of medium 13″ pizza; 4 servings per pizza)

THIN 'N CRISPY				
**Standard Cheese	340	11	22	29
*Superstyle Cheese	410	14	30	31
Standard Pepperoni	370	15	27	36
Superstyle Pepperoni	430	19	34	40
*Standard Pork w/Mushrooms	380	14	35	33
*Superstyle Pork w/Mushrooms	450	19	40	38
Supreme	400	17	13	38
Super Supreme	520	26	44	45
THICK 'N CHEWY				
**Standard Cheese	390	10	18	23
*Superstyle Cheese	450	14	21	28
*Standard Pepperoni	450	16	21	32
Superstyle Pepperoni	490	20	24	37
*Standard Pork w/Mushroom	430	14	21	29
*Superstyle Pork w/Mushroom	500	18	21	32
Supreme	480	18	24	34
Super Supreme	590	26	38	40

Roy Rogers

	Calories	Fat (g)	Cholesterol (mg)	% Fat
Hamburger	456	28	73	55
Cheeseburger	563	37	95	59
RR Bar Burger	611	39	115	57
Bacon Cheeseburger	581	39	103	60
Roast Beef Sandwich	317	10	55	28
Chicken, breast	324	19	324	53
Chicken, wing	142	10	52	63
Chicken, thigh	282	20	89	64
Chicken, leg	117	7	64	54
Potato, plain	211	0	0	0
Potato, oleo	274	7	0	23

	Calories	Fat (g)	Cholesterol (mg)	% Fat
Potato, sour cream	408	21	31	46
Potato, broccoli, cheese	376	18	19	43
Potato, bacon, cheese	397	22	34	50
Biscuit	231	12	5	47
French Fries, reg.	268	14	42	47
Cole Slaw	110	7	5	57
Potato Salad	107	6	5	50
Breakfast Crescent	401	27	148	61
Breakfast Crescent, bacon	431	30	156	63
Breakfast Crescent, sausage	449	29	168	58
Egg, Biscuit Platter	394	27	284	62
Egg, Biscuit, Bacon	435	30	294	62
Pancake Platter	452	15	53	30
Pancake Platter, sausage	608	30	94	44
Apple Danish	249	12	15	43
Strawberry Shortcake	447	19	28	38
Brownie	264	11	10	37
Hot Fudge Sundae	337	13	23	35
Vanilla Shake	306	11	40	32
Chocolate Shake	358	10	37	25
Taco Bell				
*Bean Burrito	343	12	N/A	31
Beef Burrito	466	21	N/A	41
Beefy Tostada	331	18	N/A	49
*Bellbeefer	221	7	N/A	29
*Bellbeefer w/cheese	278	12	N/A	39
Burrito Supreme	457	22	N/A	43
*Combination Burrito	404	16	N/A	36
Enchirito	454	21	N/A	42
**Pintos 'N Cheese	168	5	N/A	27
Taco	192	11	N/A	52
Tostada	156	11	N/A	63
Taco Supreme	237	15	N/A	57
Taco Bellgrande	410	26	N/A	57
Taco Light	170	26	N/A	N/A
Wendy's				
Single Hamburger	350	18	65	46
Double Hamburger	560	34	125	55
Bacon Cheeseburger	460	28	65	55
Chicken Sandwich	320	10	59	28

	Calories	Fat (g)	Cholesterol (mg)	% Fat
Kid's Meal Hamburger	220	8	20	33
Chili, 8 oz.	260	8	30	28
French Fries, reg.	280	14	15	45
Taco Salad	390	18	40	42
Baked Potato, plain	250	2	0	7
Baked Potato, sour cream	460	24	15	47
Baked Potato, cheese	590	34	22	52
Baked Potato, chili, cheese	510	20	22	35
Ham & Cheese Omelet	250	17	450	61
French Toast, 2	400	19	115	43
Home Fries	360	22	20	55
Frosty Dairy Dessert	400	14	50	32

Chart 7

BEHAVIOR MODIFICATION AND CUE ELIMINATION

EATING PLACE

Choose a specific eating place in one room of your home. This will be your *designated appropriate eating place*. It can be in the kitchen, dining room, or den, and may be different for each meal. It should be a place where you can sit down and eat in relative comfort. From now on, eat all of your meals and snacks at your designated appropriate eating place. When you have meals away from home, such as at work, or when out for a meal, the designated appropriate eating place will be just that— a place that you consider to be appropriate. This might be a table in a restaurant, cafeteria, or lunchroom.

When you eat at work, avoid eating at your desk. The object of cue-elimination tasks is to break up the association between eating and other activities such as working. If there is no place to eat other than at your desk, at least change it by adding a place mat and silverware and a real cup for your coffee. Try to make it look different. In one experimental situation, researchers discovered that a brightly colored place mat helped people designate an eating place, which later became a cue for appropriate eating behaviors. A change of this type at work or home can be a great help.

Make your eating place special—a point of luxury in your life, something to enjoy. You can include flowers, music, a comfortable seat, pretty plates, your best silverware—but most important, include enough time. All of these pleasant additions will be cues for a new eating style.

If your appropriate eating place is the dining table, change your habitual place at the table. If you sit at the head of the table, change to the side; if you sit on one side, change places with someone on the other side. This may make things a little less efficient for a while, but it also will break up a lot of longstanding cues at the table. This change need not be forever. Just try it for a few weeks, and see what happens.

ASSOCIATED EATING ACTIVITIES

When eating, only eat. Don't talk on the phone, watch television, read, work, etc. Concentrate on your food and on those with you. Really taste your food, feel the textures, and try to enjoy each mouthful—make your meals enjoyable.

STORING FOOD

Remove food from all places in the house other than appropriate storage areas such as the kitchen. No more candy on the TV, open bags of chips on the kitchen cabinet, fruit in a basket, etc. Put food in cupboards, or keep it in opaque containers that you cannot see through. Do the same for foods in the refrigerator—put everything in "see-proof" containers.

ALTERED ROUTES

Is there a bakery, sweetshop, convenience store, fast-food restaurant, or vending machine that you can't drive or walk past without making a food purchase? These are merely habits—habits which can be broken. Try taking an altered route to work. Avoid the vending machine area at work. Within 1 to 2 months, you will be freed of these annoying habits.

STRESS-RELATED HUNGER AND EATING

Most adults have at some time eaten for reasons other than hunger. Which moods cause you to overeat?

_____   _____   _____

How do you conquer this problem? By reconditioning yourself with new coping mechanisms. The most important thing to remember is that you must change the subject. *Stop.* Quit whatever you are doing (if at all possible). Do something positive for yourself.

Suggestions for alternate activities: go for a walk, go out shopping, do stretching exercises to relaxing music, take a long bath, call a friend on the phone, sew or knit, clear up a project that has waited too long to be done. *Be your own best cheering squad. Think Positive.*

BEHAVIOR CHAINS

Behavior chain-related eating is very similar to the discussion above involving stress and hunger. Behavior chains are frequent activities you pursue that always end in overeating. For example:

work a long hard day → have an ample dinner → sit down in front of the TV → watch a mediocre TV show → feel bored → walk to the kitchen → open pantry ↓

feel depressed ← cheat on your food log ← eat more cookies ← feel guilty ← eat the kids' cookies

If you have identifiable behavior chains which lead you down the path of dietary destruction, break those chains before they progress to the point of no return.

SMALLER PLATES

Research has shown that the size of the plate your food is served on has a large influence on how you perceive the amount of food you are eating and, consequently, how full you feel after the meal. Even though you know that the size of the plate does not make any difference—a spoonful of potatoes is basically a spoonful of potatoes—it seems like more food when it is served on a smaller plate. A psychology experiment demonstrated that 70 percent of the people in a weight reduction program were more satisfied with less food when it was served on a salad plate than when it was served on a dinner plate. Try eating from smaller plates; try to make them a part of your daily routine.

SET SOME ASIDE

All of us have been strongly conditioned to eat everything on our plate, and to feel guilty when we leave some behind. Whether for economy or aesthetics—or, as many of us were taught in childhood, because of all the starving children in the world—almost everyone has been taught this lesson. The implicit belief is that if we finish our meals and eat everything on our plate, it will benefit someone else. The unfortunate corollary to this is, "If I do not finish everything on my plate, somehow I am bad."

Start to break this habit—begin to free yourself of the compulsion to eat everything you are served. To accomplish this, leave food behind at each meal. Start out slowly: one pea, a spoonful of potatoes, or a crust of bread from your sandwich. It may be necessary to set the leftover food aside at the start of the meal and cover it with plastic wrap so you won't forget to leave it behind. Or, at the other end of the meal, you may find it necessary to put the leftover food in the garbage immediately, to prevent yourself from eating it. (This technique can be used later for eliminating problem foods and reducing portion size.)

SECONDS

For those eating large portions, especially at dinner, divide the food you would normally serve yourself into two servings, and go back for seconds when you finish the first half. This introduces a delay and, hopefully, a cognitive or thinking step in the middle of the meal, e.g., "Do I really want seconds or thirds?" It has the added advantage of keeping the second half of the meal warm and more enjoyable when you do eat it. Don't forget to leave some of each portion behind.

THROW AWAY

Throw away any food left on your plate immediately after the meal. Put scraps down the disposal, in the garbage can, or feed them to the cat. In this way, leftovers won't linger around to be nibbled on later in the evening or the next afternoon. If you do keep something, like a chicken wing or a serving of peas, preplan it into a snack for the next day or as part of lunch. Put it in an opaque container, and label it with its specific preplanned use, e.g., "John's lunch." Don't let food hang around the house loose and uncommitted! It will reach out and cue you to eat.

ASK FOR FOOD

Never accept food from another person unless you ask for it. Make each encounter with food a voluntary one. In restaurants, take the initiative—ask the server not to bring potatoes, or to take away the bread. If it is not on the table, you won't nibble on it while you wait for your meal.

MINIMIZE CONTACT

Try to arrange your food contacts in ways that minimize the chances for impulse eating. For example, when you fix yourself a sandwich for lunch, put away the bread, diet mayonnaise, and lite ham, and clean up the mess before you eat your sandwich. This will greatly reduce the likelihood that you will make a second sandwich. Food out of sight is often food out of mind.

Chart 8

HIGH-SODIUM FOODS TO AVOID

Salty or smoked meat such as bacon, bologna, chipped beef, or corned
  beef, frankfurters, ham, meats koshered by salting, luncheon meats,
  salt pork, sausage, smoked tongue*
Salty or smoked fish, anchovies, caviar, salted cod, herring, sardines,
  etc.
Processed cheese or cheese spreads unless low sodium dietetic
Cheese, such as Roquefort, Camembert, or Gorgonzola
Regular peanut butter
Sauerkraut, pickles, or other vegetables prepared in brine or heavily
  salted
V-8 juice
Breads and rolls with salt toppings, bread stuffing
Bacon-flavored bits
Regular salted popcorn
Potato chips
Corn chips
Pizza
Pretzels
Olives
Salted nuts
Party spreads and dips and other heavily salted snack food, such as po-
  tato chips and sticks, crackers
Canned soups, stews, and any kind of commercial bouillon
Instant cocoa mixes
Cooking wine
Italian dressing
Pickles and relishes
Celery salt, garlic salt, and onion salt
Catsup
Chili sauce
Commercial seasonings made of meat and vegetable extracts
Barbecue sauces and meat sauces
Meat tenderizers
Soy sauce
Worcestershire sauce
Baked beans
Convenience and packaged dinners
Frozen waffles

*Rinsing ham or other allowed luncheon meat and blotting dry on paper towels will reduce
  sodium content by almost half.*

Chart 9

SAVORY HERBS

	Flavor	Try with
Basil	Mildly peppery with a trace of mint and clove	Tomato sauces, salad dressings, poultry, fish
Chervil	Warm, part-anise, part-parsley flavor	Omelets, cottage cheese, green beans
Chives	Mild, sweet onion taste	Salads, omelets, potatoes, cottage cheese
Coriander*	Strong sage flavor with a sharp citrus bite	Chicken, beets, onions, chilies, curries
Dill	Slightly sweet with sharp tang	Fish, eggs, carrots, cauliflower, spinach, apples, potatoes, cucumbers, yogurt dips or sauces
Fennel	Soft, nutty anise/celery flavor	Fish, cabbage, soups, salads, breads
Marjoram	Mild oregano taste with hint of balsam	Stuffing, lamb, beef, eggplant, squash
Mint	Cool, refreshing, sweet	Tea, yogurt, fruit, carrots, peas
Oregano	Pungent, peppery, slightly bitter	Pizza, tomatoes, mushrooms, poultry, lentils
Parsley	Gentle, green flavor	Chicken, beef, shellfish, pasta
Sage	Pleasantly bitter, lemony zest	Breads, stuffing, potatoes, pork
Summer savory	Light, sweet with a peppery tang	Beans, lentils, vegetable juices, meat loaf
Sorrel	Lemonlike or vinegary sour taste	Spinach, cabbage, lettuce, fish, mixed salads, coleslaw
Tarragon	Aniselike	Chicken, fish, veal, young vegetables, vinaigrettes
Thyme	Pleasant, fresh taste with faint clove aftertaste	Veal, lamb, poultry, salad dressing, dried beans

*Also known as cilantro or Chinese parsley

Chart 10

CALORIE VALUES FOR TEN MINUTES OF ACTIVITY

	Body Weight		
	125 Pounds	175 Pounds	250 Pounds
Personal and Housekeeping			
Sleeping	10	14	20
Sitting (watching TV)	10	14	18
Dressing or washing	26	37	53
Standing	12	16	24
Making beds	32	46	65
Washing floors	38	53	75
Washing windows	35	48	69
Shoveling snow	65	89	130
Light gardening	30	42	59
Weeding garden	49	68	98
Mowing grass (power)	34	47	67
Locomotion			
Walking downstairs	56	78	111
Walking upstairs	146	202	288
Walking (30 minutes/mile)	29	40	58
Walking (15 minutes/mile)	52	72	102
Running (11 minutes/mile)	90	125	178
Running at 7 mph (8.5 minutes/mile)	118	164	232
Cycling at 5.5 mph (11 minutes/mile)	42	58	83
Swimming (backstroke)	32	45	64
Swimming (crawl)	40	56	80
Sedentary Activities			
Sitting writing	15	21	30
Light office work	25	34	50
Standing, light activity	20	28	40
Typing (electric)	19	27	39
Light Work			
Assembly line	20	28	40
Auto repair	35	48	69
Carpentry	32	44	64
Bricklaying	28	40	57
House painting	29	40	58

	Body Weight		
	125 Pounds	175 Pounds	250 Pounds
Heavy Work			
Pick and shovel work	56	78	110
Chopping wood	60	84	121
Recreation			
Badminton	43	65	94
Baseball	39	54	78
Basketball	58	82	117
Bowling (nonstop)	56	78	111
Canoeing at 4 mph (15 minutes/mile)	90	128	182
Dancing (moderate)	35	48	69
Dancing (vigorous)	48	66	94
Football	69	96	137
Golfing	33	48	68
Horseback riding	56	78	112
Ping-Pong	32	45	64
Racquetball	75	104	144
Skiing (Alpine)	80	112	160
Skiing (water)	60	88	130
Skiing (cross-country)	98	138	194
Squash	75	104	144
Tennis	56	80	115
Volleyball	43	65	94

Chart 11

BENEFITS OF VARIOUS EXERCISES

	Developing Cardiovascular Fitness	Developing Strength	Developing Muscular Endurance	Controlling Body Fat
Backpacking	...	...	....	...
Basketball	....	.	...	....
Bicycling	....	..	...	....
Bowling	.	.	.	.
Circuit training	...	...	...	...
Dance, ballet	...	...	...	...
Dance, exercise	....	..	...	....
Dance, modern	...	..	...	...
Dance, social	..	.	..	..
Football	..	...	..	..
Golf (walking)	..	.	.	..
Gymnastics	..	....	....	..
Hiking	...	..	....	...
Jogging	....	.	...	....
Racquetball	...	.	...	...
Roller skating	..	.	..	..
Skiing, downhill	.	..	..	.
Soccer	....	..	...	....
Swimming	....	..	...	....
Tennis		.	..	..
Walking, fast	...	.	..	...
Weight training	.	....	...	..

.... = excellent   ... = good   .. = fair   . = poor

Chart 12

FOOD EXCHANGE LISTS

#1 STARCH/BREAD EXCHANGES

Bread (25–30 gm.)

White (including French and Italian)	1 slice
Whole wheat	1 slice
Rye or pumpernickel	1 slice
Raisin	1 slice
Bagel	½ small
English muffin	½ small
Frankfurter roll	½
Hamburger roll	½
Matzo (6″ square)	1
Tortilla, corn	1–6″
Tortilla, white flour	¾–8″
Melba toast	4
Lite bread (40 cal./slice)	2 slices

Cereals

Bran flakes	½ cup
Cooked cereal	½ cup
Dry cereal (unsweetened)	¾ cup
Grape-nuts and granola	¼ cup
Puffed cereals (unsweetened)	1½ cups
Grits (cooked)	½ cup
Wheat germ	2 tbsp.

Crackers

Animal crackers	8
Arrowroot	3
Graham (2½″ square)	3
Oyster crackers	20
Rye wafers	3
Rounds, thin	6
Saltines (2″ square)	5
Soda (2½″ square)	3
Vanilla wafers	5

Flour	2½ tbsp.
Rice, grits (cooked)	½ cup
Spaghetti, macaroni, noodles	½ cup
Beans, baked (no pork)	⅓ cup
Bean, lima	⅓ cup
Corn	⅓ cup

Popcorn, readymade	1/2 cup
Potato, mashed	1/2 cup
Potato, white	1/2 medium
Potato, sweet yam	1/4 cup

#2 LEAN MEAT EXCHANGES

Beef

Veal, tenderloin, round (bottom, top), all cuts— rump, sirloin, extra-lean ground round	1 oz.

Lamb

Leg, rib, sirloin, loin (no visible fat)	1 oz.

Pork

Leg (whole rump, center shank), ham, smoked (center slices)	1 oz.

Poultry

Meat of chicken, Cornish hen, and turkey without skin	1 oz.

Fish

Any fresh or frozen canned salmon, tuna, mackerel	1 1/2 oz.
Crab and lobster	1/4 cup
Clams, oysters	1 1/2 oz.
Scallops, shrimp, sardines (drained)	3

Cheese

Low-fat cottage cheese	1/3 cup
Low-fat cheese	1 oz.
Dried beans and peas, cooked	1/2 cup

Eggs and vegetarian alternatives

Egg whites	4
Egg Beaters	1/2 cup
Whole egg	1

#3 MILK AND MILK PRODUCTS EXCHANGES

Milk

Skim, 1/2 of 1%	1 cup
Low-fat buttermilk	1 cup
Evaporated skim milk	1/2 cup
Dry nonfat milk	1/3 cup

Yogurt

Plain nonfat	1 cup

Cheese

Low-fat cottage cheese	1/2 cup
Part-skim milk cheeses	1 oz.

#4 FRUIT AND JUICES EXCHANGES

Apple	$1/2$ medium
Applesauce, unsweetened	$1/2$ cup
Apple juice or cider	$1/3$ cup
Apricots	3 medium
Banana	$1/2$ 6″
Blackberries, blueberries, or raspberries	$3/4$ cup
Cantaloupe (6″ diameter)	$1/4$ medium
Cherries	10 large
Cranberries, no sugar	No limit
Dates	2 medium
Figs	2 small
Fruit cocktail, peaches	$1/2$ cup
Grapefruit	$1/2$ small
Grapefruit juice	$1/2$ cup
Grapes	15 medium
Grape juice	$1/4$ cup
Honeydew melon	$1/4$ medium
Mango	$1/2$ small
Nectarine	1 small
Orange	1 small
Orange juice	$1/2$ cup
Papaya	$1/3$ medium
Peach	1 medium
Pear	1 small
Pineapple	$1/2$ cup
Pineapple juice	$1/3$ cup
Plums	2 medium
Prunes	3 medium
Prune juice	$1/4$ cup
Raisins	2 tbsp.
Rhubarb	No limit
Strawberries, fresh	$1 1/4$ cups
Tangerine	1 medium
Watermelon	1 cup

#5 LOW-CAL VEGETABLES AND FREE FOODS*

Use the following as desired. Eat at least 2 cups/day (4 $1/2$-cup servings per day).

Asparagus	Brussels sprouts	Celery
Bean sprouts	Cabbage	Cucumbers
Beets	Carrots	Eggplant
Broccoli	Cauliflower	Green pepper

*Note: Starchy vegetables are found in the Starch/Bread Food Exchange List.

Greens	Turnip	Summer squash
Beet	Mushrooms	Tomatoes
Chard	Okra	Tomato juice
Collards	Onions	Turnips
Dandelion	Rhubarb	Vegetable juice
Kale	Rutabaga	Zucchini
Mustard	Sauerkraut	
Spinach	String beans	

The following raw vegetables are especially low in calories:

Chicory	Escarole	Radishes
Chinese cabbage	Lettuce	Watercress
Endive	Parsley	

#6 CONDIMENTS, SPICES, AND BEVERAGES

Seasonings
  Flavoring extracts (vanilla, almond, butter, etc.)
  Garlic or garlic powder
  Herbs, fresh or dried
  Lemon or lemon juice
  Lime or lime juice
  Butter substitutes
  Onion powder
  Pepper
  Pimento
  Spices
  Soy sauce
  Worcestershire sauce
Drinks
  Bouillon or broth, no fat
  Cocoa powder, unsweetened baking type (1 tbsp.)
  Coffee or tea
  Soft drinks, calorie-free, including carbonated drinks
Sweet substitutes
  Gelatin, sugar-free
  Jam or jelly, sugar-free (2 tsp.)
  Whipped topping, sugar-free (2 tbsp.)
Condiments
  Catsup (1 tbsp.)
  Dill pickles, unsweetened
  Horseradish
  Hot sauce
  Mustard
  Taco sauce
  Vinegar

#7 FAT EXCHANGES

Concentrated fats
  Oil, butter, margarine, mayonnaise, salad
      dressings   1 tsp.
Low-fat alternatives
  Reduced-calorie margarine   2 tsp.
  Reduced-calorie mayonnaise   2 tsp.
  Reduced-calorie salad dressings   1–2 tbsp. (up to
                                                                     20 cal./tbsp.)

Nuts
  All nuts   1 tbsp.
Others
  Avocado   ⅛ medium
  Olives   10 small
  Bacon   1 strip
  Coconut, shredded   2 tbsp.
  Nondairy creamer   1 tbsp.
  Cream, light   2 tbsp.
  Cream, sour   2 tbsp.
  Cream, heavy   1 tbsp.
  Cream cheese   1 tbsp.
  Cream cheese, lite   1 tbsp.

#8 THE GOODIE EXCHANGE LIST*

May be used up to 4 times per week in place of 1 bread exchange.

Angel food cake   1″ slice
Cake, no icing   1½″ sq.
Cookies   2 small (1½″
                                                                     across)

Frozen yogurt   ⅓ cup
Frozen fruit bars   1 bar
Gingersnaps   3
Granola bars   1 small (100
                                                                     cal. or less)

Ice milk   ½ cup
Ice cream bars, low-cal   1 bar (under
                                                                     100 cal.)

Pudding, made with skim milk   ½ cup
Sherbet and sorbet   ½ cup
Snack chips, baked or lite varieties   ½ oz.
Vanilla wafers   5 small

---

*Reprinted by permission: Sneed and Sneed, *Prime Time.*

#9 COMBINATION AND FAST-FOODS EXCHANGE LIST

Fried chicken fillet sandwich	Average size	3 bread, 1½ meat, 4 fat
Grilled chicken sandwich	Average size	2 bread, 3 meat, 1 fat
Hamburger	Large size	4 bread, 3½ meat, 2 fat
Cheeseburger	Large size	4 bread, 4 meat, 3 fat
Cheeseburger	Average size	2 bread, 2½ meat, 1 fat
Fish sandwich (fried, fast-food type)	Average size	3 bread, 1 meat, 4 fat
French fries	Small size	2 bread, 3 fat
Danish	Average size	2 bread, 3 fat
Beef taco	Small to average	1 bread, 1¼ meat, 1½ fat

Chart 13

DAILY MENU PLANNER

Number of exchanges	Menu for Day _____	Menu for Day _____
Breakfast Starch ___ Meat ___ Milk ___ Fruit ___ Veg ___ Fat ___		
Snack _____ _____		
Lunch Starch ___ Meat ___ Milk ___ Fruit ___ Veg ___ Fat ___		
Snack _____ _____		
Dinner Starch ___ Meat ___ Milk ___ Fruit ___ Veg ___ Fat ___		
Snack _____ _____		

Chart 14

Height and Weight Tables for Adults
Desirable weights for persons age 25 and over*
Weight in pounds according to frame (with indoor clothing)

Height (with 2-in heels) ft in	Women†		
	Small frame (lb)	Medium frame (lb)	Large frame (lb)
4 10	92–98	96–107	104–119
4 11	94–101	98–110	106–122
5 0	96–104	101–113	109–125
5 1	99–107	104–116	112–128
5 2	102–110	107–119	115–131
5 3	105–113	110–122	118–134
5 4	108 116	113–120	121–138
5 5	111–119	116–130	125–142
5 6	114–123	120–135	129–146
5 7	118–127	124–139	133–150
5 8	122–131	128–143	137–154
5 9	126–135	132–147	141–158
5 10	130–140	136–151	145–163
5 11	134–144	140–155	149–168
6 0	138–148	144–159	153–173

Height (with 1-in heels) ft in	Men		
	Small frame (lb)	Medium frame (lb)	Large frame (lb)
5 2	112–120	118–129	126–141
5 3	115–123	121–133	129–144
5 4	118–126	124–136	132–148
5 5	121–129	127–139	135–152
5 6	124–133	130–143	138–156
5 7	128–137	134–147	142–161
5 8	132–141	138–152	147–166
5 9	136–145	142–156	151–170
5 10	140 150	140 100	155–174
5 11	144–154	150–165	159–179
6 0	148–158	154–170	164–184
6 1	152–162	158–175	168–189
6 2	156–167	162–180	173–194
6 3	160–171	167–185	178–199
6 4	164–175	172–190	182–204

*From Metropolitan Life Insurance Co., New York City.
†For girls between 18 and 25 years, subtract 1 pound for each year under 25.

Chart 15

FOOD AND NUTRITION BOARD, NATIONAL ACADEMY OF SCIENCES—NATIONAL RESEARCH COUNCIL RECOMMENDED DIETARY ALLOWANCES,[a] Revised 1989

Designed for the maintenance of good nutrition of practically all healthy people in the United States

							Fat-Soluble Vitamins			
Category	Age (years) or Condition	Weight[b] (kg)	(lb)	Height[b] (cm)	(in)	Protein (g)	Vitamin A (μg RE)[c]	Vitamin D (μg)[d]	Vitamin E (mg α-TE)[e]	Vitamin K (μg)
Infants	0.0–0.5	6	13	60	24	13	375	7.5	3	5
	0.5–1.0	9	20	71	28	14	375	10	4	10
Children	1–3	13	29	90	35	16	400	10	6	15
	4–6	20	44	112	44	24	500	10	7	20
	7–10	28	62	132	52	28	700	10	7	30
Males	11–14	45	99	157	62	45	1,000	10	10	45
	15–18	66	145	176	69	59	1,000	10	10	65
	19–24	72	160	177	70	58	1,000	10	10	70
	25–50	79	174	176	70	63	1,000	5	10	80
	51+	77	170	173	68	63	1,000	5	10	80
Females	11–14	46	101	157	62	46	800	10	8	45
	15–18	55	120	163	64	44	800	10	8	55
	19–24	58	128	164	65	46	800	10	8	60
	25–50	63	138	163	64	50	800	5	8	65
	51+	65	143	160	63	50	800	5	8	65
Pregnant						60	800	10	10	65
Lactating	1st 6 months					65	1,300	10	12	65
	2nd 6 months					62	1,200	10	11	65

[a] The allowances, expressed as average daily intakes over time, are intended to provide for individual variations among most normal persons as they live in the United States under usual environmental stresses. Diets should be based on a variety of common foods in order to provide other nutrients for which human requirements have been less well defined.

[b] Weights and heights of Reference Adults are actual medians for the U.S. population of the designated age, as reported by NHANES II. The median weights and heights of those under 19 years of age were taken from Hamill et al. (1979). The use of these figures does not imply that the height-to-weight ratios are ideal.

[c] Retinol equivalents. 1 retinol equivalent = 1 μg retinol or 6 μg β-carotene. See text for calculation of vitamin A activity of diets as retinol equivalents.

Water-Soluble Vitamins							Minerals						
Vita-min C (mg)	Thia-min (mg)	Ribo-flavin (mg)	Niacin (mg NE)[f]	Vita-min B$_6$ (mg)	Fo-late (µg)	Vitamin B$_{12}$ (µg)	Cal-cium (mg)	Phos-phorus (mg)	Mag-nesium (mg)	Iron (mg)	Zinc (mg)	Iodine (µg)	Sele-nium (µg)
30	0.3	0.4	5	0.3	25	0.3	400	300	40	6	5	40	10
35	0.4	0.5	6	0.6	35	0.5	600	500	60	10	5	50	15
40	0.7	0.8	9	1.0	50	0.7	800	800	80	10	10	70	20
45	0.9	1.1	12	1.1	75	1.0	800	800	120	10	10	90	20
45	1.0	1.2	13	1.4	100	1.4	800	800	170	10	10	120	30
50	1.3	1.5	17	1.7	150	2.0	1,200	1,200	270	12	15	150	40
60	1.5	1.8	20	2.0	200	2.0	1,200	1,200	400	12	15	150	50
60	1.5	1.7	19	2.0	200	2.0	1,200	1,200	350	10	15	150	70
60	1.5	1.7	19	2.0	200	2.0	800	800	350	10	15	150	70
60	1.2	1.4	15	2.0	200	2.0	800	800	350	10	15	150	70
50	1.1	1.3	15	1.4	150	2.0	1,200	1,200	280	15	12	150	45
60	1.1	1.3	15	1.5	180	2.0	1,200	1,200	300	15	12	150	50
60	1.1	1.3	15	1.6	180	2.0	1,200	1,200	280	15	12	150	55
60	1.1	1.3	15	1.6	180	2.0	800	800	280	15	12	150	55
60	1.0	1.2	13	1.6	180	2.0	800	800	280	10	12	150	55
70	1.5	1.6	17	2.2	400	2.2	1,200	1,200	320	30	15	175	65
95	1.6	1.8	20	2.1	280	2.6	1,200	1,200	355	15	19	200	75
90	1.6	1.7	20	2.1	260	2.6	1,200	1,200	340	15	16	200	75

[d] As cholecalciferol. 10 µg cholecalciferol = 400 IU of vitamin D.

[e] α-Tocopherol equivalents. 1 mg d-α tocopherol = 1 α-TE. See text for variation in allowances and calculation of vitamin E activity of the diet as α-tocopherol equivalents.

[f] 1 NE (niacin equivalent) is equal to 1 mg of niacin or 60 mg of dietary tryptophan.

Eating Compulsivity and Comprehensive Care

No book on healthy eating would be complete without considering the human being from a broad spectrum—physical, psychological, and spiritual. Although to some extent this has already been done throughout this book, below is an outline of what is generally considered to promote good health and extend life.

Both medical and lay literature were read in preparation for writing this book. And although one could occasionally find literature to support any opinion one wanted, what stood out much more was agreement in the field. This outline for good health is drawn from three main sources. They are:

1. The Bible—The Bible puts everything in perspective and must always be supreme. While it is certainly not a book on eating compulsivity, it gives important principles that apply to good health and "length of days."
2. Scientific Literature—One is usually on safer ground to go with the bulk of scientific evidence. A few books stray afar and do so on tenuous ground, but most doctors do want the best for their patients and are open to the proven scientific value of various regimens. When the bulk recommend against what seems to be an unproven extreme, beware.
3. Common Sense—Common sense has to do with godly wisdom. It relates to practical application in day-to-day living. Its essence is moderation, being cautious of extremes.

Good health has to do not only with a healthy diet and understanding factors in eating compulsivity but also with understanding the dangers of some bad habits, the benefits of some good habits, and, most importantly of all, the importance of the spiritual.

THE SPIRITUAL

One might ask what a book on healthy eating and good health has to do with the spiritual.

First, the body is the temple of the Holy Spirit, and we should take good care of it. God wants us to have an effective ministry for Him. We can do that better if we feel good and are healthy. Many scientists now believe we could live an average of another twenty to forty years if we would follow good health habits and take advantage of medical science. This may be worth at least some consideration when examining the leading causes of death (heart disease, stroke, cancer, suicide, etc.) and how often they are related to issues we could control (smoking, obesity, high blood pressure, etc.) if we just chose to do so.

Others may argue that God already knows our days (see Psalm 139:16). We would respond that God will do what He is responsible for, but His focus is not our responsibility; rather we need to focus on the human responsibility of taking care of this temple of the Holy Spirit. In early biblical days Methuselah lived to be 969 years old; Noah, 950 years old. We should at least do what we can to move a little in that direction in order to have a longer, more effective ministry for Christ.

Even so, we must ever remind ourselves of the importance of the spiritual over all else. Even one hundred years is but "a vapour" (James 4:14) compared to eternity. Every individual will spend for ever and ever and ever based on what he or she does with Christ. Knowing that Jesus Christ was indeed the Son of God—that He lived on earth for some thirty years, that He died on the cross in payment for sinners like all of us, that He arose from the grave—is not enough.

One must trust that Christ died for us! That simple decision holds the keys to eternity in Heaven. Indeed, to be healthy, to extend one's life is important, but eternity is even more so (John 1:12; 5:36 KJV).

THE PHYSICAL—A MORE PRODUCTIVE LIFE

Scientific information indicates that many Christians could minister more productively for Christ if they would take care of themselves physically. For example, 50 percent of Americans die of heart disease. In fact, heart disease is the leading cause of death in the United States. Heart disease is largely caused by arteriosclerosis. Diet is a significant factor in many cases of arteriosclerosis. A low-fat, high-fiber, low-cholesterol diet does make a difference.

Cancer is another leading cause of death. Increasingly, high-fiber diets are felt to be of help in the prevention of colon cancer.

CHOLESTEROL

Cholesterol is a waxlike substance and is the chief culprit in heart disease. It can be divided into three different types:

1. LDL—low-density lipid proteins.
2. VLDL—very low-density lipid proteins.
3. HDL—high-density lipid proteins.

Actually the HDL fraction is considered "good" and even helps prevent heart disease. Exercise, not smoking, and losing weight probably increase the HDL fraction.

As a rule of thumb the total cholesterol should be below 200 mg/dl. Cholesterol can often be lowered to this level by decreasing the fat in the diet. Individuals from countries with low-saturated-fat diets have lower cholesterol levels and a lower incidence of heart disease. Fiber also lowers cholesterol.

OBESITY

More than 50 percent of Americans are overweight, and obesity is a factor in heart disease, stroke, diabetes (adult onset), bone and joint disease, high blood pressure, and shortened life span.

Obesity may also weaken one's testimony for Christ. A story is told of a great Christian orator of the past who strongly confronted a fellow Christian worker over the sin of smoking. The Christian worker agreed to give up the sin of smoking when the orator would give up the sin of overeating.

Indeed, weight may affect one's testimony, and we need to be sensitive. We also need to realize that many factors affect weight—genetic factors, social factors, cultural factors, disease factors (hypothyroidism, Cushing's syndrome, etc.), discipline, sedentary lifestyles, set-point factors, and hypothalamic factors. Theories of obesity include the fat-cell theory, set-point theory, enzyme theory, sodium-potassium group theory, hormone theory, and activity level theory.

Maintaining weight loss is not easy because of the strong psychological factors dealt with in this book. This is probably the reason it is rare indeed for a person to lose weight and maintain the new weight. Treating the surface problem while ignoring the underlying cause does not make sense.

DIET

On the surface the basic principles seem simple. If caloric intake is reduced to less than caloric expenditure and storage, calories will be consumed, or weight (stored fat) will be lost.

As rule of thumb, at about 800 calories per day, weight will be lost at an accelerated rate. At 1,000 calories per day, weight will be lost at a fast rate. At 1,200 calories, moderate weight loss will result. However, diets and individuals are laden with variation, resistances, and dangers that complicate.

There are many kinds of diets (Dr. Atkins', Dr. Stillman's, the Scarsdale, the Last Chance, the Cambridge, the Beverly Hills, the Pritikin, etc.). Each must modify the only three basic sources of energy available (protein, carbohydrate, fat) since these are the only three variables. Understanding this really simplifies the vast array of diet data. One can raise one and lower the other two or lower all three or raise two and lower one, etc. There are only three variables with which to work. Some of the diets are more dangerous than others—none are miracles. Over 90 percent of people who go on a diet without confronting the underlying issues will fail repeatedly.

In order to understand diet better, a review of some basics should be helpful. Some practical suggestions for diet are:

1. Be sure you need a diet. A rule of thumb is that a female should weigh 100 pounds plus or minus 5 pounds for each inch above or below 5 feet in height. A male should weigh about 100 pounds plus or minus 6 pounds for every inch above or below 5 feet in height.
2. Be reasonable. Losing one to three pounds per week is a good plan for many people.
3. Use common sense in your plan: smaller protein sizes, more fiber, more fluid, small bites. Be more relaxed at meal time. Start a meal with green salad. Eat more broiled, roasted, and baked food—less fried.
4. Center your life around areas other than food: exercise, conversation, hobbies, etc.
5. Just as fat and cholesterol intake should be limited, so should sodium. Sodium can be a factor in high blood pressure in some individuals.
6. Drugs should be avoided in weight control. The two classes of drugs usually used are anorexics (like amphetamines, diethylpropsion hydrochloride, and fenfluramine hydrochloride) and thyroid hormone supplements. These drugs are potentially dangerous, do not work in the long run, and do not deal with the underlying issues.
7. Exercise, if regular and aerobic, can be of benefit when added to a diet regimen—see section on exercise.

PSYCHOLOGICAL

The psychological area is mentioned here for the sake of completeness. Most of this book has to do with the psychological aspect of good health. Its importance cannot be overstated. Again most diet plans fail because underlying issues are not resolved. Hopefully the resolution of some of those underlying issues can be taken a step further because of this book.

RECIPE INDEX

The Minirth-Meier Clinic Offices

Headquarters:

Minirth-Meier Clinic, P.A.
2100 N. Collins Blvd.
Richardson, Texas 75080
214-669-1733   800-229-4769
Metro 263-4045
    Outpatient Services
    Day Treatment Center
    Hospital Programs

Minirth-Meier, Tunnell & Wilson
    Clinic of Austin, P.A.
Centre Creek Office Plaza #100
1812 Centre Creek Drive
Austin, Texas 78754
512-339-7511
    Outpatient Services
    Day Treatment Center
    Hospital Programs

Minirth-Meier Clinic, P.A.
1701 River Run Road
Suite 901
Fort Worth, Texas 76107
817-336-6633
Metro 817-429-1634
    Outpatient Services

Minirth-Meier Clinic, P.A.
1009 N. Fourth Street
Suite 104
Longview, Texas 75601
214-753-7530
    Outpatient Services

Minirth-Meier Clinic West
260 Newport Center Dr. #200
Newport Beach, California 92660
213-515-1191   714-760-3112
800-877-4673
    Hospital Program
    Day Hospital

Minirth-Meier-Byrd Clinic, P.A.
4375 Fair Lakes Court #1050
Fairfax, Virginia 22033
703-968-3556
    Outpatient Services
    Hospital Program

Minirth-Meier-Rice Clinic, P.A.
310 Executive Court, Suite C
Little Rock, Arkansas 72205
Little Rock 501-225-0576
Hot Springs 501-623-1103
Memphis, TN 901-525-5140
    Outpatient Services
    Hospital Program

Minirth-Meier Clinic
Medical Plaza Mall, Suite I
809 Gallagher
Sherman, Texas 75090
214-892-1977
    Outpatient Services

Minirth-Meier Clinic, P.C.
The Grove, Suite 1510
2100 Manchester Road
Wheaton, Illinois 60187
312-653-1717   800-848-8872
    Outpatient Services
    Day Treatment Center
    Hospital Programs